The Shannon Navigation
978-1843511281

① ✶✶

Ireland's Waterways: Map + Directory
by Ruth
978-29

[barcode] D1093707

The Grand Canal of Ireland
978-1874675655

✶✶ Irelands Inland Waterways
978-0862818425

✶②

✶ Ireland's Royal Canal 1789-2009
978-1843511625

✶6 ✶

③ ✶
✶✶

Ireland - The
Inner Ireland
by Dwyer
1898256915

Guide to the Barrow
978-0905185019

✶✶ In Irish Waterway
by O'Regan
978 1856079150

④
✶

✶ The Inland Waterways of Ireland
by Jane Cumberlidge
978-0852884249

✶⑤

✶ Reedbound by Byford
978-1784622399

BY SHANNON SHORES
AN EXPLORATION OF THE RIVER

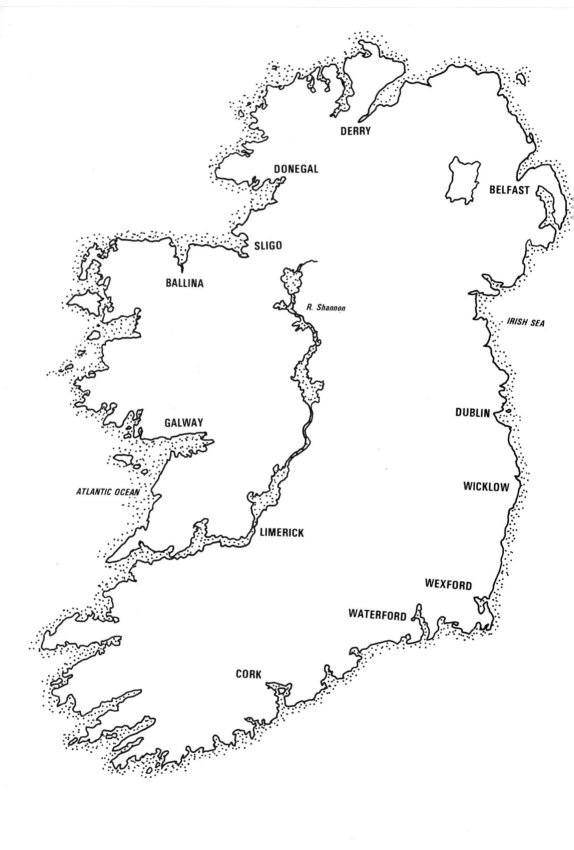

DERRY

DONEGAL

BELFAST

SLIGO

BALLINA

R. Shannon

IRISH SEA

GALWAY

DUBLIN

ATLANTIC OCEAN

WICKLOW

LIMERICK

WEXFORD

WATERFORD

CORK

RUTH DELANY

By Shannon Shores

AN EXPLORATION OF THE RIVER

GILL AND MACMILLAN

Published in Ireland by
Gill and Macmillan Ltd
Goldenbridge
Dublin 8
with associated companies in
Auckland, Dallas, Delhi, Hong Kong,
Johannesburg, Lagos, London, Manzini,
Melbourne, Nairobi, New York, Singapore,
Tokyo, Washington
© Ruth Delany 1987
7171 1526 7
Origination by Wellset Limited
Printed in Great Britain by Martin's the Printers
Bound by Hunter and Foulis

British Library Cataloguing in Publication Data
Delany, Ruth
By Shannon Shores: an exploration of the river.
1. Shannon River (Ireland) — Description and travel
Rn: Dorothy Ruth Heard   I. Title
914.17   DA990.S5

ISBN 0-7171-1526-7

CONTENTS

Contents

APPENDICES

This book is dedicated
to
the new generation of Shannon sailors
Harklow's new crew
and in particular to my daughter
Hilary

ACKNOWLEDGMENTS

I WOULD like to thank all those people who over the years were willing, and perhaps sometimes unwilling, companions in my explorations and others from whom I have learned new information about the river. I owe a special debt to Harman Murtagh who read the manuscript and advised me on matters relating to the role of the Shannon in history. I would also like to thank L. M. (Bunny) Goodbody, who allowed me to draw on his inexhaustable fund of stories; my daughter, Hilary and my brother-in-law, Alf Delany, who read the manuscript and made useful suggestions; Hardress Waller, who provided information about Dromineer Castle; Tom Maher who answered some queries for me about the north Shannon; Posie Goodbody, the source of the Traherne Holmes stories and the photograph of the 'Midge' McGrath; and Paul Kerrigan, whose articles on the Shannon defences were invaluable and who loaned me photographs and his artwork of the drawings of the fortifications.

I would like to thank Jonathan Henry for the trouble he went to in order to obtain a good cover photograph and for his help with some of the photographic reproductions; and John Gunn of Wexford Street, Dublin, for his assistance in reproducing photographs. I would also like to thank the staff of the National Library, of the library in Trinity College Dublin, and of the Public Record Office for their helpfulness at all times; and the following for permission to use illustrations: the National Library for the Lawrence plates and for assistance in photographing other illustrations, Richard Shackleton for the Jane Shackleton photographs, Alf Delany for family photographs, Rosemary Furlong for the Shannon Rally 1961 and the photograph of Harry and Cynthia Rice, Hilary Vandenberghe for a photograph of Athlone weir, John Weaving for permission to reproduce one of his 'lizards', Reggie Redmond for arranging for me to borrow the *Motor News* from the Guinness-Segrave Library of the RIAC to copy the illustration of the Clanricard eviction scene, Terence Cleeve for the shot of the boats in Meeiick Lock, W. Nixon for the photograph of Mountshannon, James Scully for the reproduction of the drawing of the opening of Banagher Bridge, the Waller family for some photographs of regattas and sailing on the rivers, Robert

Kelly for Lough Ree Yacht Club 1986 and the Simmons family for permission to use some of the late Jack Simmons's work.

Finally, I would like to thank my publishers Gill and Macmillan: Michael Gill for agreeing to publish this book and for his personal interest in its production; Brigid Lunn, my editor, who was such a pleasure to work with; Fergus O'Keeffe, who made such an excellent job of the maps, based on the Ordnance Survey by permission of the Government (Permit No. 4744); and Peter Larrigan, who arranged the layout.

How it all began

IT ALL began some thirty-five years ago when I travelled down from Dublin in the back of a very down-at-heel motor car as a member of the Dublin University Sailing Club to compete in a team race against the Lough Derg Yacht Club. It was my first sight of the River Shannon; an 'Emergency' child, my knowledge of Ireland had been limited to bicycle range around Dublin and, for me, the River Shannon was just the longest river in these islands in my school atlas.

We drove through Nenagh and followed the signpost which said 'Dromineer 6 miles'. The road twisted and turned, as indeed it still does, and

MY *Phoenix* anchored off Lough Ree Yacht Club in 1951 with L. M. Goodbody's Shannon One Design No. 61

there was no sign of water. Suddenly, we turned a corner and there it was in all its splendour with Dromineer Castle adding to the picture. The road has been altered today and the hedgerows have grown taller so you do not see the lake until you reach the harbour, but that first sight of Lough Derg is still as vivid for me today as it was all those years ago. I did not realise then how much that chance visit to Dromineer was to change my life nor what a major role the River Shannon would play in the years that lay ahead.

On that first day as we drove into Dromineer we were met by Llewellyn Marcus Goodbody, known as 'Bunny' to his friends, who had organised the fixture. I was 'rescued' by him and given a bunk on his boat, the *Phoenix*, because he considered it improper for me to spend the night in a tent. A few weeks later I received an invitation from him to accompany him and his family for the trip up the river to attend the Lough Ree Yacht Club regatta. We left Dublin by car late at night and the first streaks of dawn were beginning to light up the sky as we arrived at Dromineer. Bunny decided to assemble his tow of Shannon One Designs and set off up the lake. It was my first breathtaking Shannon dawn. It was very still as we lifted the anchor in the little bay off Kilteelagh House; the coots in the reeds reacted with a frightened chatter to the noise of our anchor chain. Behind the castle the sky

The contingent from Lough Derg at the Lough Ree Yacht Club regatta in 1951. L. to R. Edgar and Dorothy Waller, Reggie, Betty and Michael Goodbody, Jocelyn Waller, Vincent (Pompey) Delany, L. M. (Bunny) Goodbody and the author

was filled with the golden glow of the rising sun. I have witnessed many Shannon dawns since then, each one special and different, but that first trip up Lough Derg was one of those mystical occasions in life when time stands still and, maybe, just for a moment, one has a brief glimpse of eternity. I have experienced similar magical occasions on the river from time to time, just as I have had moments of fear and despair when wrestling with a sick engine in stormy weather conditions. Boating always brings with it the rough and the smooth but the Shannon has certainly provided much more of the latter for me and the pleasurable times far outweigh the times best forgotten.

On board the *Phoenix* on that trip was Bunny's wife, Betty, their two small sons and another of Bunny's friends, Vincent Delany, known to his sailing friends as 'Pompey'. I did not appreciate then what a venerable old lady I was sailing in nor that I was privileged to be making my first trip up the river in the company of the two people, Vincent and Bunny, who knew most about the river at that time. The *Phoenix* had been built by Malcolmson's of Waterford in 1872 for William Speight of Derrycastle. She was so named because his house had been destroyed by fire and the boat rose from the ashes, purchased with some of the insurance money. She was constructed of iron from the Lowmoor Pits in the north of England now long out of production; there was a very small percentage of sulphur in its composition, making it almost impervious to rust. On the death of General Speight, she was sold to Major Harry Lefroy of Killaloe. When he died she was sold to a Dublin wine merchant called Scott and he and his chauffeur, Delamere, used to go on drinking expeditions in her. Scott died and left the boat and his car to his chauffeur but he was killed in an air raid in England and Dick Lee of Limerick bought her. Bunny had subsequently purchased her from him and made her the home of his family.

Her original steam engine had been removed by Major Lefroy and replaced by an Elwee diesel. My most lasting memory of her on that occasion was the engine which was a very early type of semi-diesel started by compressed air in conjunction with a glow cartridge to assist the initial combustion. Once started, the engine recharged the air bottle from the exhaust but as the boat did not have an independent compressor the engine had to be started by using the limited quantity of compressed air in the air bottle from the previous use of the engine. This allowed three attempts at starting and after that it was a matter of waiting for the arrival of the *Eclipse Flower*, which was still trading on the river at that time, to recharge the bottle. One of the items Bunny used to start the engine was a candle to light the cartridge and he would retire below to the engine room and solemnly light his candle while a row of anxious faces peered down through the skylight. It had all the ingredients of a religious ceremony as he tried once, then twice and, finally,

The Delany family's MY *La Vague II* about 1925

The *Hark* high and dry in a field having strayed from the navigation when the river was in flood (after we sold her!)

with his last attempt, exhausted the supply of air. We did run out of air once on the way back and were marooned in Portumna for three days. Whether this delay had anything to do with it or not I cannot say, but less than two years later, Vincent and I were married. The *Phoenix* went through some bad times, her funnel was removed and her traditional wheelhouse replaced by a subsequent owner but, I am happy to say, she has now been lovingly restored by her present owner, John Lefroy, and the sight of her cutting through the water with her narrow bow brings back many memories; John's father, Ian, a nephew of Major Harry Lefroy, had repurchased the boat and passed her on to his son.

Vincent and I were destined to have only ten years together and much of that time was spent on the river in the Delany family vessel, the *La Vague II*. On one occasion we introduced a sailing friend, Douglas Heard, to the Shannon. He was instantly captivated and commissioned the conversion of a ship's lifeboat which he named the *Hark* — 'Heard's Ark'! We accompanied him on many inland waterway trips in this little boat which had the great advantage that when she went aground, one man in the water could push her off again. When Douglas sold his cruising yacht *Huff of Arklow* he decided to have a larger boat built for the waterways and he asked his old friend, Jack Tyrrell of Arklow, to design a boat for him which was a scaled-up version of the *Hark*. It seemed logical to call this boat the *Harklow* — Heard's Ark built in Arklow. It was on these three boats that I was to do most of my Shannon voyaging. Three years after Vincent's death I married Douglas and we spent

MY *Harklow* on Lough Key in the early 1960s

many happy times on *Harklow* in our years together. Now he too, like Vincent, is sailing on other waters, but I still own *Harklow* and my daughter Hilary and a new generation are learning to love the river in her.

Over the years my love affair with the Shannon has continued, whether browsing through old records, exploring new places, visiting historic sites along the banks, marvelling at its flora and fauna, swapping stories with old friends or just enjoying the peace and tranquillity. Every mile of the river has its interest and its memories for me. There are many legends as well; the line between legend and early history is a fine one but there has been a tendency in the past to give too much weight to these legends in books about the Shannon. We Irish have always enjoyed reciting our legends and they have lost nothing in the telling over the years. One or two of them are my favourites and I consider them part of the river's lore. I would like to share these with you along with my other discoveries and memories. I hasten to add that this is not a guide book. Changes and new developments are occurring all the time and so you follow me into some places at your peril. Water levels vary and silting occurs over the years. Much of our exploring was done by dinghy; weary hours trying to get boats off shoals have taught me to exercise discretion. However, I hope that this book may help those who cruise the Shannon's waters to enjoy their time on the river to the full. Above all I am writing this book because I want to write it. The best pleasures in life are shared pleasures and I feel I owe it to this great river to share some of these pleasures with you.

Douglas Heard (the author's late husband) in characteristic pose with camera at the ready

The two faces of the Shannon: a quiet bank mooring up the River Suck.

Harklow (on the right of the picture) joins the *Phoenix* and other boats locking down at Athlone between regattas in 1984.

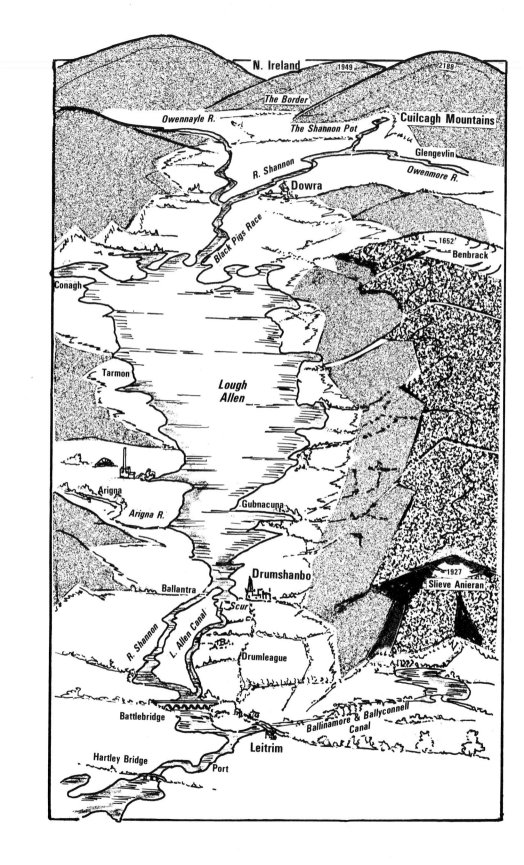

Chapter One

THE HEADWATERS
The Shannon Pot to Lough Allen

THERE is something fascinating about tracing the source of great rivers. I can remember as a child following the Liffey to its source in the Wicklow mountains with my brother and solemnly building a dam across it to halt its flow for a few moments. On my next visit to Dublin, standing on O'Connell Bridge and looking at the great river as it sped towards the sea I felt a great surge of power knowing that I had been able to halt its flow. Sometimes this search for the headwaters can become a little ridiculous; a recent programme about the River Thames on BBC TV ended with the intrepid explorer dragging his canoe over a dry field to a stone monument in a field which was said to mark the source.

In all my years on the Shannon I had never managed to see the Shannon Pot, the traditional source of the river. I had read about Richard Hayward's visit to it in 1939 and had built up a picture in my mind of this pool set in wild mountainous country. In the summer of 1985, finding myself up the north Shannon with a car, an unusual circumstance for me, I determined at last that I would seek it out; if I was to write my book about the Shannon this was one place I had to see for myself. I was accompanied by Denzil, the son of one of my good friends, who as a child had been the somewhat unwilling member of some of my exploration parties on the river, but he entered into this expedition to the headwaters enthusiastically. We set off armed with the ½ inch OS map and rubber boots; it had been one of those summers, definitely rubber boots weather.

Leaving Dowra village, we headed east to Glengevlin expecting to have to indulge in some serious map reading but our pioneering spirit received a set-back when we encountered a signpost bearing the legend 'Shannon Pot'. Dispensing with the map, we followed the signposts and eventually found ourselves driving up a tarmacadamed road to a car park where there were already a number of other cars. A short walk through a field and we were there. It was not at all as I had expected; it was just a pool in an ordinary field located a short distance off a main road in the foothills of the Cuilcagh mountains. These mountains rise to over 2,000 feet and, of course, it is somewhere up there that the real source of the river must lie. Richard

Hayward did, in fact, find a small lake higher up and threw some grass in it which duly turned up in the Pot some time later, and I have read of potholers seeking for the source in an underground cavern, using dye to establish which was the right one; in this carboniferous limestone country the whole area is a mass of underground streams and caverns. In fact, a glance at the map indicates that the Owenmore, aptly named the great river, which rises between the Cuilcaghs and Benbrack, has a far greater claim to be the source of the Shannon than the stream which it meets from the Shannon Pot. Far be it from me, however, to dispute the claim that this is the source of the Shannon; there I was, I had made it at last.

The pool itself is circular, about 25 feet across, and is surrounded by hawthorn and holly bushes. It seemed to be very deep and although its waters were still on the day we were there, despite the persistent rains at the time, it is said to bubble on occasions from its underground springs. Denzil, for all his adult years, could not resist the temptation to slither down the bank where the waters start the long journey to the sea and step across; I noticed some children doing the same thing nearby.

The Border between Northern Ireland and the Republic passes through the two highest points of the Cuilcaghs to the north east. Richard Hayward had stood here and mused about the unhappy division of the country quoting Thomas Davis's well-known lines:

The Shannon Pot

And, oh, it were a glorious thing to show before mankind
How every race and every creed might be by love combined;
Might be combined, but not forget the source from whence they rose,
As filled with many a rivulet the stately Shannon flows.

As I stood there, nearly fifty years on, these lines seemed to have an even more poignant ring.

Seeing the Pot conjured up one of the old legends of the origin of the Shannon. Cuan O'Lothchain, an eminent poet who died about 1024, wrote a poem about it, the opening verse of which when translated reads:

The noble name of Sinann seek ye from me,
Its bare recital would not be pleasant,
Not alike now are its action and noise
As when Sinann herself was free and alive.

Sinann, the daughter of Lodan, Sea God of the Gael, had come to Connla's Well in search of the salmon of wisdom. Around the well nine hazel trees grew and the salmon fed from the nuts falling into the well which were filled with the knowledge of all that is best in literature, poetry and art. Sinann approached the well furtively because she knew that it was forbidden for women to come there but she had not anticipated the anger of the great salmon at the sacrilege of seeing a woman approach. He lashed his great tail creating a wave which caused the pool to overflow. The floodwater overtook the fleeing maiden and her lifeless body was carried along by it. Thus was the Shannon created which still bears her name today. Scholars may say that Connla's well is in Lower Ormond and that the original river Sinann fell into the Shannon near the head of Lough Derg. Others may contend that the name is an anglicisation of Sean Abhainn, meaning 'old river', but for me now the Shannon will always be 'Sinann's river' as I picture the Pot welling up and overflowing down the mountainside to create the great river.

As we returned to the car several other families were arriving and we laughed at the culmination of our expedition which we had anticipated would involve a trek through the heather-covered slopes of the Cuilcaghs. We traced the course of the infant Shannon on the map; it is joined by another stream and widens into a tiny lake before passing under the Glengevlin road to meet the much larger Owenmore. From here, fed by numerous small streams, it becomes quite a substantial river before it reaches Dowra. We stopped and inspected it from the bridge at Dowra where it tumbled over shallows and the map showed that it is joined by another sizeable river, the Owennoyre, before it enters the north east corner of Lough Allen. By this time, about ten miles from the Pot, it has fallen some 186 feet and it will fall only 260 feet more before it reaches the sea at Limerick, 100

The infant Shannon at Dowra Bridge before it enters Lough Allen

feet of this in the last few miles between Killaloe and Limerick. Thus for most of its long course it meanders through the country broadening out into large lakes as it goes, a natural navigation with only an occasional place where rapids occur.

It was because it was such a fine natural navigation that the river became an important trading route from early times. Monastic settlements were attracted to its shores and to its lake islands at a time when most land routes were only rough tracks. Unfortunately, the same facility of transport it offered to the native Irish and its saints and scholars enabled invaders to penetrate deep into the country in the ninth century. The struggle to dominate the Shannon trade route from Limerick to Lough Ree was to continue on and off for nearly two hundred years.

The next invaders, the Normans, fortified strategic places along the river and must have found it a useful means of communication. In Elizabethan times its importance was appreciated by Sir William Pelham who wrote to Sir Francis Walsingham, Queen Elizabeth's secretary of state in 1580 saying that if he 'did view the commodious havens and harbours, the beauty and commodity of this river of Shannon, which I have seen from the head of it beyond Athlone to the ocean, you would say you have not in any region observed places of more pleasure or a river of more commodity, if the land were blessed with good people'. The Lord Deputy Strafford in the 1630s had proposed linking the major rivers, and the importance of the Shannon as a line of defence was appreciated by the Confederate forces in the 1640s. After the

Restoration one of the 'Instructions' issued by the duke of Ormond was that Ireland's rivers should be made navigable, and again in 1690-91 the Shannon played a role in history when Sarsfield's Jacobite forces for a time managed to keep the Williamite forces to the east of the river, giving them control of Connacht. It was not however until 1697 that the first petition came before the Irish parliament for a scheme to improve the navigation of the Shannon. The proposal evoked a favourable response and surveys were authorised but it was to be another fifty years before any work was initiated. I have told the story already of how the Canal Age evolved in my book *Ireland's Inland Waterways* — how the Irish parliament allocated grants for public works in the 1750s rather than surrender the country's surplus revenue to the English king across the water and how navigation schemes were commenced which were to give Ireland an inland waterway network she might otherwise never have enjoyed.

The Shannon benefited directly from this financial bonanza and work commenced in 1755 on the middle section of the river under the Commissioners of Inland Navigation, who two years later began the more difficult task of making the river navigable from Lough Derg to the sea. These latter works ran into considerable engineering difficulties but by the early 1770s a navigation of a sort had been achieved from Killaloe to Carrick-on-Shannon. Searching out these early navigation works is fascinating but they were not very well constructed and there are very few places where they can still be traced. Inevitably, the financial bonanza did not last for long and the commissioners were dissolved when a parliamentary inquiry revealed many shortcomings in their bookkeeping. Some of the incomplete works were handed over to private companies by the government but, while a company took over the navigation from Killaloe to Limerick, there were no takers for the rest of the Shannon. Local bodies were established to administer the waterways which remained in public ownership, but no funds were made available and nothing appears to have been done to maintain the Shannon. The Grand Canal Company, which had a vested interest in improving the navigation, took over the Middle Shannon and rebuilt the navigation works on this part of the river in the early 1800s; the canal company saw little point in opening a canal from Dublin to the Shannon unless the river itself was navigable.

The story of how the Grand Canal Company was forced to carry on negotiations over a long period before taking over the Middle Shannon is typical of the inefficiency and muddled thinking shown by public boards set up by the English administration at this time. If the Grand Canal directors had not been strongly motivated to improve the navigation in their own interest, they would never have persevered with such protracted nego-

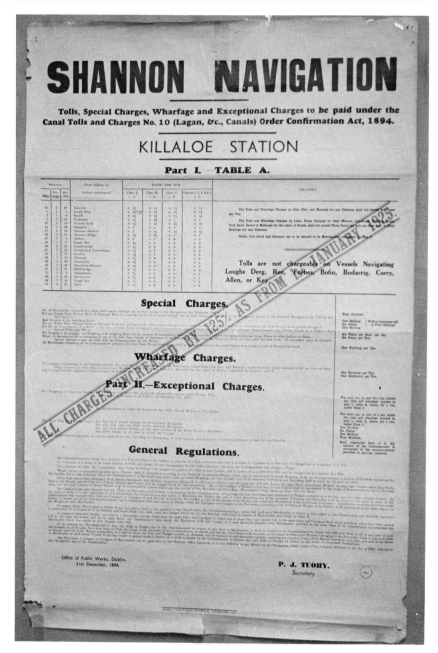

A Shannon Navigation notice indicating toll charges in 1894

tiations; these were carried out by lengthy correspondence with no attempt being made to sit down around a table to sort the thing out. Eventually, after five years, an agreement was hammered out and the company did receive part, but not all, of the money laid out on the works.

An equally ridiculous situation occurred on the Limerick to Killaloe stretch of the river. The government board, the Directors General of Inland Navigation, took over the completion of these works from the ineffective private company but the reopening was delayed for a number of years while haggling went on, during which time the completed works were obstructed by a temporary dam. Finally, the government bought out the company and opened up the waterway.

So, by the 1820s there was a moderately efficient navigation, but the absence of tow paths made progress slow on the river sections when boats had to be poled along against adverse winds. The arrival of steamers in the late 1820s changed all that, but the increasing use of the river focused attention on the shortcomings of the work already carried out and the locks proved too small to accommodate the size of steamer which was needed to navigate the larger lakes. This led to pressure on the government to improve the navigation at a time when public works to create employment were in demand. Major works were carried out in the 1840s by the Shannon Commissioners, giving us the fine navigation which we still enjoy today. Ironically, the same steam which propelled the steamers also led to the development of the railways and, even before the navigation works were finished, trade, and in particular the passenger traffic, had been seriously affected. In the years that followed there was only limited commercial traffic on the river and even this was to fall to a low ebb in the 1950s. The potential of the river as a tourist amenity was realised in the nick of time to save the navigation from strangulation by low road bridges.

Lough Allen's role in all this followed a different course. The lake is about seven miles long and three miles broad at its widest point, narrowing down at its southern end. It is almost completely surrounded by high mountains, the shore line is very regular with very few bays and there are only a handful of islands. Although the early works did not penetrate above Carrick-on-Shannon, the existence of coal and iron in the mountains around the lake provided an incentive to persevere in attempts to open it up. In 1785 William Chapman had presented a confident report to the Irish parliament that there was 'a greater Diversity of Iron Ore at Lough Allen than any Place in Britain'. It was considered that there were immense quantities of coal of the best quality for smelting the iron stone. Some half-hearted attempts were made in the 1790s to extend the navigation into the lake by Colonel Tarrant, a military engineer.

In 1794 a survey carried out by another engineer, John Brownrigg, had drawn attention to the fact that the level of the lake was then 3 feet or 4 feet higher than it had been 100 years earlier because silt brought down by the Arigna river, which discharged into the River Shannon just below the point where it left the lake, was gradually blocking the exit. He added: 'Many acres of the Lough are full of Oak Roots in four, six and ten feet of water and about forty years ago the Island of Gubnacuna was part of the mainland.' He suggested that at one time there was little difference in level between the lake and the river as far downstream as the island of Ballintrave, halfway to Battlebridge. Colonel Tarrant tried to overcome this problem of the silting caused by the winter floodwaters of the Arigna by making an artificial cut which turned the river directly into Lough Allen instead of into the River Shannon. Tarrant then turned his attention to extending the navigation into the lake. He commenced work on a short canal at Battlebridge on the west side of the river to by-pass the rapids at that place but money appears to have run out. Brownrigg reported that a local landowner, Mr Houghton, was claiming back the stone assembled to make the lock and 'there are other Claims for work done on this Canal and the People threaten they will not suffer the Works to be commenced till they are satisfied'. There the matter rested until the Royal Canal was completed in 1817.

One of the principal reasons put forward for making the Royal Canal in the first place was to provide access by water to the Lough Allen coalfields and so the completion of the canal put renewed pressure on the Directors General to extend navigation into the lake. The Directors General asked their engineer, John Killaly, to carry out a survey and he recommended making a canal on the east side of the river all the way to Lough Allen instead of using parts of the river. The plan was approved by the government and a proposal by Denis Hayes and Patrick Kelly for its construction, at an estimated cost of £14,240, was accepted; the proposal included the deepening of Acres lake, the small lake through which the canal was to pass, and maintenance for twelve months after its completion.

Work began in February 1819 but Hayes and Kelly had problems with a local landowner, Mr Horan, who claimed for damages to his land and stopped the works saying he would 'Repel Force by Force'. The problem was eventually resolved and, with commendable speed, the canal was completed and opened to traffic in February 1821. It was just over four miles long, commencing with a lock below Battlebridge which led into a small harbour. Both this lock and a second lock at Drumleague about 1½ miles up the canal were for some reason made 10 feet shorter than the Royal Canal locks, which meant that boats from the Royal Canal could not pass through. From Drumleague the canal, which was very narrow, twisted its way to Acres lake and up the last ½ mile to enter Lough Allen in a small bay at the extreme southern end, some distance from the place where the river leaves the lake.

The expected trade in coal did not materialise and only an occasional boat passed through the canal. Isaac Weld, who visited the area in the 1830s while preparing his statistical survey for the Dublin Society remarked on how little their new canal was being used; in 1831 only forty seven boats passed through. There were many shallows in the river downstream of Battlebridge and the cost of shipping the coal was high; a ton of Arigna coal which cost 7s 6d at the pithead had doubled in price when it reached Carrick a few miles downstream. In addition it was not considered as good as the 'sea coal' from England, which was shipped around the coast to Sligo and brought inland by road. Virtually none of the coal found its way to the Royal Canal and, in fact, imported coal from Dublin became one of the principal commodities to be carried on the canal, all of which made nonsense of the reason why this canal had been authorised in the first instance.

It is little wonder that the Shannon Commissioners showed a limited interest in the Lough Allen canal when the plans to improve the navigation in the 1830s were being drawn up. They did recommend a number of improvements: replacing the old road bridge at Battlebridge with a new bridge to be sited downstream of the entrance to the canal; lengthening the locks to accommodate boats from the Royal Canal and making a second lock just beyond the harbour to increase the depth of the canal; constructing a harbour at the Lough Allen end of the canal and deepening and widening the canal for its entire length. In addition, they suggested widening Tarrant's old

Battlebridge: the overgrown harbour on the Lough Allen Canal before the restoration of the canal in 1978

cut and constructing a weir at Ballantra to hold Lough Allen at a fixed level. In the event, overspending on the works downstream caused a shortage of funds and the only work carried out was some underpinning of the locks to allow the canal to take deeper draft boats, and some dredging in the canal, while Tarrant's cut was widened to divert more of the Arigna waters directly into Lough Allen. It was not until further steps were taken to control the Shannon waters following disastrous flooding in the 1860s that sluices were eventually fitted at Ballantra, designed to raise the lake 5 feet above its normal summer level. An amusing instance of public hysteria occurred in 1910, according to a report in the *Irish Independent* on 5 March:

Some alarmist spread a report, which the credulous believed, that the bridge (supporting the sluices) was in danger of giving way, and among these some anxiety was felt for the past few days. If such a catastrophe occurred, Leitrim and Carrick-on-Shannon would be swept away, but fortunately, there is not the remotest probability of such a thing happening as the bridge is so securely and solidly built that the ravages of time alone can affect it.

The construction of the Cavan & Leitrim railway in the 1880s with a tramway extension to the Arigna coalfields had further reduced the use of the canal (it is worth noting that even this railway was not successful and closed in 1959). When, therefore, a hydro electric scheme for the Shannon was being considered in the 1920s, it was decided to use Lough Allen as a storage reservoir by constructing new regulating sluices at Ballantra. This meant closing off the canal permanently because of the great fluctuations, (as much as 15 feet) which now occur in the level of the lake. Thus, when the increase in pleasure boating on the river in recent years brought a call for the reopening of the canal it was only possible to reopen it to Acres lake. The fluctuations in levels would have required designing a lock which would enable boats to lock either up into the lake or down depending on the level at the time and, in addition, the bay into which the canal opened was so shallow most of the time that a considerable amount of dredging would have been needed.

The dropping of Lough Allen to very low levels uncovered some interesting areas where crannogs, ancient lake dwellings, had been sited off the east shore and there were other indications of early habitation. At the north end of the lake there is a prehistoric ditch, known as the Black Pig's Race, extending from the village of Dowra towards the lake, which is thought to be part of an early frontier of the kingdom of Ulster. After all these years, less than 10 miles away, we still have a Border. There are a number of early

Ballantra: the sluices constructed in the 1920s to control the water from Lough Allen for the hydro electric scheme

church ruins, one on the island of Inishmagrath and two others along the west shore, at Conagh and Tarmon, indications of the importance of the lake in ancient times.

The upper road along the west side takes you through the old coalfields where the coal was worked in horizontal drifts. From this road there is a magnificent view of the whole lake and it is sad that the boats from the Shannon cannot gain access to it although, with its mountainous sur-roundings, I am sure that it is subject to sudden squalls in windy weather. A power station has been built on the shore to make use of the local coal and the Electricity Supply Board (ESB) has considered bringing additional supplies to the station from elsewhere; a suggestion from the Inland Waterways Association of Ireland (IWAI) that water transport could be used was dismissed as impractical.

The variations in water level have limited the use of this lake for all water activities. The local authority is trying to make an amenity area on the west shore near Arigna but it is not easy to make it attractive with the lake rising and falling so much. Now that the Shannon hydro power forms such a very small part of the national grid, one could question whether the ESB should continue to be allowed to monopolise the lake in this way. Extending the navigation into the lake would be of great benefit to Drumshanbo and the surrounding area. This attractive little town was an important centre for iron smelting in the eighteenth century and the local community have made the most of having the boats come as far as Acres lake by creating pleasant moorings there but many more boats would be attracted if they could reach Lough Allen.

We always enjoyed our visits to Battlebridge in the old days. Sean Nangle, the lock-keeper, would come aboard for a chat. He loved to talk about 'his' canal and was so delighted when plans for its reopening to Acres lake were announced. Sadly, he died shortly after the great day came and did not live long to enjoy the pleasure of passing boats through again.

Standing on the bridge at Battlebridge, there is very little indication that you are looking at a navigation course. The river is narrow and very shallow and the quay and entrance to the Lough Allen Canal a few hundred yards downstream are scarcely visible. It is a pretty scene with both banks wooded to the water's edge. In the field on the right there is no sign of the mill that stood there in the 1830s nor the millrace which passed through the small arch of the bridge. Looking west to the crossroads, there is little left of the thriving community of over a dozen houses that was here at that time. When we used to come here in the 1960s there was a little shop at the crossroads but on my last visit even this had closed down.

The embrasures in the bridge, which were for pedestrians to step into to avoid the coaches thundering across, are an indication of its antiquity. The name infers a battle but I have never discovered what this battle was. There were skirmishes here and also at a number of places further upstream, when Humbert's forces pushed east after their victory at Castlebar in 1798. When Thomas Rhodes was surveying this place for the Shannon Commission in 1839 as already mentioned, he suggested re-siting the bridge: 'under-

Battlebridge: one of the oldest bridges and the limit of the river navigation

standing that it is intended to pull down the existing dilapidated bridge at Battlebridge, and that a new one is about to be erected by the adjoining counties...' but these plans did not materialise and, thankfully, the adjoining counties failed to get around to replacing the 'dilapidated' bridge.

Thomas Rhodes is a name which will occur frequently in my story of the river. It is thanks to his vision that we enjoy such a fine navigation today. He was an English engineer, a relative of Cecil Rhodes, and he had worked on the construction of the Caledonian Canal where he had learnt the uses that could be made of the new discovery of steam power to operate pumps and dredgers. He was invited to survey the Shannon in the 1830s and it was his plans which were adopted by parliament. His meticulous drawings are a great source of information both about the early navigation works as he found them and about the new works.

Heading downstream from Battlebridge, the river is narrow and fast flowing with a number of bends, the wooded banks making visibility difficult. In fact, it used to be a great deal more tortuous but the Shannon Commissioners reduced the number of bends by cutting canals across the natural curves, creating small islands. The entrance to Leitrim comes into view and it is important to come down past the island before turning in; we have spent some time helping people get their boats off the shallows when they tried to enter by the channel to the north of the island.

Although it gives its name to the county, Leitrim is only a village. Little remains of O'Rourke's fort into which O'Sullivan Beare and the remnants of his people staggered on 14 January 1603. The agile can climb the old wall and read the inscription commemorating the march of 300 miles from Glengarriff in Co. Cork. He was pursued and harried all the way and we are told that of the one thousand who started out with him, some of them soldiers, 'only 35 remained, 16 armed men, 18 non-combatants and one woman, the wife of the chief's uncle, Dermot O'Sullivan'. Our paths will cross again, in the course of this epic journey, far downstream near Portumna.

This short stretch up to Leitrim village was artificially straightened in the 1840s as part of the Ballinamore & Ballyconnel Canal works. During the Canal Age it had always been the dream of canal entrepreneurs to provide a navigable link right through the country from Belfast to Limerick. When the Ulster Canal was completed in 1841, joining Lough Neagh and Lough Erne, one final link remained to be achieved for the great through route — a waterway from Lough Erne to the Shannon. Sadly, by the time this had been achieved a number of factors had jeopardised its chances of success. The Ulster Canal had proved far from satisfactory: there was a constant shortage of water on its summit level and the locks were too small to accommodate boats from the other Ulster waterways. Even though there was no railway

13

Leitrim: where the Ballinamore & Ballyconnell Canal begins; John Weaving dredging out a passage with his canal boat *Peter Farrell* during a work-in rally in 1972

along the route of the B & B canal at this time, railways were expanding rapidly throughout the country and coastal steamers were operating regular services, so it was unlikely that goods would be sent via the long inland waterway route between Belfast and Limerick and, with the disappointing coal trade from Lough Allen, there was little demand for local traffic. The result was that this waterway, a government scheme, one of the many aimed at creating employment, became a white elephant. It was never really completed properly because there was no demand for it and the unsatisfactory condition of the navigation did little to encourage people to use it. The official records indicate that in its short working life from 1860-69 only eight boats passed through it which paid tolls, a poor return for the expenditure of £¼ million of public money.

With the growth in pleasure traffic on the Shannon and the Erne today, this unwanted waterway could yet come into its own. An EEC report has indicated that its restoration should be a priority project and it would be a very useful cross-border scheme, bringing potential employment and tourists to these border counties which have suffered so much from the conflict in recent years. It is well worth taking a dinghy through the road bridge at Leitrim and up the canal to the first lock. This is the first of eight rising locks to the summit level at Lough Scur. The chambers which are a good size would accommodate most boats on the river today and the condition of the stonework is remarkable.

Downstream of the junction to Leitrim, the Shannon rapidly becomes a much larger river and the wooded banks give way to the more characteristic open fields. There is a strong flow entering the S-bend of Port which used to be a fording place. A monastic site was established here and it was subsequently guarded by a fort. An early attempt was made to by-pass the ford by cutting a channel across the bend but this was later abandoned by the Shannon Commissioners who dredged a channel through the ford.

Hartley Bridge comes into view where the navigation passes awkwardly through a channel near the east bank. It is an ugly bridge but is of interest to the industrial archaeologist because it is a very early example of the use of reinforced concrete, dating back to the 1930s. A rail type section, called a 'moss bar' was used as reinforcement, the parapets act as beams, spanning between the supports, and the bridge was constructed to extend out over the floodplain on the west side. Once through the bridge, the river again changes in character widening out almost into a small lake, fringed with reed beds, as it approaches the junction with the Boyle Water. In the seven short miles from Battlebridge the Shannon has grown from a small fast-flowing river into the more characteristic great wide one which will flow lazily across the central plain, widening out occasionally into lakes and here and there gaining momentum temporarily as it passes through narrow channels.

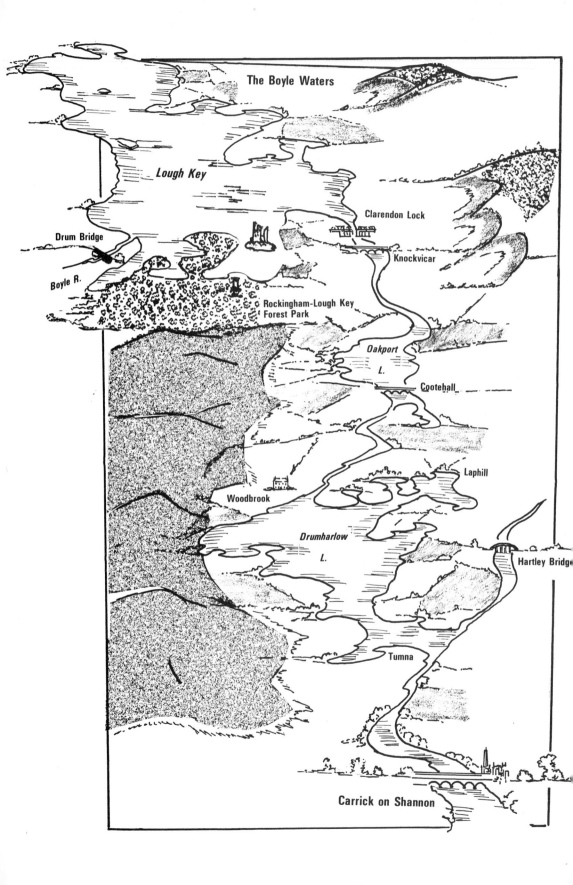

The Boyle Waters

Lough Key

Clarendon Lock

Drum Bridge

Knockvicar

Boyle R.

Rockingham-Lough Key
Forest Park

Oakport
L.

Cootehall

Laphill

Woodbrook

Drumharlow
L.

Hartley Bridge

Tumna

Carrick on Shannon

Chapter Two

ENCHANTED WATERS
The Boyle Waters

BEFORE heading downstream we turn to starboard and pass upstream again to explore the Boyle Waters. There does not appear to have been any attempt made to improve the navigation of this river until the 1840s, although boats carrying a small amount of cargo did work their way up to Cootehall over the shallows. The first obstruction was at Tumna which was formerly a fording place and where even today the passage is narrow. On the west shore there is the small ruined church and graveyard of St Eidin's. Samuel Lewis in his *Topographical Dictionary* published in 1837 records that seven gold balls, the size of eggs, were dug up here. I quoted this piece of information in the *IWAI Shannon Guide* and, the last time I went by here, I was amused to see someone busy with a metal detector. It is good news that the law is to be strengthened to deter the modern treasure hunter.

Once through the Tumna shallows the navigation opens out into the broad waters of Lough Drumharlow, originally called Lough Eidin. It is a fine lake and it was here in the 1890s that some early yacht racing took place under the burgee of the North Shannon Yacht Club in 15 to 20 ton keel boats. We have spent many hours exploring this lake, tucking ourselves behind Inishatirra away from the madding crowd. The channel around the island has now been marked but our favourite anchorage in the innermost bay near the old schoolhouse of Laphill is completely remote from the main navigation. It is prudent to keep some distance off the shore entering this bay and there is one large shoal at the entrance but it is clearly visible; it needs to be given a wide berth because it extends out some distance underwater.

Back in the navigation course there is another attractive bay to the north of the woody promontory of Drumharlow, the townland which has given its name to the lake. On several occasions we spent a few days anchored quietly here observing a pair of great crested grebe. They are a shy bird but are becoming more used to modern boat traffic. They circle around a territory feeding from the bottom and resurfacing here and there, but if startled, they immediately dive and then it is difficult to spot where they resurface because they can travel long distances under water. We had noticed that this pair had three young chicks and Douglas was very anxious to try to film the parents carrying them on their backs. He reckoned that they would accept *Harklow* as part of the scenery after a couple of days but as so often happens when other boats see a boat at anchor, they come and anchor nearby and so our plan was frustrated. Douglas would get up at dawn and sit quietly with camera poised but they never came near enough for him to get a shot. Seeing grebe at other places along the river always brings back memories of those birdwatching dawns in Drumharlow when the lake waters were like glass and a faint mist lay over the reed-lined shore, while gradually the birds woke up and started their busy day and the chorus grew louder. We may not have the pictures on celluloid but it has left an indelible image on my mind. I recommend Shannon dawns when the weather is fine and the breezes light.

Drumharlow wood is full of interesting wild flowers. I learnt a good deal about Shannon wild flowers through a game we used to play if we had a young crew aboard. The children were put ashore for an allotted period to gather as many different types of wild flower as they could find and this was followed by prizes for the winner and hours of poring over the wild flower book to try to identify their finds. It was quite amazing how many different types they found. These areas of scrubby woodland are very ancient and undisturbed, with willows, alder and birch trees, and some of the even older oak woods have hazel and holly.

Some years ago, in 1974, a Scotsman called David Thomson wrote a book called *Woodbrook*. I read it with enormous pleasure, partly because of its connection with this little bay at Drumharlow; Woodbrook House is near the shore of the lake here. David Thomson had come to Woodbrook at the age of eighteen in 1932 to act as tutor to Phoebe, then aged eleven, the daughter of Major and Mrs Kirkwood. He stayed for ten years and wrote the book describing his years in Ireland, the many places they visited and people they met. It was a world of horses and house parties, 'only the landlords had bathrooms', the *Irish Times* — always yesterday's — came by post each day at lunchtime, the postman, who had sounded his arrival with a post-horn in previous generations, now announced himself with the crunch of gravel under his bicycle. The author builds up a fascinating picture of an Anglo-Irish family against the background of the history of that period and of earlier centuries, using that great historian, Lecky, as his principal source. Interwoven, in a most sensitive way, is the author's developing love for his pupil. He was to meet her again some years later only to lose her for ever when she died in the following year. In an epilogue he relates returning to Woodbrook in 1968. The Kirkwoods had sold off part of the estate to the local golf club, the wings of the house had been demolished, and a local family, the Maxwells, who had formerly worked on the estate, had bought what remained and lived in a few rooms at the back of the house. The

18

Maxwells' forebears had owned this land and like many others at that time they resented the fact that they had been dispossessed by the plantation of English settlers, although Anglo-Irish families like the Kirkwoods would have been the last to question their own 'Irishness'. Ironically, having gained possession of the place, the Maxwells no longer wanted it and in 1970 they sold it to John Malone who still lives there today.

The description in the book of the house, the estate and the little 'canal' down which they brought the boat to go rowing on the lake, filled me with a great curiosity to see the place for myself. We rowed ashore and made our way up to the house, knocking on the door to apologise for our intrusion. There was no reply but we had the strong feeling that we were being inspected by unseen eyes; we were probably not the first people to come on a similar pilgrimage. The place was not at all as I had imagined; the house, bereft of its wings, was small and unkempt. I was sorry I had gone to look at it at all and would have preferred the picture I carried in my imagination.

Leaving Drumharlow, before entering the river again, the navigation passes through a tiny deep pool. In the old days we often anchored here particularly in windy weather because it offered a sheltered haven, but today the wash of passing boats would make it untenable. The large boulders lining the banks along the next stretch of river are an indication of the dredging required to deepen it. This was Annalecky ford and a short distance upstream there was another obstruction, known as 'The Doctor's Weir' where there had been eel weirs in the past. I do not know who the Doctor was and whether he had some connection with either the Coote family of nearby Cootehall or the local landowner, the Rev. Thomas Gough. The presence of a ringfort on the west shore, just where the river expands into the small lake approaching Cootehall, would indicate that these shallow places were important fording places in the past.

A floating jetty was installed in this little lake some years ago. We much prefer to lie here than at the bridge at Cootehall; it is better for swimming and sailing. In addition, a section of old road, where the local authority had altered the line near the jetty, makes a fine hard tennis court, although it is necessary to have active ball boys to fish the balls out of the lake! The IWAI have frequently tried to persuade the Office of Public Works to put up more of this type of jetty in quiet mooring places in preference to the customary costly concrete harbours. How many such jetties could be made for the price of one concrete one? But the maintenance-free concrete is always preferred.

A short walk up the nearby lane leads to Oakport lake and a quiet amenity area; wild strawberries grow in the hedgerows of this lane. It was formerly the road from Cootehall, climbing up over the hill and running along beside Oakport lake before reaching off to join the main Boyle road but the new road was made around the hill in the 1840s. At this time the Shannon Commissioners replaced the old eight-arch bridge at Cootehall with the present fine three-arch structure. It was originally planned to site the new bridge further downstream nearer the little lake, with an opening span in the centre arch and to realign the road but, as already mentioned earlier, a much heavier expenditure than anticipated further downstream forced them to severely curtail their north Shannon plans. The bridge was erected on the same site as the old one and the awkward road approach remains. Plans to dredge the river were also curtailed; for many years there was a shoal in the centre of the river below the bridge and the west arch was the only navigation arch. This created some near misses when boats met here and made approaching and leaving the quay a difficult manoeuvre. In recent years the shoal down the centre of the river was removed and today the boats can speed through their respective arches creating a nasty wash for boats moored to the quay. One day we might see speed limits imposed on stretches such as this?

There was the inevitable castle here commanding the bridge erected by the Coote family in the seventeenth century. Charles Coote had come to Ireland as an army captain in 1600 and fought with distinction at Kinsale. He was rewarded by receiving estates in the Roscommon and Cavan area and, later, as Sir Charles Coote, he became known for his uncompromising behaviour in supressing the 1641 rebellion. He was killed in action in the following year and his son, Sir Charles II, acquired an equally horrific reputation as a Cromwellian general. However, he had the good sense to support the restoration of the monarchy at the right moment and his reward for this change of heart was the earldom of Mountrath. The castle at Cootehall was within a quadrilateral enclosure with towers at each corner. It was attacked and burned by insurgents in 1798 and by the mid-1800s it was reported to be largely in ruins with only three of the four towers and a few of the buildings intact. Parts of these buildings were converted into a farm dwelling house and were acquired, together with much of the surrounding estates, by Hugh Barton Esq., a rich Dublin wine merchant.

The decline in the fortunes of the castle did nothing for the village, which Lewis in 1839 referred to as 'old Coot Hall's wretched dependent village'. John McGahern, a native of these parts, conjures up very vividly the atmosphere of the village in the 1940s in his novel *The Barracks* which traces the terminal illness and death of the sergeant's wife and her utter loneliness even though she is surrounded by people. It makes one realise how much life has changed in small rural villages since then. Today the pleasure boat boom on the river has brought new vigour to the place and the 'Water Splash' shop and pub by the quay does a good trade with its Beer Garden and singing sessions. In IWAI circles, passing through Cootehall without 'stopping for milk', as it is euphemistically called, is unheard of. This usually ends in a darts match in 'Henry's' up the village; such sessions were dear to the heart of the late Seamus Kelly, better known as 'Quidnunc' of the *Irish Times*. A one-time colleague of Seamus's, Patrick Campbell, wrote a most amusing story, which he entitled 'Ireland is not England', about meeting an English couple further down the river at Roosky who had, in fact, stopped early one morning for milk and inquired of him if it was a holiday because all the shops were closed.

Oakport lake is dominated by Oakport House built in two periods by the Mulloy family, of Great Mulloy fame. The woods of the demesne make this a most attractive little lake but beware of anchoring because we have always found the holding poor here. Once through the lake the river becomes much narrower and winds its way towards Knockvicar. It is a lovely stretch of river with trees down to the water's edge on the west shore and then, suddenly, rounding a bend Knockvicar Bridge comes into view, framed in the green of the surrounding trees. The bridge is the same design as Cootehall; here, too, Rhodes had recommended moving the site of the bridge downstream a short distance to permit realigning the road but, as at Cootehall, the cheaper option of erecting the new bridge on the old site was adopted. There was a mill on the west side of the bridge in those days and the old millrace can be traced in the grounds of the millhouse above the bridge. The fine stone quay erected by the commissioners shows little sign of the shortage of funds which dogged the later stages of the works.

Cootehall: the Shannon Rally assembled at the quay in 1984 with John Weaving in the *Peter Farrell* in the foreground.

The stretch of river from the bridge to Clarendon Lock is one of the prettiest on the entire navigation. Here the commissioners constructed a lock, naming it after the Lord Lieutenant of the time, and beside the lock they built an open weir. It makes a most attractive picture as you approach from downstream. In the 1845 report it was stated that 'since the commencement of the works at this station, the conduct of the men employed has been most exemplary, no dissatisfaction has been evinced amongst them, and they have been throughout industrious and peaceable'. It must have been back-breaking work; two pairs of pumps had to be kept working by eighteen men, day and night, to remove the water from the area which had been dammed off. From time to time there were problems with the water bursting through and, in October 1846, it was reported that 'another sudden and unexpected burst' had occurred, drowning two of the unfortunate labourers.

They did a good job; the lock looks as solid today as the day it was built but in the 1950s things were different: the place looked neglected and over-grown, one of the tailgates was chained because it was unsafe to open it and the other gate looked very shaky. Harry Rice, one of the founders of the Inland Waterways Association of Ireland, came up here in 1955 with a small flotilla of open boats. His purpose in coming was threefold: he wanted to publicise the wonderful potential of this navigation which very few people appreciated; he was trying to draw attention to the dangerous condition of the lock and demand his right to navigate through it and, thirdly, he wanted to claim for the people of Ireland the right to land on the shores and islands of Lough Key despite a notice at the lock advising them that landing was pro-hibited. Harry resented the fact that people were expected to go cap-in-hand to seek permission even if they wished to drop an anchor in Rockingham Bay. Sir Stafford King Harman was known to extend a welcome to some of those who approached him and Tom Rolt and his crew were wined and dined and offered baths but others had not been so lucky. It had been Rolt's book *Narrow Boat* about the English waterways which had awakened interest there in the 1940s and he had come to Ireland in 1946 to visit our neglected waterways. Following this visit, he wrote *Green and Silver* which became the classic of the Irish waterways creating a similar awakening in this country. It was his title, *Green and Silver*, conjuring up the silver river running through the green fields of Ireland, which prompted the newly formed Inland Waterways Association to adopt this theme for its emblem and this burgee still flutters at many a masthead.

Harry Rice's campaign bore fruit, new gates were installed in 1958 and, as we shall see, the fates took a hand in solving his quarrel with the King Harmans. He would scarcely recognise the scene at Clarendon Lock today: the lock is constantly in use and by the time one set of boats has been locked

Lough Key Forest Park: the Moylurg Tower which was erected on the site of Rockingham House

through a new batch has arrived, a new quay stretches up towards the lake and it is a busy spot at all times in the season. Shannon boat rallies organised by the Athlone and Carrick branches of the IWAI were to become an annual event on the river commencing in 1961 when over seventy boats participated; since 1976 there has also been an annual rally organised by the Lough Derg branch on the lower Shannon.

It is always a breathtaking moment as you move out on to the lake and the wooded islands come into view. When we first came here, Rockingham

Lough Key: during the Shannon Rally in 1961 after the house had been badly damaged by fire

The yard and farm buildings. *Lawrence*

The Rock, Castle Island. *Lawrence*

Rockingham Estate seen through the lens of the photographer, William Lawrence

The police barracks. *Lawrence*

The harbour. *Lawrence*

House dominated the lake as you turned into the bay and approached the shore. Today, a structure called the Moylurg Tower occupies the site where the house once stood. Most people will agree that the Forest and Wildlife Service, who administer the estate today as a forest park, have done a first class job in preserving the atmosphere of the place, but I have never heard a good word said about the Moylurg Tower; it should never have been put there. There is an excellent guide book available at the centre and a copy of this is essential to learn about the history and to appreciate the flora and fauna of the park.

So how did all this change come about since Harry's expedition in the 1950s? Fate took a hand: Rockingham House was badly damaged by an accidental fire in 1957 and the entire estate was bought by the government two years later to become one of Ireland's first Forest Parks. The "Plain People of Ireland" — the P.P.I. as Myles na gCopaleen used to call them — could now enjoy their ancient right, demanded by Harry, to enjoy this most beautiful of lakes.

Possibly because I first wandered around the estate in the early years shortly after the Forest and Wildlife Service took it over, when the burnt-out shell of the house still stood there and the estate was much as it had been, it has always conjured up for me a picture of the large country estate and I could readily imagine what it all must have looked like in its heyday. Lawrence, the photographer, who has left us such a wonderful pictorial record of our country in the early years of the century, visited Rockingham and captured the atmosphere perfectly.

To appreciate it all fully it is necessary to understand something of the background history of the place. This was MacDermot territory right through from the twelfth to the seventeenth century and there was a settlement on the shores of the lake with a fortress on the nearby island, known as The Rock, which is now called Castle Island. *The Annals of Loch Cé*, which commence in 1014 and end in 1590, chronicle the history of the MacDermot family and the many battles which were waged around The Rock. In 1578, when times had become slightly less turbulent, it is recorded: 'The great regal house of the Rock was begun by Brian, the son of Ruaidhri MacDiarmada, and he had this work and the head (roof) of the monastery of the Trinity, and the bawn of Dungas, in progress together'; the latter is thought to have been a house on the mainland where the aforementioned Moylurg Tower stands today.

The MacDermot lordship of the area was soon to decline and their lands were granted to Sir John King in the seventeenth century. His grandson, Robert, built the first Rockingham mansion on the site of the old MacDermot house in the 1670s. This house was subsequently destroyed by fire and, in 1810, the great great grandson of the earlier Sir Robert, Robert Edward King, Lord Lorton, commissioned John Nash to design a new house for him. A two-storey house was built surmounted by a large dome but in 1820 Lord Lorton had the dome removed and a third storey added; it is said that he felt that Nash's design was less imposing than the houses of some of his contemporaries. The addition did nothing for the house, making the ionic portico look out of proportion. Yet another disastrous fire in 1863 led to a further reconstruction which again did nothing to improve the appearance of the house. David Thomson, who visited it with the Kirkwoods when the King Harmans were in residence, referred to it unkindly as 'a top-heavy mausoleum in a green graveyard' and it was this house that succumbed to fire once again in 1957.

Even as a ruin it was imposing, but the blackened walls and twisted remains of pipes and radiators were evidence of the severity of the fire and it was obvious that it would have been a gigantic task to restore it or even to preserve it simply as a ruin. In spite of the efforts to fence it off, the temptation to inspect it at close quarters was very great, and in the end it was considered to be so dangerous that the only practical thing was to demolish it. Few will argue with this decision but I have yet to meet anyone who could defend the monstrosity erected in its stead. Intended as a viewing tower, there must be a fine view from it but on each occasion we have been there it has been bolted and barred.

A feature of Rockingham House was the servants' quarters and working area, which had been constructed underground so as not to impair the stately appearance of the house. This basement area remains, with two underground passages opening off it. One of these led down to a quay, known as the turf quay, passing under the front lawn, with store-rooms opening off it, so that goods and fuel could be landed and transported to the house without being seen by the people 'upstairs'. Many a time we inspected this passage and its dark recesses with a torch. The second passage leads down at an angle to the old harbour and the ice-house. These were a common feature on estates in this period, but it makes one wonder whether the winters were harder in those days because there are few winters now that would provide a supply of ice.

Nearby is the shell of the estate church rebuilt by Lord Lorton in 1833 so that the family could worship in private. This was the period when worshipping was principally for the wealthy, the aristocracy often had their own churches built on their estates and most of the gentry had boxed-off pews for which they paid an annual rent, while the common people were permitted to stand at the back or in the gallery. Some of the fine old quadrangular farm buildings have been retained together with the small gazebo jutting out into the lake, known for some reason as The Temple.

Out on MacDermot's Rock, Lord Lorton built a sort of fairy castle using parts of the old castle which were still standing. Francis Grose included a drawing of the Rock made in 1792 in his *Antiquities of Ireland* which gives some idea of how it looked before the new castle was built. The entire island is shown as a fortified structure with massive walls built right out to the shoreline and with the ruins of the castle within. He described it as follows:

The island is circular and fortified with a wall fourteen or fifteen feet thick, so that there is no landing on the isle but at a breach in this wall. It contains, with much wood, a square castle, so covered with ivy that not a stone can be seen on the outside; and the inside is so ruinous, that no judgment can be formed of the mode of building or workmanship. It obtained its present name (MacDermot's Island) from one of the Toparchs of this country, who through jealousy, always confined his wife in this sequestered island while engaged in warlike expeditions. Her lover, however, despising every obstacle that sea and walls presented, swam frequently from the main land to visit his insular fair one.

Lord Lorton's new castle was lavishly furnished and used as a guest house but it, too, was badly damaged by fire and never restored although it still presents a pretty picture from the shore. It has a sad air about it, pervaded by the spirit of Una MacDermot. The usual version of her story does not tally with Grose's account.

She was said to be the daughter of one of the last of the great MacDermots, who fell in love with Thomas MacCostello, the son of her father's mortal enemies. Her father would not allow them to meet and kept his daughter immured in the castle. When she fell ill, he was too proud to send for the one man who might have given her the incentive to live and so she died and was buried on nearby Trinity Island. There her lover came secretly each night to be with her, but one night as he crossed to the island he was drowned. Too late, her father relented and allowed him to be laid beside his daughter. The grave is said to be in the north east corner of the island and over it two trees grew which became intertwined, but so many people used to visit the place that one of the stewards at Rockingham cut down the trees to conceal where the grave lay. I have never managed to find any trace of it.

Trinity Island had been given by the MacDermots to the White Canons of St Francis, Premonstratensian Canons, in the thirteenth century. They remained on the island until the suppression of the monasteries in the early 1600s. The generosity of the MacDermots in erecting buildings for the abbey was rewarded because it was here that the *Annals of Loch Cé* were written which have left us such a wealth of information about the family. The original book is in the library of Trinity College Dublin and the annals trace the history of the area and of the abbey. It is recorded that a fire caused great damage on the island in 1466, the cause of which was a lighted candle carried by the wife of one of the canons; celibacy does not seem to have been practised in those days. We have often anchored off here to explore the island and look at the old abbey ruins. I have never managed to find the grave of Sir Conyers Clifford which is said to be near the abbey. He was killed in a battle in the nearby Curlew hills in 1599 and his Irish adversary, Red Hugh O'Donnell, recognising his bravery in battle, instructed Brian MacDermot, one of his own officers, to give his headless body a decent buriel.

There are endless interesting walks through the estate; the western promontory was turned into pleasure grounds by the great Lord Lorton. He cut two ornamental canals through the isthmus, spanned by attractive bridges. One of these, called appropriately the Fairy Bridge, was constructed with stones of strange and fascinating shapes from the lake shore; the limestone had been eaten away by the acidic waters of the lake. Tom Rolt recorded that he saw a large insect drowning in the lake near here which he thought to be a Great Pine Sawfly. One evening standing on the Fairy Bridge I saw a truly enormous dragonfly. I am not sure if it was the same species but it reminded me of the Rolts' visit to Lough Key, when his little boat dragged her anchor and ended up on the rocks near the old turf quay. The wind has a habit of filling in from unexpected directions in this bay. I remember *Harklow* dragged her anchor there one night, blowing in broadside on to the rocks and it was a long frightening struggle in the dark laying out anchors to kedge her off.

There is a magnificent avenue of red cedars between the canal bridges, and the old bog garden containing many interesting plants and shrubs has been beautifully restored. The favourite haunts and hiding-places for children used to be the bamboo plantation near the turf quay, which is no longer there now, and the climb through the curving branches of the great tree nearby.

Amongst other things Lord Lorton had a canal constructed from the south east corner of the lake to a neighbouring bog to bring down supplies of turf. We had tried on a number of occasions to find the entrance to this canal from the lake without success and so one day I determined to set off on foot to try to strike the canal further inland. I was ill prepared for such a search with neither map nor a clear idea of where to go. I set out from the new carpark by the old harbour and headed off through the estate gate deciding that if I kept turning left I would be bound to cross the canal. My persistence was rewarded and I was delighted not only to find the canal but to come upon it at an attractive bridge with a small lock. Lord Lorton obviously enjoyed all these construction works and he even built a mock castle wall around his

The lock and bridge on Lord Lorton's private canal for bringing down turf from the adjacent bog

gamekeeper's house on Cloontykilla Point so that it would look well from the lake, though it can hardly have given the unfortunate gamekeeper a very bright abode.

We love to cruise around Lough Key in calm weather, keeping well clear of the shoals and the rocky shoreline. Blackheaded gulls and terns enjoy the rocks jutting out of the water and seem to sense that we will not come near. There are some delightful anchorages in this most beautiful of lakes: you can anchor off Doon and climb the lower slopes of the Curlews for a breathtaking view of the lake studded with its many wooded islands or moor in the lee of the islands to explore them; there are ruins on both Church and Hermit islands but dense undergrowth and brambles defeated our best endeavours to find them. One of our favourite places is tucked away in the north west corner of the lake protected on all sides by the rising shores. Over the hill less than two miles away lies Lough Arrow, its waters discharging into Sligo Bay while the brackish waters of Lough Key have to travel many miles southward to reach the Atlantic.

People chartering boats are not encouraged to explore the lake but are instructed to stick to the main sailing courses. This makes the Boyle River a popular destination. The Shannon Commissioners removed the bends and dredged the river up to Boathouse Ford, which is two miles from the town of Boyle, but they did not attempt to extend the navigation any further because there is a rise of 34 feet from here to the bridge of Boyle. When we first visited this place there was a very dilapidated wooden jetty here and Drum Bridge was closed to traffic because it was falling down. So few were the visiting boats at that time that it was the custom to carve the boat's name on the jetty. Today there are always a number of boats here which, when the river is running hard, can make this a tricky place to turn a large boat like *Harklow*. It is a good idea to warp the boat around in an unhurried manner when you arrive, but for some reason we never seemed to be able to accomplish this manoeuvre without a great deal of shouting.

The walk into Boyle is a very pleasant one; the commissioners made this attractive road along the river which is a more direct route into Boyle than the old road across Drum Bridge. The town has an old world atmosphere and there are extensive ruins of a Cistercian Abbey, founded in 1161 on the site of an earlier religious settlement; the MacDermot family were closely connected with this foundation and some of the family joined the order. Although it survived the dissolution of the monasteries in the reign of Henry VIII, it did not escape in Elizabeth's reign and the lands finally came into the possession of the King family. The ruins require an unhurried visit for they contain some interesting architectural features not usually associated with the austere style of this order. The abbey buildings were subsequently used as a military barracks by Cromwellian soldiers who showed scant respect for their hallowed surroundings and did much damage.

I always have a feeling of regret as I leave Lough Key. It is to me a magic place with its wooded islands and its rich history, but I always know that some day soon I will be back.

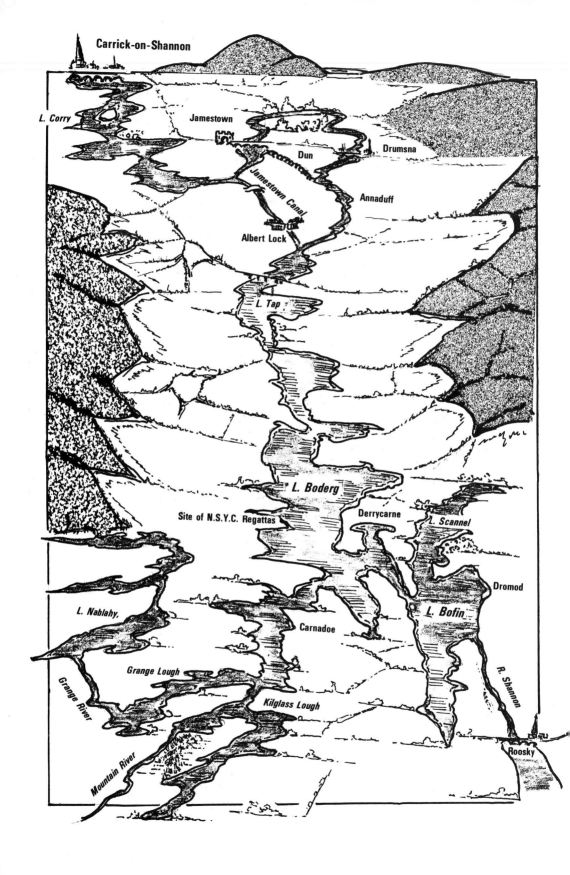

Carrick-on-Shannon

L. Corry

Jamestown

Dun

Drumsna

Annaduff

Jamestown Canal

Albert Lock

L. Tap

L. Boderg

Site of N.S.Y.C. Regattas

Derrycarne

L. Scannel

Dromod

L. Nablahy,

Carnadoe

L. Bofin

Grange Lough

Grange River

Kilglass Lough

Mountain River

R. Shannon

Roosky

THE GREAT LOOP
Carrick-on-Shannon to Roosky

LIKE Boyle, Carrick-on-Shannon has retained its old world atmosphere. It is easy to imagine the stagecoach thundering down the road from Boyle, taking the bend on to the old eleven-arch bridge, passing up the narrow main street and pausing outside the old thatched-roofed Bush Hotel before proceeding on to Dublin. The bridge had been erected in 1718 to replace an earlier one; the local landlord, Sir George St George, had enjoyed the toll rights on the first bridge in return for keeping it in repair and he was probably also involved in the construction of the eighteenth-century bridge. The St Georges appear to have been good lordlords. In 1786 Samuel Clifford addressed a poem about the Shannon to Richard St George and in the introduction he spoke about his patron in glowing terms:

I beheld with pleasure your beautiful improvements on the banks of the Shannon, and how your happy tenantry, basking in the sunshine of prosperity, see their annual rents returning into their own hands; nor can complain that their landlord is an absentee.

The poem itself, entitled *A Poetical Description of the Shannon*, is a wordy and lengthy work of doubtful poetic quality written in Miltonian style as the following example shows:

> But, above all, may Irish patriots strive
> To make thy inland navigation thrive!
> May commerce fill thy stream from shore to shore
> Spread the broad sail, and ply the well-tim'd oar.

John Brownrigg, who later became the engineer to the Directors General of Inland Navigation, surveyed the river in the 1790s and remarked: 'A Boat of Burden cannot in summer pass the Bridge of Carrick.' He said that the fifth arch from the west side was the best for navigation but it was only 28 ft 6 in. wide with about half the headroom of the present bridge. These comments suggest that some boats were using the river north of Carrick even though the navigation works had not been extended above the town.

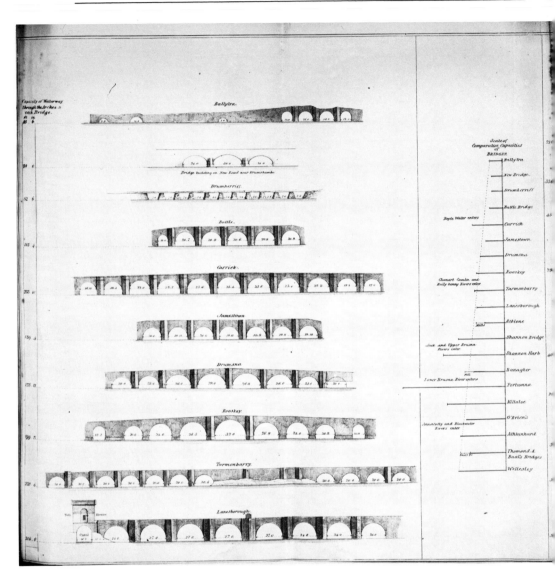

Upstream of the bridge a harbour had been excavated in 1829 on land donated by the St Georges and this was approached by a narrow channel. Looking out over the harbour was the eighteenth-century courthouse, which is still there today, and beyond the courthouse there was a large gaol built to the polygonal design common at that time. Lewis records that it had 'ten wards with some eighty separate sleeping cells for each prisoner and a good tread-mill: the prisoners are taught reading and writing by the master and

34

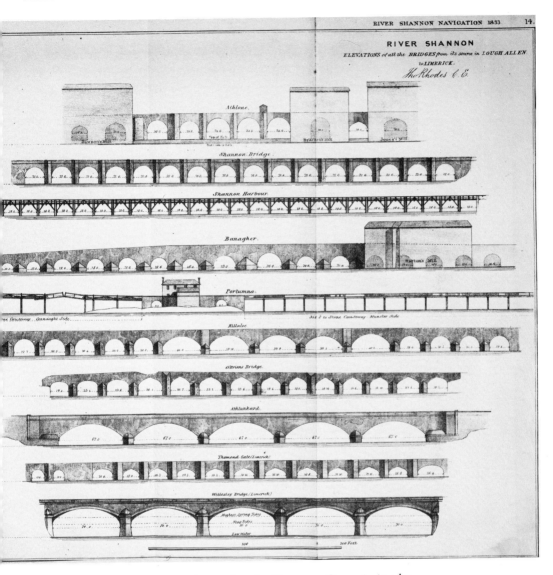

RIVER SHANNON NAVIGATION 1833   14.

The bridges on the Shannon drawn for the Shannon Commission by
Thomas Rhodes in 1833, showing them as they were before the commissioners
commenced work

the matron'. There was a hospital, a condemned cell and gallows and two
places of worship. Most of these buildings were still there when we first
visited the town by water in the 1950s and they had a distinct air of gloom

about them. They were eventually removed to make way for the marina development by the imaginative local authority who succeeded in attracting some of the largest boat hire businesses, bringing to the town a new wave of prosperity. The Carrick people have always shown an awareness of the river; the local rowing club goes back over a century and has recently produced a world class oarswoman.

In the 1830s, when Rhodes was surveying the river for the Shannon Commission, Carrick was a town of some 2,000 inhabitants. The commissioners decided to replace the old bridge and it was blown up in 1845. A shaft was driven into the centre of each pier, sunk to the level of the springing arch, and in each a 125 lb wad of gunpowder was placed: 'when fired the explosion was most successful'. The original plans envisaged an opening arch in the new bridge but in the end there were no opening spans made upstream of the Jamestown Canal because of financial constraints. However, fine quay walls were built and the old harbour above the bridge was enlarged. There were problems with the dams erected to dry out the old harbour area. It was reported in 1845 that 'the floods, which came down in October from the mountains, suddenly burst the dams, and it was with great difficulty the workmen were able to escape'.

Rhodes's plans showed a hotel on the narrow road near the bridge and this old hotel, Church's, was till there in the 1950s. I remember staying there with my husband, Vincent, who was a member of the Junior Bar on that Circuit and who had come to appear in a case concerning the navigation, of which more anon. Our room, in the manner of Irish hotels at that time, contained a large double and a single bed. After we had gone to bed, the Junior appearing on the other side arrived in our room and proceeded to sit on the bed and discuss the case. This was my first insight into the behind the scenes workings of the Irish legal system and I felt that it was most improper; I was further disillusioned by the proceedings in the court the next day which had a Gilbertian quality about them. I subsequently was told that the room we had been in was haunted but at least we were spared that sort of visitation!

We had been unable to book into the Bush Hotel because the learned members of the Senior Bar were monopolising that establishment. Since then I have come to know the Bush and its owner, Tom Maher, very well because Tom is one of the stalwarts of the IWAI in the area, and he is most knowledgeable about the Shannon and its history. The hotel has been in his family for six generations and I like his story about his grandmother, Ellen MacDermott, who applied to the Lord Lieutenant in 1900 for permission to transfer her licence to a temporary premises while the thatch-roofed inn was being replaced by the present building. She was granted her request and the licence was transferred to, of all places, the former Temperance Hotel.

With stores replenished by helpful shopkeepers, who will even deliver them to the quayside, it is time to head off downstream. I always associate the next stretch of river with the railway which follows the river closely from Carrick to Lough Bofin crossing it just below the Jamestown Canal. Although it is only visible from time to time, the roar of the diesels can be heard, especially at night when goods trains shatter the peace of the river. This was the old Midland Great Western Railway, which proved such a disastrous competitor to the Shannon Navigation, with its line to Galway crossing the Shannon at Athlone in the early 1850s and this line to Sligo, through Carrick, completed in 1862. The sound of the trains always reminds me of the tragedy of this really fine engineering achievement of the commissioners in constructing a navigation to accommodate the large steamers which had found their way on to the river, while even as they were presenting their final report to parliament in 1850, railways were radiating out from Dublin heralding the end of the Canal Age. They would, indeed, be happy to see their great navigation work coming into its own today.

Lough Corry is really three small lakes connected by wide stretches of river. The water is shallow outside the navigation channel, five to six feet in most places but we have never found any rocks here except close to the shore. It is not a lake we often stop in, except in fine weather, because there is little shelter from the surrounding countryside. South of Lough Corry, on the east bank, Klaus Mayr and his wife have opened a restaurant with mooring facilities. The river then widens out into another small lake with dense reed-beds around its shores, where there is more shelter from the land and it is a pleasant anchorage, despite the nearby railway and road.

South of this little lake, the river turns to the east and begins its great loop, part of this loop is not navigable and is by-passed by the Jamestown Canal. Just downstream of a small island to starboard, the river passes over an ancient fording place. Christine O'Brien Kennedy had mentioned to me that she had found signs of an old road leading down to the river here on the north bank and I noticed the turbulence passing over this shallow on the last occasion when we went down with the river in flood.

Christine and her husband, Brien, chose Jamestown Bridge to establish one of the very first boat hire businesses on the river. Brien had been working abroad and they decided to come back to Ireland and build their own small fleet which included a couple of sailing boats. This was back in the days before Bord Fáilte had become aware of the tourist potential of the river and so there were no grants to help firms to build up fleets for hire. The O'Brien Kennedys had the vision and courage to blaze the trail but in the end they found themselves competing with the large grant-aided concerns and they were forced to sell off their boats. They still live at Jamestown Bridge which is the limit of navigation for boats down the loop, although it is astonishing how many people have tried to take boats through this bridge, despite the smallness of the arches, the end-of-navigation notices and warnings in the guide books. In fact, the O'Brien Kennedys have found that there is never a dull moment between boats going through the bridge or being swept on to it by the stream while trying to round up for the quay.

The Shannon Commissioners found that they had to replace the bridge here and it subsequently suffered damage in the 1920s when one of the arches was blown up; approaching from upstream the arch that was substituted is still clearly visible being of a lighter colour than the rest of the bridge. If boats do go through this bridge by mistake they end up very quickly on the weir. This weir was built by the commissioners who first of all had to remove old mill works before building their open weir wall. By diverting the river down the Jamestown Canal, they succeeded in completely drying out the river with a dam while these works and the new bridge were being built.

The removal of the old mill works was supposed to improve the flow of water and prevent flooding upstream but, subsequently, there was much controversy about the shape and location of the commissioners' weir. It had been part of their brief to try to prevent flooding by their new works but later it was revealed that those aimed at relieving flooding had been curtailed because of overspending on the navigation works; while it was agreed that the flooding problem had been improved, there was criticism of the measures taken. It was suggested that the horseshoe shape had been adopted by the commissioners in the mistaken idea that it would allow more water to pass over it when, in fact, a straight wall would have been equally effective; the quantity of water passing over a weir is limited by the width of the river's channel above it. It was also suggested that the weir wall was constructed higher than the original plans approved by parliament. Studies carried out in the 1860s into the alleviation of flooding recommended the re-siting of this weir at a location upstream of the bridge where the approach channel would be less constricted but this was not implemented because of the cost and, instead, sluice gates were eventually fitted in the 1880s so that the flow could be regulated.

There is a good view of the weir from the main road on the far side of the village, a short walk from the bridge. Jamestown is an attractive little village but suffers from a constant stream of mainroad traffic passing through it. In the time of James I this place was made an important stronghold using the natural defences afforded by the river. It was granted a royal charter and surrounded by a wall 20 feet high and 6 feet thick; the area encompassed by the wall was a small rectangle about 300 yards by 100 yards, commencing about 150 yards from the bridge and extending to the remains of the old arch, part of which still stands today. Crenellations were added to it at the end of the eighteenth century by a local proprietor, Hugh O'Beirne. Spanning such a busy main road, it became an increasing traffic hazard and as juggernauts grew bigger, something had to be done with it. It was suggested that it should be taken down and re-erected in another location but, instead, it was decided to remove the upper portion of it. Maybe some day the village will be by-passed and it can be restored. Sir Charles Coote built a castle within the walls in 1822 but it changed hands several times and eventually the defences were thrown down by Sarsfield's army. There are fragmentary remains of this castle by the river. Jamestown had also been the site of an ancient Franciscan friary; a chapel lay inside the walled area but the old graveyard and ruined church, still visible today, were outside the walls.

The history of this area goes back a great deal further than these seventeenth-century activities. In prehistoric times the land enclosed by the fast flowing river offered a good strategic site. Using some natural high ground near the present bridge, an earthwork rampart was raised across the base of the loop. It is thought that this bank, known locally as 'The Dun', was 16 feet high and 100 feet wide at the base. Clear indications of it can still be traced by walking back towards the main road from Corlara Bridge, the bridge about halfway down the Jamestown Canal. The road from the canal to the main road actually passes at right angles through a gap in the old earthworks

Jamestown: the surviving arch of the old wall which formerly surrounded the place photographed by Mrs Shackleton in 1899; the top was removed in recent years

and they can be seen extending in both directions from this point. With the fast flowing river providing an excellent defence behind it, the Dun enabled quite a large area to be secured and traces of six raths have been found which were probably the sites of homesteads.

The early navigation engineers took the obvious course of making a canal to by-pass the rapids in the river, parallel to the old Dun but some distance beyond it. This canal was completed in the 1770s; it was S-shaped with a lock about halfway between Corlara Bridge and the present lock. When John Brownrigg inspected it in about 1794 for the Directors General of Inland Navigation, he remarked that they had been forced to make bends in the canal because of the hard rock which had been encountered. There was a fall of 5 ft 3 in. at the lock, which was 66 ft 6 in. long and 14 ft 3 in. wide, about half the size of the present lock. He said that the stonework was in good condition but like all the Shannon locks, by this time, the gates were 'greatly out of repair'. He was concerned about the condition of the banks of the canal, fearing that the water would flood out into the nearby Black Lough: 'It is apprehended that much mischief will be done here in the ensuing winter, when the Shannon rises three or four feet higher — for there is no person now empowered to lay out a shilling to prevent it.'

Eventually the traders, who were trying to operate on the upper Shannon, succeeded in persuading the Directors General to carry out some work. The gates were replaced, the lock was raised 9 inches and the banks of the canal strengthened. However, the complaints continued and in 1824 the Directors General wrote a plaintive letter to Mr Richard Purdy of the Mining Company of Ireland, who was operating the Arigna coalfield, explaining their difficulties in maintaining the canal banks which they said were originally formed upon a treacherous foundation. They added: 'The Board are ready to afford every Assistance in their Power towards the Extension and Application of the Capital of Ireland, and of affording employment to the People, consistent with due Attention to the Public Economy which is periodically and strictly enjoined them,' sentiments which have a familiar ring today. Brownrigg assured the navigation board that 'the Disposition to work the Mines in the Neighbourhood of Lough Allen with increased Spirit which has latterly arisen gives Promise of an encreased Trade upon the Shannon.' Some further work was carried out but the condition of the upper Shannon remained unsatisfactory.

The Shannon Commissioners decided to enlarge and straighten the canal when they commenced the major works in the 1840s; by this time the techniques of blasting through hard rock had been greatly improved. Rhodes used the spoil from the canal to fill in the Black Lough and he moved the site of the new lock further down the canal. Having studied Brownrigg's reports and Rhodes's plans, I decided to see if I could find any sign of the old canal works. It was obvious that the old lock would have disappeared completely in the widening operation but there might be some remains of the old canal where it had curved around to avoid the hard rock. I set off from the quay at the head of the canal and, crossing the road, I quickly came on the old canal excavations, which gave a good impression of its dimensions. Below Corlara Bridge I did find some traces of the other loop of the old canal on the east side but these were less discernible.

We always enjoyed passing through the Albert Lock because of the great chats with Mattie Bourke, the lockkeeper. He represented the old style lock-keeper but he moved with the times and became their shop steward. Even when the traffic increased and there were queues of boats assembled above and below his lock, he still moved at the same pace, leaning on the beam of the gate and letting the water in and out of the lock quietly. He would relate all the gossip of the river to us and he had a keen sense of humour and loved to tease the unsuspecting foreigners in chartered boats, telling them the most outrageous stories with the straightest of faces. On one occasion I came upon him chuckling away to himself and he told me that he had just told a German visitor that the reason why Douglas had such a large deck on *Harklow* was so that he could be picked off it by his helicopter! He had a wonderful turn of phrase, describing the impatient visitors as 'fidgety',

Jamestown Canal: Thomas Rhodes's plan showing the line of the old canal and the location of the original lock

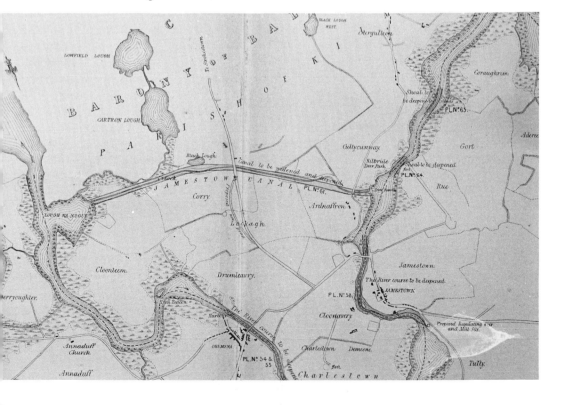

The late Mattie Bourke, the popular lockkeeper at Albert lock on the Jamestown Canal for many years

adding wryly: 'The Lord knows 'tis difficult to be so high-sterical.' Mattie retired in 1981 and moved from the lockhouse, where he had lived most of his life, to a new house on the nearby road but, sadly, he did not live long to enjoy his retirement.

The fast-moving visitors on the hire boats often miss out one of the loveliest little stretches of river, the other end of the great loop up to Drumsna. The river winds up past Annaduff Church, an attractive nineteenth-century Church of Ireland church with a backdrop of trees built on the site of the eighth-century Annaduff Abbey; the ruins here, however, relate to a later period. Between the church and the river lies the busy main road with cars speeding to and fro, making the voyager on the river truly grateful for the gentle pace of water travel. On the west bank of the next bend there is, I am told, a ringfort and a short distance upstream of this the eastern end of the great Dun meets the river. Rounding the next bend, Drumsna Bridge comes into view with the fine new quay and old harbour which is the limit of navigation. This bridge was not replaced by the Shannon Commissioners and was just underpinned and so it is therefore much older than the bridge at Jamestown; some years ago part of it succumbed to the heavy traffic and had to be rebuilt.

Anthony Trollope was stationed in Drumsna for a time as an employee in the postal service and drew on Headford House, the ruins of which are nearby, as the setting for the opening of his novel *The Macdermotts of Ballycloran*. He was later to move to another Shannonside post at Banagher and once again he drew on his experience of life in this small country town and of travel by passage boat on the Grand Canal. There is an amusing description of Drumsna in the log of a boat called the *Lally* owned by Ralph Smyth of Athlone which was cruising on the river in 1911:

It is the most godforsaken looking place I ever put foot on. I went into the stationer's shop, forgive the libel, and asked for a picture postcard of the bridge. The young woman opened her eyes and mouth and said 'Whaate'. I repeated the question. 'Noa, we doant keep the likes here'. The grass was growing over the cobblestone pathways. We were able to get two loaves of bread at 4d each.

How these little Shannon villages have changed since then. On one occasion, many years ago now, we decided to take the dinghy and try to work our way over the shallows and up through the bridge to see whether we could get up to Jamestown weir. The outboard was barely able to drive us against the stream but once through the bridge the river increased in depth and the current lessened. It was a delightful trip along a densely wooded stretch of river to where it widens out below the weir. I remember well the return trip down through the bridge as the current caught us and hurtled us along. If we had grounded on a shallow or struck the bridge travelling at this speed we would have more than likely capsized. In the boat was my small daughter, who was the only one wearing a lifejacket, my elderly husband, the dog and Paul, a young man with steady hand and nerve at the helm. I remember wondering which one to try to grab if we did go over and thinking that of us all, the dog had the best chance of survival. Nothing was said at the time but Paul did confide in me afterwards that he had been scared stiff, although nothing in his demeanour had betrayed this. How casual we were in those days about safety and the wearing of life jackets; some tragic accidents involving small boats in recent years have made us more conscious of the dangers of boating.

Having unwound itself from the great loop, the river broadens out into three lakes, the first one, Lough Tap, is very small but the other two, Boderg and Bofin are a considerable size. At the entrance to Lough Tap there is a railway bridge and although it was not built until the 1860s, for some reason the railway company were obliged to fit an opening span even though the

Roosky Bridge:
Rory O'Hanlon's
Firedrake passing through the
bridge in 1952; these bascule
bridges, designed by Thomas
Rhodes, have all been replaced

fixed bridges in the canal just upstream restricted the headroom immediately above it.

In the 1950s the Shannon navigation was threatened with strangulation because some of the local authorities wanted to replace the old opening bridges with fixed structures; they thought that the low volume of traffic on the river at that time did not warrant the extra expenditure involved in installing opening spans. While some of these bridges would have been sufficiently high to allow good headroom the others were so low that the navigation would have been virtually closed. This was the crisis situation which was to bring about the formation of the Inland Waterways Association of Ireland.

In 1952, two years before the association was formed, Rory O'Hanlon, encouraged by Harry Rice and my late husband, Vincent, decided to bring his yacht, a dragon class boat called *Firedrake*, up the river to draw attention to the problem and to make a gesture of defiance by demanding his statutory right of navigation through bridges that had not been opened for many years. He made the journey down the Grand Canal to Shannon Harbour using a 1½ hp outboard motor while his mast followed on board a CIE (Irish Public Transport) canal boat. Knowing that it was not mechanically possible to open Athlone road bridge, he decided not to ask CIE to open the railway bridge here either and so he did not step his mast until he had passed through both these bridges. He sailed across Lough Ree, Lanesborough bridge was duly opened, which involved disconnecting the water main, much to the delight of the local parish priest who said that it would flush out all the dirt in the pipes, and progress up river continued with Tarmonbarry and Roosky bridges being swung without incident. Rory had notified CIE that he would be seeking to have the railway bridge at Lough Tap opened and, when he arrived there, he found no less than 23 railwaymen sent down by special train from Dublin standing by to open the bridge. The mail train was allowed through and then the men set about working back the rails to enable the bridge to be swung. By this stage Rory's expedition was quite a movement; *Firedrake* was accompanied by Jim and Maureen Browne in the *Maga* and by Sean MacBride in his boat. With the bridge open the *Maga* commenced towing the dragon through but, despite the fact that everyone thought that she had sufficient headroom, her mast fouled telegraph wires overhead and she swung around and damaged her stern against the bridge.

Honour was satisfied, *Firedrake* was disentangled and they headed down-stream because, in any event, the fixed bridges in the Jamestown Canal made further progress upstream, with the mast stepped, impossible. Both Sean MacBride and Vincent, being lawyers, immediately began to think in terms of taking an action against the Minister for Posts & Telegraphs for obstructing navigation with his wires and causing the boat to be damaged, a case which would also have the advantage of focusing attention on the threatened closure of the navigation. It was this law case which had brought us to Carrick-on-Shannon and our stay in Church's hotel. In the event, the case was won in the Circuit Court but the Minister appealed and eventually the decision was reversed, the judge maintaining that the owner had failed to take reasonable precautions to ascertain if he had enough headroom to pass under the wires; the judge chose to ignore the wider issue of whether the Minister was infringing Rory's statutory right to navigate with a mast. At this stage Rory was far from pleased with his legal friends for involving him in considerable costs because the damage to the boat had, in fact, been negligible.

The navigation passes through the small reed-lined Lough Tap before opening out into Lough Boderg. Ahead and to the left are the trees of Derrycarne Forest Park. The west shore is more open and on the raised ground about halfway down the lake the tents for the North Shannon Yacht Club's (NSYC's) annual regatta used to be erected in the early 1900s. As

Jamestown Canal: unloading Water Wag dinghies into the canal in 1903; they had travelled down from Dublin to the nearby station

already mentioned the NSYC was formed in 1896 with racing on Lough Drumharlow but soon they moved south to Boderg for the annual regatta because this was a more convenient venue for the boats from Lough Ree and Lough Derg which came north for the regatta each year. The racing was in 15 to 20 ton keel boats, halfdeck centreboard boats and 18-foot open boats, all of miscellaneous sizes and shapes. They were even joined for the regatta by a fleet of Water Wags from Kingstown (as Dun Laoghaire was then known) from 1903-6; the Wags were brought down by rail to nearby Drumsna station and launched into the Jamestown Canal from handcarts.

The *Lally's* log described the scene: 'Boderg looks quite festive with yachts, steamers, motor boats and house boats, and the hill covered with tents.... We had a grand day, the yacht races were very good.' They returned down river with some of the boats and the Grand Canal Company's *Portumna* towed fifteen of the yachts, 'it was very exciting getting through the locks.' I can just imagine the scenes and the shouting. The movement of boats between regattas is well described in the log of the *Truant*, an 8-metre yacht owned by Paddy Murtagh of Athlone. The log which was written by his son, Dermot, records the scene in Athlone in 1923 where the tow of boats was assembled for the trip south to Lough Derg and it goes on to give a graphic description of encountering a storm on that lake when the fleet became dispersed and ran into difficulties with the boats under tow.

The 1914-18 War had brought a temporary cessation to the regattas and

Lough Boderg: a North Shannon Yacht Club regatta in about 1903

A group at a North Shannon Yacht Club regatta in
about 1914: standing (L to R) R. H. (Tulip) Newland,
Jocelyn Waller, Edgar Waller; seated (L to R) George
Devenish, Mrs Bob Devenish, Major Villiers Hunt;
seated on grass Mrs Jocelyn Waller, Mrs Edgar Waller
and Bob Devenish

when they were resumed in 1919 the venue was moved to a site on the west shore at the southern end of Lough Bofin. The north Shannon regattas continued through the 1920s with the new Shannon One Design making its first appearance in 1922 in an effort to make the open boat racing more evenly matched. In the 1930s support from the southern clubs was declining and in 1929 the venue was moved further downstream to Lough Forbes but this lake proved too small for keelboat racing. The regattas in the 1930s were small affairs and the last one was held in 1938. It is a measure of the increased interest in sailing in recent years that the NSYC was revived in 1984 and an annual event is held each autumn at Dromod with a good fleet of visiting SODs and a few local boats.

Opening off Lough Boderg are the Carnadoe Waters, one of my favourite places on the navigation course. I remember vividly the first time I penetrated into this world of narrow channels and waving reeds, as the boat threaded its way deeper and deeper into places remote from the outside world. I still feel the same thrill every time I come in here. Harry Rice used to call it 'pygmy country' and it is easy to imagine little men with bows and arrows lurking in the rushes. Harry's description sums it up best:

Here amongst the reed beds that sway like ocean rollers in the breeze, one might easily imagine meeting a hippopotamus or a reed buck venturing out timidly at dusk, apprehensive of a hungry lion creeping silently upon its trail. One could picture encountering a pygmy in a loin cloth or a ragged 'Trader Horn', complete with musket!

For me this offshoot of the navigation evokes all that is best about the Shannon. Here nature still seems to be in accord with man and it grieves me greatly that these waters are not a nature reserve; this means that men can come here with their guns and shoot the birds. Efforts by the IWAI to have this area declared a reserve were defeated by local interests that make money by providing accommodation for these sportsmen.

It is safe to wander in and out of the little bays and around the islands for there are no rocks here; the rushes mark the limit of deep water, the dark green rushes indicating deep water and the light green the shallower places. We love to come in here and anchor the boat 'Shannonstyle', driving her bow up into the rushes and leaving her stern in deep water while we spend the day quietly enjoying the varied bird life around us.

The Shannon Commissioners opened up these waters, replacing the bridge at Carnadoe with a higher navigable arch and making a good quay here. Once through the bridge and past Donal Conroy's yard (he is a wizard at fibreglass repairs), the reed-lined shores make it difficult to see where you are on the chart and it is easy to become confused about which way to go. Often there does not seem to be any way opening out ahead until you move up closer, but it does not really matter if you do take a wrong turn and find yourself in a cul de sac. After weaving your way through narrow channels and little lakes to the southern end of Carnadoe lough, there are two courses open to you, one passage leads into Grange lake and the other into Kilglass. Just by the entrance to Grange lake we have once or twice stolen a root from a fantastic bed of white water lilies. While the yellow ones are fairly common on the Shannon, there are only a few places where white ones are to be found; another place where they thrive is on Lough Key near the Rockingham canals.

The course through Grange lake to the quay in the Grange River is more open and straightforward. We usually prefer to dig into the rushes opposite the entrance to the Grange river instead of using the quay or the new harbour of the Silver Eel. Grange was formerly quite a busy station with goods for nearby Strokestown but when Harry Rice visited here in the 1950s he remarked on the fact that there were a number of houses and stores all in good condition but with their windows boarded up and no sign of life; today there is no longer even any sign of these buildings.

Several times we have set out on an expedition here with the dinghy to try to work our way up the Grange river. Many years ago Peter and Maureen Denham had launched a canoe into Lough Nablahy and had come down through the maze of little lakes into the Grange river. We hoped to get through to these lakes but the first part of the river was too shallow to float us in the dinghy and so the crew had to wade through the bridge and up the first stretch of river pushing the dinghy. It was still shallow up to the next bridge about a quarter of a mile upstream and for some distance above this, but then the river became quite deep. Unfortunately, when we reached this far we ran out of time and had to turn back before we arrived at the first lake and, on our next attempt, we encountered a formidable barbed wire fence under the second bridge which we were unable to get through. Maybe some day we will make it.

For many years it was not possible to get into Kilglass lake because the Carrigeen Cut had silted up at the entrance. We did manage to get through on one occasion in *Hark* when the water was high. I remember there was a man waving wildly on the shore trying to indicate to us that we were not following the correct navigation course, he did not realise that we were exploring. Once over the bar we found the cut was deep and clear with every detail on the bottom visible. We continued into the lake and up the Mountain river until the road bridge was in sight where there is a good pool for turning; now that the entrance has been dredged, boats can pass freely into this lake. I had always assumed that this was a natural channel opened out to make it navigable but I discovered that it is an artificial cut made by the Shannon Commissioners who closed off the original channel from Kilglass lough which had formerly discharged into Grange lake.

Kilglass jetty used to be a very rickety affair, sloping at an alarming angle. You came alongside in a gingerly manner and stepped on to it at your peril. Then in 1971 John Weaving put in a good floating jetty marking a rock with a 'boat aground' symbol in typical Weaving style. John Weaving is a most remarkable character, who knows more about the Shannon than the rest of us ever will. He is one of nature's philosophers who many years ago opted out of the rat race and went to live on a canal boat. A stickler for accuracy, John insists on the use of the term 'canal boat' which was that used by the old Grand Canal Company men, who never called their boats 'barges'. Since then he has travelled the river installing jetties and dredging out harbours. When the hire boat business expanded, he became the expert at hauling boats off rocks and he is constantly on call for this operation. He is particularly knowledgeable about the flora and fauna of the river having lived in harmony with nature all these years. Although he has been up and down the river so often he must know every yard of it, he will tell you that he learns new things about it every time he travels its waters. In his own quiet and unassuming way he has done more than anyone to help river users, often marking dangerous waters and helping to provide facilities. It was his extremely accurate charts which formed the basis for the Shannon guides of the past. He has a very lively sense of humour and some years ago when he was working on the navigation charts for one of the Shell Guides to the Shannon, he received a communication from the publishers asking for details of hazards on the river. Due to a typing error this reached him as a request for information about 'Shannon lizards' and he obliged with a beautiful selection of prehistoric monsters! He has an endless fund of stories, an evening listening to John reminiscencing is a memorable experience.

We usually opt for our customary Shannon moorings in the rushes opposite the jetty and it is a pleasant walk up the hill to the little post office-cum-shop from where there is a magnificent view of the group of lakes. We penetrated through the rushes in the dinghy into the upper end of the lake on one occasion and landed on the shore for a stroll but had to beat a hasty retreat back to the dinghy when we saw a large irate bull bearing down on us at speed. There always seems to be so much to do here that I have never had time to look for the ringfort which is on the tongue of land between Kilglass and Grange lakes; this is an indication that early man lived in this area.

Back in the main navigation, we often go up the southern arm of Lough

Fallon

Magnum Bicapulia
Often seen to take a jar
With clients in Sean Fitgs bar
By Athlone Docks.

One of John Weaving's Shannon 'lizards'

Boderg where there is a pleasant anchorage at the top of the bay and a quiet lane to walk along. There was an important fording place at the Derrycarne Narrows in the past; a skirmish took place here between a Williamite contingent and a group of Sarsfield's forces, and a mound known as 'James's Heap' marks what probably was the mass grave of those who fell but I have never succeeded in finding this. Lord Harlech chose this lovely spot to build a house, facing south, looking down Lough Bofin. The Nesbitts lived here for a time, then the Kiernan family, who were known for their hospitality and, eventually, it was purchased by Commander Mack, RN, who had the reputation for being sharp with people who landed on his property. When the yacht *Firedrake* was making its progress downriver after the contretemps with the telegraph wires, Rory wanted to spend the night here; one of the crew was sent ahead by car wearing his RNVR (Royal Navy Volunteer Reserve) tie to seek permission. The ruse worked and not only were they allowed to put up a bell tent on the front lawn but a bucket full of fresh milk arrived down from the house. When the Macks left, the property was bought by the Land Commission and today it is a forest park with a carpark on the site where the house once stood. The two black beacons are connected by a submerged weir wall and so it is dangerous to approach the 'boathouse quay'; the attractive old boathouse has now been removed. The water is shallow also at the quay around the corner and we usually anchor and row ashore to enjoy the walks.

There is a tendency to hug the east shore moving down Lough Bofin and we have several times managed to strike a shallow near the first black stake. Again the southern arm of Lough Bofin provides an opportunity to get off the main navigation but it is not as easy to get in close to the shore and there is a busy main road at the head of the bay. Vincent always said there were shoals in the bay called Lough Scannel but an aerial survey of this lake did not show anything. However, it is close to the railway and main road and so we have never ventured in there to see if he was right. Lough Bofin is not a deep lake, averaging 8 or 9 feet, and it is particularly subject to sudden squalls because of the configuration of the land around it.

In the 1960s we always chose to overnight in the little harbour at Dromod in preference to staying at Roosky. It was a delightful haven in those days and apart from the family living in the little house at the harbour, we never saw a soul. This harbour was constructed in 1829 for the sum of £194 7s 0d; Francis Nesbitt of Derrycarne gave the land free and contributed £69 14s 8d towards the cost. I never cease to wonder when I turn up these figures how they arrived at these precise amounts. The house was formerly a store and the marks of the double doors are visible in the gable wall. The Board of Works lowered the wall of the harbour to suit the modern cruisers by pushing back the top few feet and then, more recently, constructed a new harbour beside it. It is a fine big concrete affair with a breakwater to deal with the swell that rolls in with south westerly winds. Even with all this space you have to pull in here early in the afternoon to get a berth for the night; local boats permanently moored in this harbour and at other new harbours on the river are causing a problem, forcing the Board of Works to consider taking action against them. Gone are our quiet evenings at Dromod and our peaceful haven but I suppose we should have realised that we were in a Catch 22 situation, we could not expect to preserve the navigation and keep it to ourselves.

Drumsna Bridge photographed by Mrs Shackleton in 1899

North Shannon Yacht Club regatta on Lough Bofin in 1920

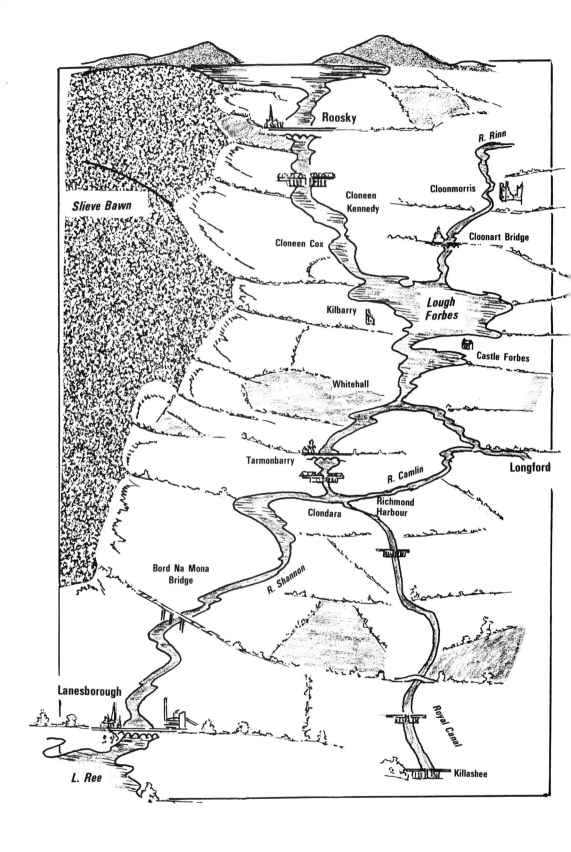

Roosky

Slieve Bawn

Cloneen
Kennedy

Cloneen Cox

R. Rinn

Cloonmorris

Cloonart Bridge

Kilbarry

Lough
Forbes

Castle Forbes

Whitehall

Longford

Tarmonbarry

R. Camlin

Clondara

Richmond
Harbour

Bord Na Mona
Bridge

R. Shannon

Lanesborough

Royal Canal

L. Ree

Killashee

TERMON LANDS

Roosky to Lanesborough

THE OLD canal which originally by-passed the shallows at Roosky bridge is of particular interest because it is the only section of the old eighteenth-century navigation works which remains exactly as originally constructed; all the other locks on the river were either altered or replaced at one time or other. The canal was entered by a channel west of Pigeon Island, the small island upstream of the bridge at Roosky. It ran parallel to the river on the west side rejoining it near the present lock. The old lock was at the lower end

Roosky: Thomas Rhodes's plan showing the old canal; the lock was at the downstream end

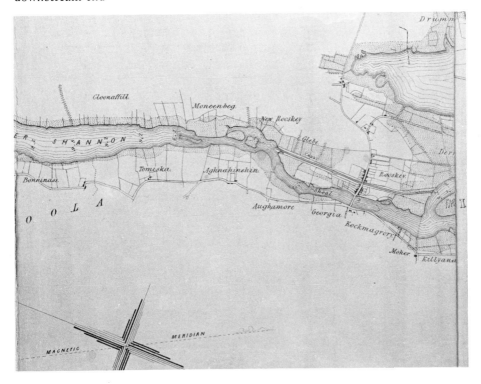

of the canal and it is probably best approached from the village down along the towpath. The time that we went to look at it our boat was moored above the present lock and rowing across the river we worked our way across a field and a drainage channel to find it. This exercise called down the wrath of the lockkeeper's wife who was still recovering from the shock of having seen two visitors swept through the sluices a few days earlier, fortunately without any ill effects except some damage to their dinghy. They were indeed fortunate to survive such an accident; it is easy to be unaware of the close proximity of the weir and to get caught in the pull from the sluices, particularly when there are a good number of the gates open. We knew about the weir and kept well up river away from it but I expect it should be admitted we were not setting a good example using our dinghy in this area of danger.

I found the old lock fascinating even though it was greatly overgrown. The stones used in its construction were much smaller and more irregular than those used in later locks but apart from this there was very little evidence of its great antiquity; it would have been built about 1769. There had been a lockhouse but this was allowed to fall into disrepair and was demolished by a very contentious local millowner called Mr Tredennick. He had built his mill in the village in 1797, after the construction of the canal, and his millrace ran parallel to the canal between it and the river. Because of the small amount of traffic using the canal, he reckoned that no one would notice if he increased the volume of water to his mill by rolling a few stones into the canal to reduce the amount of water passing down it. The result was that boats ran aground in the canal until the Directors General were prevailed upon to remove the obstructions. They decided reluctantly that it was futile to take the miller to law over the incident.

They also carried out some repairs to the lock and it was reported to them that there was 'flagrant abuse and imposition being practised in the conduct of these works'. John Nesbitt of Derrycarne was the overseer and with the approval of the engineer in charge, Mr Murphy, he had removed men to help him with his harvest while still returning them as working for the Navigation Board: 'that several others are returned by Murphy who hardly worked at all, that the carpenters do but very little, and that no Public Business was ever carried on with less attention'. Nesbitt was fired but Mr Murphy survived the exposure of these irregularities.

The canal continued to give trouble and Rhodes reported finding a vessel aground there in 1833. This boat, belonging to Mr Farrell of Clondara, had left Killaloe on 20 July for Lough Allen but there were frequent delays in the canals and the boat constantly had to be lightened by off-loading some of her cargo to get her through so that in the end she did not arrive back until 1 October.

At first Rhodes recommended widening the canal and rebuilding the lock to larger dimensions with a swivel bridge in the village. He also proposed replacing the old nine-arch bridge and making a U-shaped weir above it. This plan was eventually dropped in favour of abandoning the canal, dredging out the river channel and making a new lock and weir downstream of the village. Rhodes made use of steam-operated bucket dredgers which he had designed and perfected on the Caledonian Canal; three of these dredgers were built for the Shannon works, patriotically named *Victoria*, *Albert* and *Prince*.

Although the opportunity to obtain work must have been appreciated at this time of famine, there were problems with the work force at Roosky when some troublemakers stirred up the men to stage a 'combination' to seek higher wages. A report in 1844 suggests that this trouble was shortlived:

The conduct of the workmen during the past year had been generally satisfactory. Some bad characters attempted at the commencement of the works at Roosky to prevent the peasantry of the surrounding district from working at the usual liberal rate of pay given by the contractor and by threats and violence they succeeded in their efforts for some days, but the energy displayed by the magistrates and constabulary soon restored order, and everything since has proceeded in a quiet and satisfactory manner.

The 'liberal' wages ranged from 1s to 2s per day depending on how much work the labourer achieved. Each man worked in a gang of 10 or 12 getting from 5d to 7d per cubic yard; at first some resistance had been offered to the introduction of 'piece work' instead of a fixed daily wage but soon the men realised they could earn better wages that way. In the five-year period from 1842-47 an average of about 2,000 men per day were employed on the works throughout the entire length of the river but it is ironic that by 1846, famine and emigration had so decimated the work force that it was becoming difficult to find labourers during the harvest period; for example, one report stated: 'Labourers were scarce in consequence of the lateness of the crops, which delayed operations considerably.'

In 1847 the water was diverted down the old canal, a dam was constructed and the river bed was dried out, but the operation was not without its problems:

Early in August the work was unwatered and the necessary arrangements as regards pumps were almost completed when, on 23 August, the upper stank burst, and flooded the work; it was immediately repaired and the pits unwatered again in a few days. The excavation was carried on by night and by day, and by the exercise of great care and watchfulness, it was completed on 27 September, and so great were the difficulties to be contended against, that the workmen and their tools were scarcely removed from the enclosure before the dam burst in three places and the whole was flooded.

A new bridge was constructed and an opening span inserted on the east side to a design by Rhodes himself and made by Mallets of Dublin. A quay was made on the west side, and the shallows, which were about halfway between the bridge and the new lock, were removed; and the new lock and weir wall were built.

The commissioners subsequently leased the fishery at the outfall of the weir and the lessee erected a wickerwork obstruction to catch the fish. In the 1860s when bad flooding occurred the local people "gathered en masse to take away the wicker work' which they reckoned was preventing the flood waters from flowing away but the magistrates prevailed on them not to take the law into their own hands. This obstruction was probably removed in the 1860s when bad flooding occurred the local people 'gathered en masse to flow of water to be controlled, as was done at Jamestown weir.

John Cowan who had surveyed the river way back in the 1790s, published a chart and *A Description of the Upper Part of the River Shannon* in 1795. He described this stretch of river between Roosky and Tarmonbarry as: 'prettily diversified with woods and well enclosed fields, presenting a scene somewhat paradisaical to a mind susceptible of rural beauties'. Another visitor, Alfred Webb, one hundred years later in 1895 brought his 17-ton yacht down the Grand Canal for a trip on the river. He was so impressed that he wrote a little book entitled *Irish Navigable Inland Waterways* in which he expressed surprise that they were 'little spoken of and rarely visited by the ordinary tourist'. He summed up his overall impression of the river in this way:

Upon these water there is no scenery specially grand or sublime — there are no mountains much above 2,500ft high, no beetling cliffs, no waterfalls. But I never saw lovelier colouring, more tender views of hill and mountain, more beautiful wooded islands, wider expanses of varied level country, more glorious skies and sunsets; never felt softer balmier, more health-giving air.

Mrs Jane Wigham Shackleton, well known for her pioneering photography in the 1890s, visited the Shannon with her sons in 1899; she was a relative of Alfred Webb's and may have had her interest awakened by his account of the river. They brought their 18-foot Norwegian-built boat by rail from Leixlip to Carrick-on-Shannon and spent 10 days on the river rowing downstream to Killaloe, paying 4s for her permit. She must have been an extremely unusual voyager on the river at that time and she records in her log of the trip that they were greeted at Roosky by 'the lockkeeper, an aged man, and very much the worse for drink, who was very complimentary addressing me as "My Lady" and "Duchess". W. and J. had to open and close the lockgates as he was quite incapable'. She remarked on the small number of boats encountered on the trip: 'rowing on a mile or so (just below Roosky) we passed a canal boat *The Pride of Westmeath*. It was moving slowly along propelled by two men pulling, with a sail up to help them. This was the only sign of traffic we saw between Carrick and Athlone'. Her generation were expert letter writers and kept very detailed diaries and her log is full of some most interesting observations:

In these days when almost everyone travels, our thoughts during the winter evenings are often occupied with plans as to where our next summer holiday will take us. Then comes Cook, Dr Simm with their beautifully illustrated pamphlets on travel, and tempting tours arranged so economically, and many are thereby tempted to go further afield without turning their attention to the attractions of our native land. I am not one of those who think that encouraging streams of tourists, especially the 'tripper' kind, to over-run Ireland, will be of any real advantage to the country or its inhabitants, but I do think that our countrymen might often do better instead of running with the crowd to English, Welsh or foreign tourist resorts, if they devoted what time they could spare to exploring the beautiful scenery with which Ireland abounds and which possesses an indefinable charm peculiarly its own.

We always used to stop at Roosky to get some rashers in the village at the bacon factory shop. Attempting to do this recently, I was told that it was not possible to buy rashers from the factory any longer, they are all dispatched to suppliers and the vacuum-packed ones available in Roosky come in to the village from a different factory. Such is progress. It was here in Roosky that another of the very early boat hire businesses was set up when Dick McGarry built up a small fleet of boats for hire but, like the O'Brien Kennedys, he was unable to compete when the large companies moved in.

A fine wide stretch of river below Roosky is followed by the fords of Clooneen Kennedy and Clooneen Cox. Eel weirs had been erected at these fords and when the eighteenth-century navigation works were being carried out these two places were by-passed by two short canals. However, the traders continued to experience difficulty here and complained to the Directors General about Clooneen Cox: 'There is an annual Patron near that Place the latter end of summer when the water is low, and the Country People regularly on that occasion refill the Place to make a fordable Passage between the two Counties.' The Shannon Commissioners abandoned the two side canals, dredged out a channel in the river and removed the eel weirs. They appear to have partly removed two islands halfway between the two old fording places which are marked today by two red stakes in midstream, with the channel close to the east shore. I have seen a large boat high and dry here; possibly, the helmsman, blinded by the sun, went the wrong side of the first one and then tried to pass between them to get back on course. This is one of those places where the channel is unusually far over to one side of the river and should be marked by pairs of markers, black and red, making it very clear that the channel lies between the markers. It is easy if there is an inexperienced person at the helm for them to become confused when confronted by a marker of just one colour.

The 'patron' referred to was probably at Kilbarry which lies a short distance from the shore on the west side. I have never tried to approach it from the river, it might be difficult to get into the shore because of the dense beds of reeds, but I have driven to it, taking a turning off the road from Roosky to Tarmonbarry. This was a monastic settlement, founded originally by St Barry, on an island of high ground with marshy land all round it making it easier to defend from attack. There were originally seven churches here and Richard Hayward said that he traced the ruins of three of these and the base of a round tower. I waded through the long grass in the little graveyard to the ruins of the main church but there was no sign of the other churches or tower and I did not have time to search for them. There is a local tradition that a night spent within the walls of this ruin could bring about a cure for mental illness. St Barry is said to have arrived on the east shore of the river and failing to find any boat to make the crossing, he stepped on to a large boulder which floated him across. St Barry's 'ferry-boat', a stone 5 feet by 4 feet and 3 feet high was later identified and removed to the nearby church at Whitehall.

When preparing the text for the IWAI Shannon guide, I included all this information and received an irate letter from a gentleman who lives on the other side of the river who said that 'No one believes these Kilbarry fairy tales.' He upbraided me for omitting all mention of the ancient twelfth-century abbey church at Cloonmorris, about a mile's walk from Clonart Bridge on the River Rinn, where there is an interesting ogham stone. He added that I would have been better employed mentioning that George Calvert, Lord Baltimore, the founder of the state of Maryland and the city of

Baltimore, came from Johnston's Bridge, the second bridge up the River Rinn. The River Rinn was dredged and opened up as far as Clonart Bridge in 1970 and, although this is the limit of navigation for cruisers, it is possible to reach Johnston's Bridge in a dinghy where, in addition to being the place George Calvert came from, there is an adjacent pub to make the journey worth while.

Leaving the mouth of the Rinn one morning in dense fog, Douglas insisted that it would be a simple matter to steer a course across Lough Forbes, pick up the navigation channel on the far bank and follow the shoreline downstream. Using the wake to steer by, we set off but failed to reach the far shore in the anticipated time. Douglas was prevailed upon to drop the anchor and wait for the sun to burn up the fog; it is a very usual occurrence on the Shannon to have dense fog like this in fine weather which is quickly burnt up by the sun during the forenoon. When the fog did lift, we discovered that we were right back near the entrance to the river where we had started out from: he had actually steered around in a circle. It was a salutary lesson in the importance of carrying a compass aboard if you intend to navigate in fog.

Lough Forbes is shaped like an egg timer with a narrow passage separating the upper and lower lakes. Passing through this passage there is a brief vista of Castle Forbes which is sited at the end of a long avenue of trees. These lands were first granted to Sir Arthur Forbes by James I in 1619 and he built a castle here which was enlarged in the nineteenth century. There is a sharp

Castle Forbes. *Lawrence*

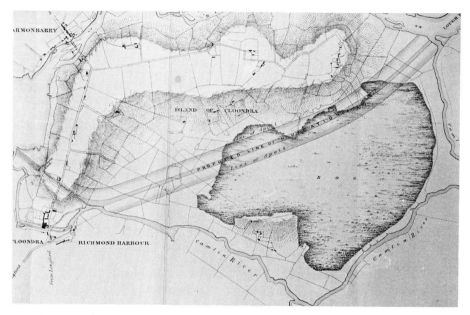

Clondara: Thomas Rhodes's plan showing the old navigation via the River Camlin and his plan to make a new canal which was later abandoned when he decided to use the river

Richmond Harbour: the Delany fleet, the *Changsha*, The *La Vague II* and the *Oudra* laid up for the winter about 1928

contrast in the view on either side of the lake: to the east there is the fine wooded estate of Castle Forbes and to the west the land is low and marshy.

The next stretch of river to Tarmonbarry is narrow and fast flowing. It had so many shoals that it daunted the early navigation engineers and they decided to by-pass it by using the River Camlin which ran parallel to the Shannon here and which could be linked by two short lengths of canal. When the Shannon Commissioners came along, they considered that it would not be practical to try to widen the Camlin route and they contemplated making a new canal from Lough Forbes to Tarmonbarry. In the end, however, they decided that it would be better to tackle the shoals in the river. Some of these were removed by using the dredger but where there was a large accumulation of rock, coffer dams were erected and the area was dried out with pumps so that the men could work at breaking up and removing the rock. Today the old Camlin navigation has been opened up again providing an alternative route for boats. It is a very attractive stretch of waterway but we found it narrow and twisty with overhanging branches; we swept our chimney off on one of them and there was a certain amount of discussion about what we would do if we met a boat coming the other way.

At Clondara the River Camlin was linked with the Shannon by a short canal with one lock; this became the terminus of the Royal Canal which was completed to here in 1817. The occasion was marked by the attendance of the Lord Lieutenant of the day, the Duke of Richmond, and the harbour named Richmond Harbour in his honour. Although the Royal Canal is closed to navigation, access to the harbour from the Shannon has been restored and boats can lock up via the Camlin and enjoy the nineteenth-century atmosphere which has been carefully preserved; the old stores and offices have been converted into dwellings with a pub on the corner, the dry dock has been refurbished and beside it is the lock down into the Camlin with its typical Royal Canal lockhouse with recessed windows. Without a map it is rather difficult to see how the navigation links up with the Shannon. Standing at the lock and looking north, beyond a line of trees, the canal down into the Shannon branches off to the left, while the Camlin route to Lough Forbes continues on under the new bridge and, looking south, the river passes over a small weir to create a millrace for the distillery before rejoining the Shannon. In the 1830s 70,000 gallons of whiskey per year were produced here with a work force of about seventy people and it subsequently became a corn mill. The cars now speed across the new by-pass bridge at the head of Richmond Harbour, leaving Clondara with its narrow bridges in peace; a contrast between the urgency of today's travellers and the more leisurely days of the canal passage boat.

The story of how the Royal Canal Company was authorised by the Irish parliament to build this canal, running parallel to the Grand Canal, has fascinated canal historians over the years. I have told this story in detail in *Ireland's Inland Waterways;* suffice it here to say that the idea is supposed to have come from a disgruntled director of the Grand Canal Company, who was a retired shoemaker, and who felt he had been insulted by his fellow directors. I have identified this man with a fair degree of certainty as one, William Cope, who was aided and abetted by his business partner, John Binns. They were both to lose a great deal of money in the venture as indeed did many other shareholders; William Cope was declared a bankrupt and John Binns died a broken man. In the end the government was forced to take over the task of completing the canal, using public funds in an effort to save something from a venture which had already been heavily subsidised and to protect, so far as possible, the interests of the many small investors. Once completed it was handed over again to the reorganised company but the canal was never very successful and was eventually closed to navigation in 1961. Happily, the story does not end there because in recent years a campaign to save the canal was launched which has met with such interest and support from local authorities and the communities who live along its route that it is hoped to open it again to navigation in about ten years. A walk back along the line from Richmond Harbour will give some indication of the problems which have to be overcome at this western end; Rinnmount lock (the 45th from Dublin) is less than ½ mile from the harbour, not far from the lock Bord na Mona have made a temporary crossing and a mile further along the rather overgrown towpath is Begnagh Bridge where a culverted road crossing has been driven through the bed of the canal with the old hump-backed bridge lying rather forlornly alongside.

Back in Clondara, in the grounds of the Catholic church there are the ruins of an ancient church; this had been the site of a monastery and hospice for the poor. The word 'termon' means 'fenced off lands belonging to the church', so the land around here would have been the church lands of St Barry's community. In the churchyard, facing out towards the road, there is a gravestone dating back to 1793 on which is inscribed the following sobering piece of verse:

> Stay Passenger
> See where I be
> As you are now
> So once was I
> And as I am
> So shall you be
> Prepare for death
> And follow me.

On the road by the bridge over the canal leading out into the Shannon from the River Camlin there is a little two-storey lockhouse which was built in about 1760 to a design by Thomas Omer, one of the principal engineers of the Commissioners of Inland Navigation. Unfortunately, this house has now been empty for some years and it will be sad if it is not preserved. There are a number of Omer's houses at other places down along the river and on the Grand Canal and Lagan Navigation. Thomas Omer was attracted to Ireland by the spate of canal building in the mid-eighteenth century; he had been engaged in navigation works in England but it is thought that he originally came from Holland. He and another foreign engineer, William Ockenden, were entrusted by the commissioners with carrying out most of the works at this time in preference to using Irish talent, but the commissioners' faith was to prove misplaced; most of the early works had to be reconstructed and some of them were eventually abandoned. The lock leading out into the Shannon is the original eighteenth-century Shannon Navigation lock but it probably received some attention when the Royal Canal was opened and was further restored by the Shannon Commissioners, after which it was difficult to identify the older parts of it.

When the Shannon Commissioners decided to abandon the Camlin route and run the navigation down the Shannon from Lough Forbes to

Clondara: the early Shannon navigation lockhouse designed by Thomas Omer which was built about 1760

Tarmonbarry, it was their original intention to underpin the old bridge at Tarmonbarry but when they dried out the piers it was found to be in such a dangerous condition that a new bridge had to be erected with an opening span on the west side of the same design as the opening bridge at Roosky. The area for the new lock was surrounded with a coffer dam and when the lock had been completed, work on the weir commenced. The final section of the weir was not closed off until all the work upstream had been completed, so that this whole difficult stretch of river could be kept at a low level. There were problems from time to time as this report for 1844 indicates:

The excavation for the lock pit was commenced in April, and a steam engine erected for unwatering the same; the work was successfully carried on until the month of August; on the sixth a sudden and heavy rain came down, which lasted for several days; the rise in the river was very great, and, notwithstanding the exertions made to raise and strengthen the works, the water overtopped them, and the dam at the south end of the lock gave way; thus a stop was put to the operations until September, when the water in the river having fallen considerably, the work was resumed.

They obviously had bad summers occasionally in those days as well.

Tarmonbarry lock about 1920

In *A New Oarsman's Guide*, published in the 1890s, the description of Tarmon is not very complimentary and it adds: 'The only inn is a miserable little pot-house.' Today things are different. At the top end of the village is the old dance hall. This was one of the original 'ballrooms of romance' and was a very popular venue in the 1950s and 1960s when the dancing craze took the country by storm. Richard Hayward tells of meeting an old man at Kilbarry, nearby, who showed his concern about these dens of iniquity in words reminiscent of O'Casey:

Of late I arose in the public assemblies to make the heavens ring with my distaste of the temples of Terpsichore, and they, filled with the sound of idle feet shuffling to the savage patterns of negroid tom-toms.

Two most unlikely enthusiasts at the Tower ballroom in those days were Dr and Mrs Delany, my in-laws. He was a much-loved GP and county coroner for Longford but as he grew older he took to moving out to Tarmon for the summer to live aboard the *La Vague II*. Here they gave a great welcome to visitors arriving by water and he even held 'surgery sessions' for the local people. His paid hand for many years was a man called Mick Donlon, known to everyone as 'The Pirate'. Mick had lived a very eventful life including driving a locomotive somewhere in the Middle East for a period during hostilities there. He was my husband, Vincent's, early mentor and taught him to sail and other nautical accomplishments. The Donlons came from Garrykennedy, a little place on Lough Derg on the south Shannon. His

Mick Donlon and his father 'ould Mick'

brother Tom was skipper of the canal boat 102B which belonged to the Wallers, maltsters of Banagher, and his father, 'ould Mick' also worked the boats and was a giant of a man.

For many years the lockkeeper at Tarmon was John Bourke, a brother of Mattie's, and he always had a special welcome for any of the Delany family. His assistant, Tom Feeney, who is the lockkeeper now, is a modest man who risked his life a number of times trying to rescue people who went too close to the weir and were swept through the sluices. All too predictably, it was not until a young visitor from Germany lost his life that steps were taken to place a boom across the river to prevent such tragedies.

The river is very shallow between Tarmon and Lanesborough and the multiplicity of markers indicates how important it is to stay in the channel. It is an open and exposed stretch of river with great tracts of bog stretching away to the west and in the distance Slieve Bawn which, although it rises to only some 800 feet, is a prominent landmark when coming upstream all the way up the middle Shannon. Away to the north the mountains around Lough Allen are receding, an indication of how far the river has travelled south. Ahead, the Lanesborough power station appears on the skyline and the river passes beneath a new bridge, built in 1957, to bring the turf from the bog to the power station. In a normal year 300,000 tons of powdered turf and 110,000 tons of sod turf are used and all this activity on the bog and in the power station has brought great prosperity to this area although the bad summers of 1985 and 1986 raised the threat of lay-offs.

Ireland has shown the way to the rest of the world in the techniques of utilising turf (or peat as it is called outside this country) to create electricity. Over the years there was considerable experimentation in using artificial means to dry the turf but in the end it was realised that the most efficient method was to let the air dry it. Given our climate, that system has its drawbacks and so when the weather is good the bogs become a hive of activity. Machines have been developed which skim the turf off the surface in powdered form and it is then left to dry and gathered up into mounds to await transfer to the power station. Some of the turf is cut into sods which are also left to dry before being brought in. Passing in a boat you can watch the carriages full of turf being conveyed aloft by lifts and then tipped into the furnaces while the milled peat is blown into the furnace at pressure. These power stations were not built to last very long because, in time, the bogs will be worked out; already experiments are being carried out to find the best use for these large tracts of land in the future.

Lanesborough owes its name to George Lane, later Lord Viscount Lanesborough, who received extensive grants of land in this area in the seventeenth century. He chose Rathcline Castle, about two miles to the south on the east shore of Lough Ree, as his seat, enlarging and embellishing the original tower house there. The importance of Lanesborough as a river crossing is borne out by the role it played in Sarsfield's defence of the Shannon. There was a most interesting paper written on this episode in history by Henry Mangan in the *Irish Sword* in 1949, based on letters written at the time. He explained how in the winter of 1690-1 Sarsfield was trying to hold the country west of the Shannon while the Williamite forces were dug in in the area around Mullingar. Sarsfield gave instructions for the approach from the east to be fortified, while at the same time four boats were being prepared in Mullingar by the opposing forces which were to be conveyed over land to the Shannon. An advance party under Lord Lisburn arrived unexpectedly on 1 January and surprised the Jacobites, 'killed several of them on the bridge and found large quantities of corn and other provisions by the river side and about 3,000 head of cattle'. The bridge had been partly broken down and he claimed that if the guns and the boats had arrived he could have secured 'their broken bridge and pass without any, or little opposition'. Instead, he was ordered to withdraw to Mullingar because William's commanders did not feel able to support him in holding this Shannon crossing. William was disgusted with the lack of purpose of his commanders and recalled three of them, holding them responsible for allowing Sarsfield to hold the river for the rest of that winter. This one episode in that campaign gives some idea of the importance of the river as a line of defence in those days.

There is evidence that a bridge with nine arches was built at Lanesborough in 1706 but it is not clear whether this was a new bridge or only the old one repaired. The eighteenth-century navigation works here consisted of a short canal on the west side by-passing the shallows in the river. There was a'fall of only 1 ft 5 in. and so instead of a conventional lock, there was just a single set of gates, or flash lock, through which boats had to be hauled upstream or be allowed to pass downstream on the current. A two-storey lockhouse, of the same design as the one at Clondara, was built astride this flash lock but it must have suffered from damp because by 1813 it was reported to be uninhabitable. These were troubled times. In the previous year it had been reported that there were 'atrocities committed by those deluded people called "Threshers" by breaking open the stores at Lanesborough, until they were discomfited by the military'.

Upstream of the bridge a harbour was made in 1820 on the site of an old barracks, but there was very little trade through here, the Athlone trade all went south to the Grand Canal and it was quicker to send goods by road to meet the Royal Canal at Killashee than to send them upstream to Richmond Harbour. Commander Wolfe, who was a RN officer responsible for preparing a chart of Lough Ree in 1837, said that the lockgates here were rarely opened 'except for the purpose of allowing some small pleasure boats to pass up and down'. He added: 'Lough Ree is but little used in a commercial way, not a trading vessel of any description crosses the surface.'

When the Shannon Commissioners came along later in the 1840s they laid the piers of the bridge dry with a view to underpinning it, but they decided it would have to be replaced by a new one. The present seven-arch bridge, therefore, dates from this time and it had an opening span on the west side to the same design as those at Roosky and Tarmonbarry. In addition to replacing the bridge, the commissioners did away with the canal and lock, removing the outer wall which separated it from the river and deepening the channel; the old lockhouse would also have been removed at this time. It was not too difficult to remove the outer wall which was about 500 feet long because it was said to be 'almost entirely demolished being carried away by Boatmen as Ballast upon discharging their cargoes of slates from Killaloe'. It is just possible to trace some signs of the early works but there is not much left to indicate what they were like.

In the early 1900s an Englishman called Scott James wrote a book called *An Englishman in Ireland* about a marathon trip he made across Ireland by canoe from Belfast to the Shannon, transporting his canoe by horse and cart from Belturbet to Lough Allen. He worked his way down the Shannon to Lanesborough assisted by a tow from a steamer owned by 'Mr & Mrs L.' which might have been the Lefroys' *Phoenix*. He had to resort to having his canoe carried aboard the *SS Portumna* across Lough Ree because the weather was so stormy, and from Athlone he paddled downstream to Banagher from where he sent his canoe back to Athlone for some repairs and completed his journey to Killaloe in a passenger steamer. His book is entertaining because of the adventures and conversations he had with people along the way. A bit of a philosopher he quotes Shelley's comment in a letter to his friend Peacock: 'Rivers are not like roads, the work of the hands of man; they imitate mind, which wanders at will over pathless deserts, and flows through nature's loveliest recesses, which are inaccessible to anything besides.' He records a wonderful conversation with a local man in Lanesborough who told him about the days of boycotting and evictions when Lanesborough Bridge was often the scene of 'cattle-driving' in the dead of night when small farmers who could not get ownership of land had to graze their cattle where they could. This man had travelled the world in the British army and was obviously finding life back home a bit humdrum; he told Scott James:

But mark my words, there's not much chance for vice in a place like

Lanesborough, whatever a person does is sure to be known and will reach the ears of the priests; and I can say, they are terrible down on immorality. They keep on preaching morality Sundays and week-days alike. Some time ago there was an attempt to start an immoral house near here, but the priests put it down.

Today the influx of boating visitors together with the prosperity engendered by Bord na Mona and the ESB have transformed Lanesborough but I venture to suggest that the chances of finding 'an immoral house' are still unlikely. The opening span of the bridge has been replaced by a fixed arch, the quay above it has been extended and the old harbour renovated to cater for the new pleasure traffic. The notice on the bridge warning boats to travel in company in bad weather is a warning that the lake which lies ahead can be very stormy on occasions.

ROYAL CANAL HARBOUR,

BROADSTONE, DUBLIN,

day of Nov. 1828.

SIR,

We beg leave to acquaint you, that We will convey any Goods committed to our care, to and from Dublin and Athlone, at SIXTEEN SHILLINGS per TON—Land Carriage from the Navigation Harbour, Athlone, to the place of delivery, included.

We have the honor to be,

Sir,

Your most obedient Servants,

The Royal Canal Company did try to encourage its Shannon trade in 1828

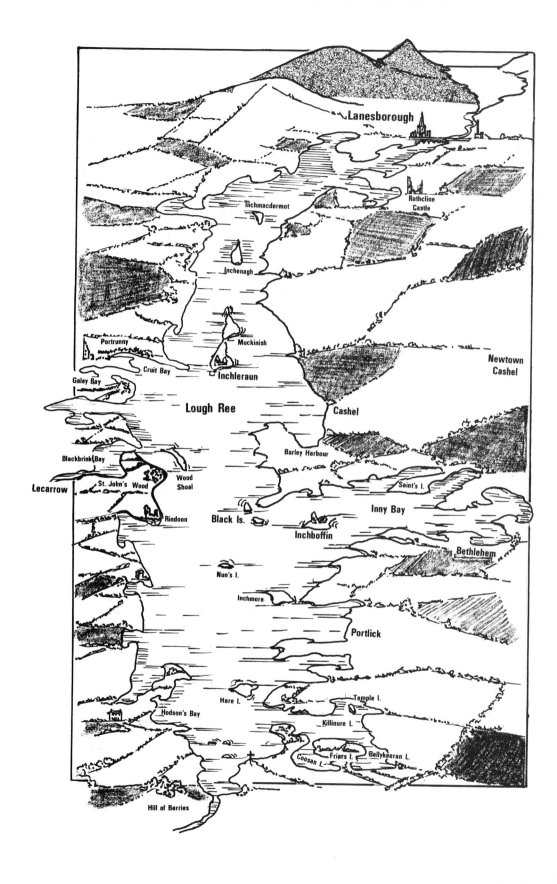

Chapter Five

THE LAKE OF THE KINGS
Lough Ree

JOHN O'DONOVAN, translator of the *Annals of the Four Masters*, that irascible scholar who was involved in the preparation of the ordnance survey in the 1830s and who devoted much of his attention to the interpretation of Irish place names, said that he had heard that Lough Ree was so called because of twenty seven kings who lived at St John's Point about halfway down the lake. He, however, dismissed this theory out of hand: 'This is not worth attention, it being one of those fooleries got up by ignorant people to account for names in the absence of history.' Harry Rice referred to the fact that in Ptolemy's second-century map of Ireland the lake was already called Lough 'Ribh', he added that many people interpreted this name as the 'Lake of the Kings' and that some said the name sprang from seven kings named John who ruled at Carlan on the Connacht shore. So we are really none the wiser as to who the kings were who gave the name to the lake back in those early days.

While there appears to have been little use made of the lake in the midnineteenth century except by some pleasure boats and yachts, this was not the case in early history. There are a number of interesting references to boats on the lake in early annals. During a storm in AD 756 it was said that 'thrice nine vessels and three of the Gamhanraighe' were shipwrecked and 'there escaped of them with life except alone the crew of one vessel'. It is recorded that in 843 the Dane, Turgesius, used the river to penetrate deep into Ireland, dragging his boats over the shallows. He held a hosting on the lake and from here they plundered into Connacht and Meath and all the monastic settlements they could find until his reign of terror came to an end when he was captured by Maelshechlainn I and drowned in Lough Owel.

Alfred Smyth in his book *Scandinavian York and Dublin* has followed the exploits of the Vikings using references to them in the annals. He says that after Turgesius there was no Viking presence on Lough Ree for nearly one hundred years but the monastic settlements were not free from attacks by Irish raiders for it is recorded that Hare Island was plundered in 899. In 922 a group of Vikings set up a strong base near Limerick and made a number of incursions up the river in the following years; their fleet on Lough Ree was attacked by the Dublin Vikings in 924 but they warded this off successfully. The Limerick Vikings under their leader Olafr also extended their sway to Lough Neagh and Lough Corrib, using the waterways to establish control over the areas around them. From 931 to 937 there was a continuous Viking presence on Lough Ree; in fact Olafr even brought his longships to Lough Erne in 936, returning with them overland in mid-winter to arrive back on 'Great Christmas night'. In that year the Viking lord from Dublin, who was also called Olafr, determined to try once again to gain control of the Shannon from his rival. He struck out for the river and raided Clonmacnoise; it was also attacked by the king of Munster in that year although, as so often was the case, much greater emphasis was given to the attack by the invaders in the annals. He then turned his attention to the Lough Ree fleet and in the following year he scored a victory, destroyed the boats and brought the leader captive to Dublin. This brought to an end the Viking rule on the lake but the plundering of the island settlements and Clonmacnoise continued; there are references to 'great fleets' amassed by Irish chieftains who sacked the islands and did battle with each other. Brian Boru's brother led an attack on Clonmacnoise, Brian himself raised a fleet to contest control of the lake and some years later he found himself competing with Maelshechlainn II for mastery over Ireland. This time he sailed up the Shannon with a fleet of 300 ships to do battle. Eventually, reason prevailed and the two kings met near the mouth of the River Inny on Lough Ree and agreed to a truce.

The lake continued to be the scene of plunderings and battle in the eleventh and twelfth centuries. We are told that in 1089 the fleet of the men of Munster commanded by Murtagh O'Brien sailed up the Shannon to Lough Ree and plundered the islands. His retreat was cut off by Rory O'Connor who 'caused two fords to be stopped' and they were forced to return to Athlone and surrender but were magnanimously allowed to return to Munster with their boats by the king. In 1137 'A fleet was conveyed by Turlough O'Connor upon the Sinainn and Loch Ribh. This was, indeed, a brave expedition for him against the fleet of the men of Breifni. . . . and against the fleet of the men of Meath . . . where there were 200 vessels, and he had but 20 ships.' Another shipwreck was recorded in 1190 when one of the King of Connacht's ships foundered with the loss of 36 lives.

Harman Murtagh, who has written many interesting papers on the role of the River Shannon in history, has noted that in medieval times a galley was maintained to help to impose control on the country bordering the lake. In Elizabethan days, a water bailiff was appointed; it was recorded 'that the great number of boats and cots on the river had facilitated robberies from the banks and had been used by the proclaimed rebels Sir Edmund Butler and Owen and Coghe Madine. The bailiff had authority to destroy, upon the finding of twelve honest men, all unnecessary boats, none to be allowed on the river without his brand, and is to have two galleys to scour the river, one above and one below Athlone'. The water bailiff enjoyed the fishing and fowling rights of the river and also its swans 'in like manner as the overseer of the swans on the Thames'. The river was also used for the dispatch of mail at this time: a letter sent from Dublin on 18 July 1580 came by road to Athlone and then by water to Limerick, arriving on 23 July. Letters have been known to take longer today.

A manuscript from a collection made by Sir Thomas Phillips in England in the nineteenth century, written by N. Dowdall Esq. and entitled 'A Description of the County of Longford, 1682' is quoted in the *Ardagh & Clonmacnoise Antiquarian Society's Journal*, 1932. It gives an interesting picture of Lough Ree at that time:

this Loch Ree hath many islands in it.... It is well replenished with fish viz. Pike, Salmon, Trout, Eel, Bream, Roach, etc. The Pikes are an incredible bigness being some above four foot in length. It is navigable for boats of about 10 or 12 tuns, but the vessels most made use of for fishing, portage of goods, etc., are made of one big tree like a trough, flatbottomed and some of them so large that they will carry 60 or 80 men, and are called cotts. They usually carry horses and other cattle in them, besides they make great use of them for carrying timber from the adjacent woods and by laying of long poles over across the said cotts and fastening great beams of timber across the said cotts they will carry 20 tun of timber or more.

We have already seen that boats were part of the Williamite equipment during the campaign of 1690-1. Paul Kerrigan, who has made a detailed study of the measures taken to meet the threat of a Napoleonic invasion from the west, has found mention of gunboats on the river and it is known that Napoleon's plans for the invasion of Ireland included boats for fording the Shannon.

The evidence of Commander Wolfe that there was virtually no traffic on Lough Ree in the 1830s is borne out by another account. Henry Inglis in his *Journey throughout Ireland in 1834* describes how the Inland Steam Navigation Company politely offered him the exclusive use of a steamer to make a trip on Lough Ree because there was no regular service north of Athlone. It was a beautiful day 'calm, sunshiny and warm' but he added: 'I regret to say, that not one prow clove the waters of the loch but my own. In place of being in the very heart of a fruitful and civilized country, we might have been navigating a lake in the interior of New Holland.' However, the

A boat registration certificate, 1860

authorities did sometimes use the lake. In 1835 a letter was received from the Excise Office in London seeking from the Shannon Commissioners free passage for their revenue police boat through Athlone lock to patrol the lake, and in the 1840s during the famine years when food became very scarce and raids on grain boats were common, there was a gunboat on the river, a sailing ship called the *Pluto*. At that time all boats on the river had to have their names and registered number painted on them and there is a record of several boatowners being summonsed for failing to do this; they had fines of 2s imposed on them. Earlier, in Elizabethan times, all boats had to be stamped with the letters ER and pay a fee of 12d per quarter; those people today who resist registration and talk of the traditional freedom of the river do not realise that it is not as 'traditional' as they think. In 1835 Francis Sproule complained that his pleasure boat was delayed at Athlone lock but an inquiry revealed that he had arrived outside the regulated hours and 'what was a matter of favour was demanded in a manner which furnished an excuse to the lockkeeper'. This incident has a familiar ring, the Shannon lockkeepers today are usually very helpful when approached as 'a matter of favour'.

Lough Ree is once again used by a large number of boats and some of the visitors complain that the navigation marks are difficult to find. I am reminded of the comment of Syd Shine some years ago when the call for more markers was first made. He suggested that they would not be happy until they had a handrail all the way up the lake. Syd who lives aboard the *Fox*, which was formerly the Board of Works maintenance boat, has over the years been responsible for introducing many young people to the river, always keeping 'open boat' for those who wanted to join him. Many of these people now have their own boats to bring their families on the river and I am sure they will never forget the debt they owe to Syd.

The navigation channel passes to the east of Inch MacDermott and

Inchenagh although at one time the marked channel lay to the west of these islands affording better protection from the prevailing westerlies. The course continues down the east shore past Clawinish and Muckinish to Inchcleraun, where there is usually good shelter to anchor and go ashore to explore this interesting island. It is also known as Quaker Island because for many years a Quaker, called Fairbrother, lived here. When John O'Donovan visited the island in 1837 he recorded that the 'tasteless follower of George Fox' was then eighty years old. O'Donovan tells the tale that when Fairbrother first arrived on the island he removed a corner stone from the ruined church on the hill to build his house but when he returned with his horse and cart for a second load, the story continues:

St Diarmuid smote the beast with the bolt of his holy revenge which caused him to run furiously, untameably, terribly, outrageously, irresistibly mad, and the Quaker, fearing for his own safety, was obliged to shoot him. All the beasts on the island (from the cow down to the mouse) also exhibited symptoms of madness but it subsided soon when the Quaker had formed a fixed resolution of touching no other stone of St Dermot's Clogas.

St Diarmuid, the founder of a monastic settlement here, appears to have continued to keep an eye on his island because O'Donovan's boatman told him that he himself had observed 'a man of tall stature walking on the water towards Athlone' whom he assumed to be the saint. The ruins of Fairbrother's house lie in behind the cottage which was formerly occupied by the Farrells and to my unpractised eye there seem to be a number of stones in the walls which look suspiciously like those to be seen in the ruins.

The story of this island goes back to the early days when history and legend have become inextricably bound together. The island is called Inchcleraun after Clothara, sister of the legendary Queen Maeve. The latter's involvement in the famous Cattle Raid of Cooley, chronicled in a twelfth-century manuscript, is said to have led ultimately to her death on her sister's island here in Lough Ree. Maeve appears to have been an Amazonian type with an insignificant husband, Ailill, King of Connacht. In trying to prove she owned, in her own right, as much property as her husband, she found that she was short by one bull because one of her bulls had transferred to her husband's herd. With female obstinacy she set out to find herself a comparable bull and learning that there was one in Ulster, she carried it off in the famous raid and returned with it to Connacht. The two bulls were matched against each other to prove which was the stronger and honour was satisfied when Ailill's bull was killed. After the death of her husband she retired to her sister's island and made herself a bower there but, while enjoying the sun one day, she was killed by Forbaid, the son of the Ulster king from whom she had stolen the bull. He had practised diligently with a sling until he was able to cast a stone accurately from the mainland, a distance of some 1,500 yards. Tradition even points to the place where she died, in the field facing towards the Longford shore below the Clogas, the church on the hill. Sitting there today on a fine sunny day, it is easy to picture the scene but it needs a good imagination to believe that anyone could sling a stone so far, and we are still left wondering what the real facts were behind this ancient Irish legend.

While these legends suggest that the island was already a place of importance in pre-Christian times, it was not until the arrival of St Diarmuid in the sixth century, that a monastic settlement was founded here. Some grave slabs date back to this time as do the banks of earth and stone surrounding the later buildings. The tiny Temple Diarmada is traditionally associated with the saint and could possibly date back to those days. An indication of its antiquity are the corner buttresses, or antae, which project out in imitation of the projecting timbers, a feature of the earlier wooden churches; its flat headed dorway is also a feature of these early stone buildings. The Christian settlement was plundered both by the Vikings and by Brian Boru's forces from Munster and it was not until the twelfth century that a house of the Canons of St Augustine was established here. The large church beside Diarmuid's little oratory and the other ruins date back to this period. There are two fine tall narrow lancet windows in the east gable of Temple Mor which the experts say are of a slightly later date and they have the puzzling feature that, while they both appear to be the same from the inside, viewed from the outside only one has elaborate moulding around it. Attached to the church are the remains of fifteenth-century monastic buildings. Harry Rice unearthed a legend that any woman who worshipped inside the walls of Temple Mor would die within the year so it's not an advisable place for females to pray. This legend is supported by the location of the women's church outside the enclosure to the south although it was customary for the women to be excluded in this way. There are two other ruined churches within the original enclosure but the most interesting ruin is the Clogas on the highest point of the island.

To reach the Clogas we usually walk up past the Farrells' old cottage and look at the Quaker's house behind it on the way. The Farrells lived here until the late 1950s and it is sad to see their house in ruins. It's hard to imagine how anyone would want to leave such surroundings but it must have been lonely and difficult living here in winter. Mary Banim, who wrote a series of articles in the *Weekly Freeman* in the 1890s which were subsequently published in a book called *Here & There Through Ireland*, was shown over the island by

Dan Farrell and his wife, 'a handsome woman of eighty-five'. They entertained her with the many legends associated with the place and told her about some of the problems of island life. On one occasion, 'a few summers since' a wedding between one of the family and someone from the mainland had turned into a disaster when one of the boats capsized, drowning the occupants. Tucked away in the corner of the island near the isthmus which connects Inchcleraun and Muckinish is the ruined home of the Walshes. I believe, with the perversity which is part of human nature, the two families had little time for each other.

Having climbed up through a couple of fields past Maeve's bower, it is difficult to find a way through the brambles into the enclosure surrounding the Clogas. It is called the Clogas because of its belfry but it is thought that the tower was a later addition. There is also a strange staircase in the north wall which must have led to some sort of loft. From the top of the Clogas there would have been a fine view in all directions to watch out for the approach of enemies and sound the warning bell.

The level of Lough Ree varies a good deal depending on the amount of rainfall and we have been on the island when the water was exceptionally low. It was fascinating to walk along the exposed foreshore, half expecting to find some long-covered object connected with the island's past history, but all we have ever found were indestructible objects of our modern consumer

Inchcleraun: the Clogas

society, plastic containers and broken bottles. On one very still day I saw three otters making their way in towards the shore some distance away. All I could see were the three humps of their backs as they swam in line and, for a moment I did not realise what it was. I remembered hearing stories of fishermen who claimed that they saw a strange humpbacked monster in these waters and I wondered if this could be the explanation of the Lough Ree monster.

The island was used as a refuge by some 'anti-treaty' men in 1922. Bob Devenish and Kieran Delany were travelling down the lake in that year and they were taken prisoner by these men who had mistaken them for military personnel because of their yachting caps. They were subsequently released when they established that their only mission was to attend the local regatta which, in fact, was actually abandoned when news of Michael Collins's death broke. The Free State authorities were uncertain how to dislodge these men without bloodshed and when it became known that they were stopping passing boats for food supplies, a Grand Canal Company boat was commandeered, the hold was filled with soldiers and, when the men came out to intercept the boat, they were easily overpowered.

The parish of Cashel is on the mainland to the east from where the bold Forbaid cast his fatal stone. There is a quarry here where some of the stone was obtained for the new bridge of Lanesborough and the Athlone works in the 1840s. In behind Priest's Island, where masses were said in penal times, there was a harbour for shipping out the stone, St George's Harbour, but we have never tried to get in there because it looks very shallow. In addition to the Cashel stone, they also used two other quarries, one near Lecarrow and the other at Killinure, and also stone from Clerhaun, about nine miles downstream of Athlone near Clonmacnoise. O'Donovan had an interesting comment about the people of Cashel in the 1830s. He remarked: 'The people on this side of the lake know more about Elections than Hagiology, which argues the decay of superstition and the upswinging vigour of political intelligence.' Later he made another interesting comment: 'As soon as one crosses the Shannon, he observes a great difference in the pronunciation of the primitive language, and in the physiognomy of the people, from which it may be fairly inferred that they are different races of people.' How much modern Ireland has changed since those days of the mid-nineteenth century.

It is a straight run across from the anchorage at Inchcleraun to Barley Harbour. The hire firms do not like their boats to use this harbour and private boatowners are happy to encourage the idea that these are dangerous waters. It is one of our favourite harbours and the small housing development here has been carefully designed to blend with the surroundings. Michael Casey, a wood carver, has his workshop here where he makes

Barley Harbour: the Silver Jubilee cruise organised by the Athlone Branch to celebrate the 25 years of the IWAI

Barley Harbour: a group at the Silver Jubilee cruise: L. to R. Alf Delany, Cynthia Rice, Rosemary Furlong and Pat Delany

beautiful objects using the strange shaped pieces of oak found in bogs. Some of our more energetic crews have even walked up to Newtown Cashel, three miles away, where they always managed to meet some obliging local in the pub and persuade him to drive them back to the boat. I must admit we have bounced on a number of rocks along the shore on our way to and from this harbour and there is a large shoal in the middle of the harbour itself but these hazards have never kept us away.

Equal caution is required entering Cruit and Galey bays but the Board of Works has recently put some navigation marks here which are a considerable help. The shoals across the entrance to Galey Bay are called the Louisa shoals because the yacht *Louisa* went aground here many years ago. This bay was the venue for an annual regatta in the days when she sailed the lake and the tents were erected in the field by the ruined castle. An ancient Irish song records that William Boy O'Kelly invited a great gathering of poets, bards, harpers and jesters to a feast here on Christmas Day 1351 and it is a strange feeling to sit there today and imagine what the scene would have looked like then.

The old ruined boathouse on the shore is a reminder of the later nineteenth-century aquatic events. William Bulfin gives a wonderful description of a regatta day here in the early 1900s and the goings-on of the gentry. He relates watching two society women meeting, shaking hands 'over an imaginary five-barred gate in that high elbow top storey fashion so much in vogue in high circles'. Their conversation betrayed their complete ignorance of the world around them as they wondered why the 'country' people took such little interest in their regatta, their 'Union Jackery and denationalisation'. His description of the race was even more scathing:

I observed several committee men leaving the marquee in a body. Their leader carried a double barrelled shotgun across his arm. He had a pencil behind his ear and a sheaf of papers protruded from his breast pocket. He marched with a firm tread to where the blue signal flag was flying, hauled it down, and then fired a shot, after which he and his comrades retired for refreshment. The hauling down of the flag and the firing of the shot gave the signal for the departure of the two yachts on a race around the lake. They went away at a spanking pace but their movements excited little interest.

Portrunny is at the head of Cruit Bay. The 'Port' in the name belies the place; efforts by the local authority to create a harbour here were hindered by the shallow nature of the site chosen but there are plans to make it a better place for boats to berth by extending jetties out into deeper water.

The *Harriet*

A tea party aboard the *Harriet* owned by Major Reeves about 1914

Blackbrink Bay to the south is free of all obstructions and the IWAI mooring buoy tucked in under St John's wood is a very sheltered anchorage with the high ground around the bay providing shelter from most winds. Jimmie Furey lives in a little house on the north shore of the bay. He is a carpenter *par excellence* who can produce things of beauty from pieces of wood. The craft of building wooden boats is unfortunately a dying one and Jimmie's boats are much in demand.

The Lecarrow Canal opens into the north west corner of the bay. This is the canal which was constructed by the Shannon Commissioners in the 1840s so that stone could be brought from the nearby quarry for the building of the bridge and lock at Athlone. The Lecarrow Canal was actually extended further than originally planned in 1842 to provide employment 'at a period of great distress'. When commercial traffic declined on the river, the canal became silted up and it was reopened again in 1966 to provide a harbour of refuge halfway up the lake for the increasing number of pleasure boats on the river at the time and it is now being enlarged by the Board of Works.

The boats carrying the stone from Lecarrow to Athlone used the passage between the Wood Shoal and the shore which was marked in those days. Vincent always used this passage in *La Vague* but he had been given leading marks on the shore by some of the boatmen which would take him safely through; it is not to be recommended without extreme caution because the shoal extends a long way to the north. The Wood Shoal passage also has memories for me of a nightmare journey some years ago. Marine diesel engines are extraordinarily reliable if given diesel fuel free of any air or water. We had been having a great deal of trouble with our engine which was eventually traced to rain water leaking in through the filler cap on the fuel intake pipe. Setting out to cross the lake in windy conditions to make a rendezvous with friends up the north Shannon, the rolling of the boat with the water swilling about in the tank caused the engine to stop every half hour. Each time we had to anchor and bleed the fuel line. *Harklow*, because of her high freeboard, will not ride head to wind at anchor and trying to bleed an engine with the boat rolling wildly is not a pleasant experience. Douglas was not able to work on the engine because of his arthritis and so I had to carry out the operation under his instructions. I am not very mechanically minded and each time I bled the engine I tightened up the 'bleeding screws' as hard as I could. Eventually, with repeated opening and closing I managed to strip the thread so that the screw would not tighten and the engine kept sucking air. Just off the red buoy at Rinnagan Point we could not get the engine restarted and finally had to admit defeat.

By this time it was dark and blowing hard from the south and the boat was lying uneasily at anchor. I set off in the dinghy with my small daughter, leaving Douglas aboard, even though I knew there was little he could do if the anchor dragged. We made for Lecarrow where I knew there was a telephone and halfway up the canal the outboard packed up. I rowed the rest of the way and went ashore to phone for someone to come to help us the following morning. I had to row back in the dark, down the canal, across Blackbrink Bay and through the Wood Shoal passage against the wind. All the time I was praying that *Harklow* would not have dragged her anchor. We eventually made it and spent an uncomfortable night peering out from time to time to check that the anchor was holding. Through those sleepless hours I puzzled with the problem of the engine and by morning I had come up with a solution. I suggested to Douglas that we should try a lilo plug instead of the screw and I expect at that stage he felt we had nothing to lose by trying it. Much to my amazement it worked and we were able to work our way up the lake to a more convenient place to meet Trevor Tomsett from Roosky who has always answered our calls for help with a cheery smile. The whole nightmare episode was just one of those bad times which all those who go boating have to cope with from time to time and, while I have always been opposed to the modern trend to have VHF radios aboard, I must admit that there are occasions like this when one would be very useful.

St John's Wood extends from the south arm of Blackbrink Bay to Rinnogan Point; it is a very old area of wood and contains some interesting plants. From here a small bay opens up to the next point to the south, Rindoon Point. This is the narrowest part of the lake; it is only a little over a mile across to the Longford shore. Because of its commanding position, Rindoon, the point of the fort, was probably occupied as early as the Iron Age. An early Christian hand bell and a crucifixion plaque were found here (now in the National Museum) suggesting that there was a monastery here at one time; they were found near the ruined Church of Ireland church at the base of the peninsula, near the road, so this is assumed to be the site of a settlement, but the finding of such objects does not necessarily prove the existence of a community here. If it did exist, it may have evolved into the later house of Premonstratensian canons which was established here in the twelfth century when the Irish Church was reformed and the monastic system was replaced by a diocesan administration. Although the Vikings probably had a fortified position here, the ruined castle dates from much later when the Normans established a settlement, the first to be based west of the Shannon.

The area of the bay near the castle is called Safe Harbour. It is not a harbour but it does provide a safe anchorage in the prevailing west or south west winds and the IWAI have put a useful mooring buoy here. Following the path along from the castle ruins which leads to the road, it is possible to find traces of a defensive wall, with a number of square towers and a gatehouse, which stretched across the peninsula to protect it from land attack. A second line of defence was provided by a moat which could be flooded with water from the lake and an arm from this moat encircled the castle enclosure. Within the walled settlement there was also a priory of the medieval hospital order of Fratres Cruciferi and ruins of their church can be found near the castle. Some people have referred to this as the church of the Knight Hospitallers of St John but the experts say that this is incorrect. The Rindoon order was not a military one and the confusion may have arisen because both orders were dedicated to St John of Jerusalem.

Rindoon Castle in the 1840s

The castle was built in 1227 and enlarged six years later. It had to be restored several times in the thirteenth century, following attacks by the Irish. A new hall was erected nearby at this time and there are signs of modifications in the sixteenth and seventeenth centuries to cater for changing methods of warfare. The castle enclosure was many sided, roughly triangular in shape, with a portcullis gateway and barbican on the opposite side of the moat. The rectangular keep formed part of the north curtain wall and I always feel when I look at the vaulted dungeons that many stories of misery could be told about these dark places. The ruined castle had occupants in recent times; a rough cabin was built within its walls and an old man and his wife lived here up to the 1940s. The remains of this dwelling, which incorporated one of the castle fireplaces, can still be seen.

I had often been to Rindoon but never found time to look for the 'windmill' which is located further out along the point. A few years ago I was invited to join Sheila and Reggie Redmond for a weekend's cruising and although they know Lough Ree and its places of interest better than most, they had never seen it either, so we decided to seek it out. We had read an article by Tony Claffey about this building, which stated that some people have suggested it might be a medieval windmill and therefore unique. Peter Harbison in his *Guide to the National Monuments of Ireland*, a most excellent publication which no boat should be without, is circumspect, describing it as 'a round tower of uncertain use and date'. It is marked as a 'windmill' on seventeenth-century maps and, while the Norman settlement must have had its own mill, it has never been established whether this building was the mill used at that time. It was because of this mystery that we were anxious to see it for ourselves.

Reggie and I discussed how best to find the building and decided to follow the shore around and then strike inland to avoid having to pick our way through undergrowth. We did this and found it very easily, raised up on a small artificial mound. We had hardly discovered it when we were amused to see Sheila arriving; she had walked without any bother through the trees from the castle. It is roughly 20 feet in diameter and to my unpractised eye it looked far too modern to be a medieval windmill but the two doorways facing each other are characteristic of the early type of mill giving access to the building from either side when the sails were in motion. There are two strange flues or vents which splay inwards and downwards, the purpose of which is hard to determine. Tony Claffey suggests that they are a residual feature of the early post mill which had vent holes to inform the miller of changes of wind direction but they seem to be too elaborate for this purpose and I wonder if they were chutes down which the corn could be poured into the grain boxes.

The article about the 'windmill' which had aroused our interest had been in *Irish Midland Studies*, published in 1980 by the Old Athlone Society in commemoration of William English. Billy was a local historian who had died in his fifties before he had had time to write his *magnum opus* on Lough Ree. He had even sent me a list of chapter headings at one time but he had continued to discover new information and follow fresh leads and it is a great pity that the book was never written. The Old Athlone Society volume is a fitting tribute to him, which he would have appreciated, containing interesting articles by many of his friends concerning local history.

The main channel down the lake passes to the west of a group of seven small low islands, the Black Islands. Richard Hayward describes visiting here in the late 1930s when he found three families living on the largest of the islands, King's Island: two families of Hanleys and one of O'Haras. He was amused by the description of the cottages being 'on the same street', the street in these parts being the forecourt of the cottage. A small cottage was pointed out to him which had once been a pub in the days when more people had lived there. They relied on farming, swimming the cattle from island to island to graze, but they also derived income from eel fishing. These people

Rindoon: one of the puzzling chutes in the 'windmill'

on the Black Islands held out for a long time against accepting the ESB's offer of compensation for the loss of these earnings from what was for them a traditional way of life until they were forced to surrender in the 1950s.

The Board of Works has now marked the passage into Derry and Inny Bay and many private boatowners, who have had this area to themselves for so long, have greeted this news with a certain amount of dismay. We have long navigated these waters with the assistance of the Admiralty chart which was made by Commander Wolfe and Lieutenant Beechey in the 1830s and which is very accurate once you establish the relative level of the water in the lake. The chart makers used 4 ft 6 in. on the sill of the old lock in Athlone, but this lock is no longer there. However, by doing some calculations this works out to be about 6 ft 6 in. on the sill of the present lock and as the normal summer level of the lake is about 7 ft to 8 ft (123 ft-124 ft OD) on the sill, that means that there is usually a little to spare over the soundings on the chart. Obviously, the actual level of the lake is slightly higher than the reading at the lock because of the fall in the river to Athlone and the ESB do have a gauge at the south end of the lake as well, the readings of which can be ascertained by a phone call, so having ascertained the level at either of these places you can use the chart with confidence.

The channel lies to the north of Inchturk and south of Inchbofin; the best anchorage for visiting the latter is off the small boat pier about a quarter way up the east shore. From here it is a short walk to the old monastic site at the north end of the island. This settlement was founded by St Rioch in the sixth century but some early graveslabs are all that remain of this period. It is recorded that Brian Boru's Munstermen raided the island a number of times and some other objects found here would suggest that the Vikings visited it as well. The surviving ruins date from a later period when it was almost certainly a house of Augustinian canons.

There are two churches set inside a low wall enclosure and there are indications of a larger enclosure in the outlying fields. The more southerly ruin is a simple nave and chancel church with a well preserved chancel arch, round headed windows and a pointed door in the south wall. The other building, known as 'The Monastery', has a nave, with a transept added later, at the north end. Beside the ruined altar in the north wall, there is a fine twelfth-century Irish Romanesque window and opposite it on the south wall there is a piscina; this was a basin for washing the sacred vessels, complete with drain hole. The transept has two beautiful fifteenth-century traceried windows and it is worth looking at these from the outside because one of them is surmounted by the mitred head of a bishop or abbot. The sacristy, which is also a later addition, is used as a store to preserve graveslabs because these could so easily be stolen; the fear of theft from these monastic sites is the reason why jetties for boats have not been encouraged.

Saint's Island is now connected with the mainland by a causeway but there is a local tradition that in the past coffins were floated out to the island for burial on a large stone. W. J. Nash told the story in his booklet *Loughree and Around It* that in 1820 during a period of severe frost, the mourners were bringing out a coffin across the frozen lake when the ice gave way and about 120 people were drowned. I have never been able to trace his source for this story but, undoubtedly, the lake did ice over completely on a few occasions. The annals record that in 1156 Rory O'Conor was able to draw his boats across the ice from Galey Bay to Rindoon, a distance of 5 miles and I have heard accounts of a horse and cart being driven across the main lake in more recent times and reports of the deafening noise of the mini-icebergs grinding together when the ice was breaking up.

The Priory of All Saints was founded here, probably about 1200, by the Dillon family, the predominant Norman family in the area. There is a ruined church with some fragments of the cloister arcade scattered around and to the north are traces of the domestic buildings. The church has a fine switch-line traceried window, which is probably fifteenth century, and there are remains of a transept leading off the south side of the nave. It was a prosperous priory and noted for its scholars and it is thought that it might have survived the period of the dissolution of the monasteries because of the patronage of the Dillons, who remained true to the Catholic faith. John Colgan, the noted early seventeenth-century Franciscan scholar, who wrote so much about the lives of the early saints, was able to obtain manuscripts from here. If you chance to arrive here bearing a grudge, then a drink from the spring is to be recommended which is said to cure malice from people's hearts; a monk, driven from the island in the days of King John, fell on his knees and asked God to pardon his enemies and a fountain of clear water sprang from the spot.

Across the channel from Saint's Island is the strangely named Bethlehem Point, so called because nearby there was a house of the Poor Clares, called Bethlehem Convent. It was established in 1631, again under the patronage of the Dillons, and in the troubled times which followed the rising of 1641, soldiers from Athlone destroyed the convent. This outrage was avenged; on their return to Athlone the soldiers, sixty in number, including a captain and other officers, were murdered as they revelled. It is suggested that some of the nuns managed to escape to a small island in the middle of the lake which is still called Nun's Island today. There is a ruined church there but the window would date it as a medieval church of a much earlier period. I have never been ashore there but Harman Murtagh says there are signs that the church was adapted for use as a dwelling place. He considers it unlikely that the nuns would have made for the island from which it would have been difficult to escape if they had been attacked further and thinks that the name may relate to an earlier period when the Bethlehem convent might have farmed the island. Henry Inglis visiting the lake in 1834 remarked that it was 'partly under tillage' but I understand that it is greatly overgrown today. There are two graves on the island which are reputed to be those of two of the nuns who took refuge there.

The entrance to the River Inny is shallow but once over the bar the water is deep. We took *Harklow* in there many years ago just after the drainage scheme on this river had been completed. Both sides of the river were lined with banks of spoil, making it very unsightly, but these have probably mellowed by now. We tied up to the bank a short distance up the river but I believe you can navigate up to the first road bridge. Here you would be only some three miles from the Royal Canal. You might well ask why this canal was continued all the way to Clondara instead of entering the Shannon here. The answer to this question is just another part of the saga of this extraordinary canal. When the engineers reached the point where they could see Lough Ree so tantalisingly close, they tried to persuade the government to allow them to lock down into the Inny instead of continuing on for another fifteen miles to the north Shannon. However, the directors of the Grand Canal Company raised their voices in protest. They did not want another canal entering the Shannon at Lough Ree, where it might interfere with their Athlone trade, and so they insisted that the canal must follow the route authorised at its incorporation. It will be remembered that the principal reason put forward for the construction of the canal had been to provide water transport from the coalfields at Lough Allen and this was why it was laid out to enter the Shannon so far to the north. In addition, it was judged that it was not practical for a canal to enter the river at Lough Ree, where bad weather conditions could hold up boats for long periods — it must be remembered that this was before the days of steam navigation and the boats would have had to be sailed across the lake. I have often wondered whether now, in the different circumstances which exist today, a case could be made for linking up the canal with Lough Ree via the Inny; it would create a wonderful addition to the restored Royal Canal but there would be a fall of 77 feet to be overcome by locks.

Leaving Inny Bay and heading south there is a good sheltered anchorage in Portlick Bay. It is also possible to approach Portlick from the south through Rinardo Bay but, having been there with the Redmonds, when the lake was exceptionally low, and seen all the shoals, I am well aware of the need to use the Admiralty chart carefully here. It is always jokingly said that the soundings on the chart for this area are particularly profuse because one of the two naval officers, R. B. Beechey, was courting one of the Smyths of

Portlick, whom he subsequently married; he later became well known for his marine paintings. I was rather puzzled by this story because one of the branches of the Smyth family was called Wolfe Smyth which led me to wonder whether it was James Wolfe that she had married but I recently got to the bottom of the mystery. Portlick Castle was originally another Dillon castle and it was purchased by the Rev. Smyth who came to these parts to take up an incumbency. The 'Wolfe' in the name of one branch of the family had been introduced some years before the arrival of the two surveyors, when one of the Smyths had been a ward of court and had adopted the name Wolfe, which was that of his guardian. It is many years now since I visited Portlick. There was an attractive old house adjoining the Dillon castle where Harriet Simpson (née Smyth) lived with her husband, Norrie. The castle was roofed at that time and in very good repair; Norrie had fitted up a workshop for himself in the great hall. The Smyths are all gone now and the estate was later sold to the government and transferred to the Forest and Wildlife Service.

Beechey and Wolfe used the traditional names for the shoals and rocks on their charts whenever they could find them out. For example, the Adelaide rock had been struck by a boat called the *Adelaide* and the Slate rock was so called because a canal boat had foundered here carrying a load of slates from Killaloe. Inchmore, as its name suggests, is the largest island on the lake; there is a ringfort at the southern end of the island, which indicates that it was inhabited from early times. St Lioban founded a settlement here, but all that remains is a featureless ruin at the north end of the island. There used to be some 200 people living here and on neighbouring Inchturk but they gradually moved to the mainland. The Marquis of Westmeath had built a lodge for himself in the centre of the island and the ruins of this house and the old kitchen garden are still there today. He was supposed to have played an active role in the defeat of Napoleon in Egypt and W. J. Nash, in his little book called *Loughree and Around it*, told the story that the marquis tried to make the islanders pay him rent but they claimed to be freeholders. Nash told how one of them, Celia Kindleton, had chased him with a pitchfork and she was later pointed out to him by his father as 'the woman who defeated the man who defeated the great Napoleon'. The ruined cottages, the old schoolhouse and the remains of a road were the only signs of this colony but today people are moving back to the island and establishing holiday homes there. It must be remembered that the islands are all privately owned and, while the owners do not object to people visiting places of archaeological interest, the increase in boating on the lake has led to a problem with people landing and causing damage to property and livestock.

The passage between Inchmore and the Napper Rocks was a tricky one requiring a dog's leg course but it has now been marked, and out in the main lake the vicinity of the Hexagons and the Long Shoal, which is a large area of shallow water marked by black buoys at either end, should be avoided. While the names of many of these shoals and islands are self-explanatory, I have often wondered how Fathead Island earned its name and I feel there must be a good story about it somewhere.

On the west shore of the lake there is a fine new quay at Hodson Bay which is a good berth in the prevailing winds but should be avoided if the wind is from the east or north east. The marking of this bay causes visitors much confusion. Many people coming in from the north mistake Hodson's Pillar for the Pinnacle Rock and try to pass inside the island, with disastrous results. Some people claim that Hodson's Pillar marks the geographical centre of Ireland, but there is also a stone pillar at Kilkenny West, in the Goldsmith country to the east of the lake, which carries a similar claim. The Hodson family obtained large grants of land in this area in the seventeenth century but the house has been a hotel now for many years.

Steering straight across the lake from Hodson Bay, Hare Island seems to merge into the mainland. To the uninitiated the marks around this island are most confusing because the Shannon Navigation Authority, the Board of Works, will not accept the need for introducing some sort of middleground or island buoy. In the main navigation channel the red marks are situated on your port hand when proceeding upstream and the black on the starboard hand and this is reversed when coming downstream. This works well until you come to the lakes, where entering a bay is considered heading upstream and leaving it is downstream, but the difficulty is that you have to know whether you are, in fact, still in the main navigation channel or entering a bay. The result is that when you approach Hare Island to pass to the south of it you leave the black buoy off Crow Island on your port hand because it is a main channel buoy, then you pass between a red and a black, this time leaving the black on your starboard hand because you are now considered to be entering a bay. You then see a black buoy straight ahead marking a shoal off Killinure Point. Which side of it are you supposed to go? That is a good question and one which a great number of visitors answer incorrectly; you actually must leave it on your port hand if you are turning into the Inner Lakes. In fact, if you were to make a circuit of Hare Island, you would leave the black off Crow Island on your port hand then three reds on the same side and, when you come around and see the black buoy off the Hexagon Shoal, you could be forgiven for not knowing which side to pass. It is, therefore, of great importance for visitors to follow their charts carefully on the lake.

Hare Island is another of my favourite places on the river but once again it is privately owned and you should ask the Duffy family if they would mind if you paid it a visit. There is a little boat harbour in the south east corner, called the Lord's Harbour. The 'Lord' in this case was Lord Castlemaine, a member of the Handcock family, the previous owners of the island, who built a lodge here and planted the island with many interesting trees and shrubs which give it a special charm. As with so many places around the lake, it was the Dillon family who held sway here in earlier days and some members of the family are buried here. They would have been patrons, and possibly founders, of the twelfth-century House of the Canons Regular of St Augustine and the ruined Romanesque church near the harbour dates from this period. An earlier Christian settlement was founded here by St Ciaran in 541 after he had studied on Inchcleraun, under St Diarmuid.

Walking along the shore of the island, I always think of the story which is told of how one day Ciaran told his fellow monks to welcome their new abbot whom they would find down by the shore. They found an unimposing young man there but, under Ciaran's tutelage, he soon became fit for the abbacy and Ciaran was able to set off downstream in search of a place to found a new settlement. He chose the site of what was to become one of the greatest of all European monasteries, Clonmacnoise, but he was to spend only a few short months there before his death and it must have been here at Hare Island that he enjoyed his best years.

Hare Island: the Lord's Harbour

Landing-Place at Hare Island,
Lough Ree.

A hoard of gold and silver ornaments was found on Hare Island in 1802 which has since completely disappeared. J. A. Graham-Campbell in an article in *The Antiquaries Journal* engages in a fascinating piece of detective work into the fate of this find. A letter from an Irish antiquary dated in the same year, 1802, referred to seeing the ornaments in a silversmith's shop having been bought by the latter 'from a countryman'. Charles Vallancey in his *Collectanea de Rebus Hibernicis* stated that the articles found were: 'ten gold bracelets, a number of silver anklets with some ingots of silver', he included drawings of some of them and indicated that they were then (in 1804) in the possession of a Dublin goldsmith. Then in 1812 a London silversmith exhibited some gold ornaments to the Society of Antiquaries in London which the late Marquis of Landsdowne had previously purchased in Dublin. These were destined for the melting pot, because of the intrinsic value of the gold which was said to be about one thousand guineas. Graham-Campbell concludes that these were the Hare Island gold ornaments because it would seem that a suggestion that drawings should first be made of them may have been adopted and a drawing of one of the bracelets exists in the society's archives and is of a similar design to Vallancey's drawings. He describes the ornaments as of a Hiberno-Viking type, suggesting that they were probably deposited on Hare Island some time during the second half of the ninth or the first half of the tenth century and it is sad to think that this unique find was lost to posterity in such a callous way.

The channel between Hare Island and Coosan Point is marked today with a red and a black buoy but in Harry Rice's day there were no marks here and people were constantly going aground. He put a red and white striped barrel on the Hare Island shallow, which was known locally as Pott's shallow because William Potts, the proprietor of *Saunders Newsletter*, had gone aground there in the *Audax*. The shoal on the Coosan side Harry marked with a stake and he called it the Godiva Shoal, this was because when they were trying to fix the stake on the rock, the boat drifted away and his daughter, Betty, had to strip off quickly and swim after it. Not only did Harry personally mark a number of unmarked hazards on the lake at that time but he prepared detailed charts of the lake using a lead line from a rowing boat, and then put all his experiences down in his classic book *Thanks for the Memory*.

Harry had served in the RAMC in France during the 1914-18 War and then spent a further twenty-five years in the Indian Army. Invalided out of the service, he had returned to Ireland and bought a Nissan hut to make a home for himself and his wife on the shores of Lough Ree, calling it, appropriately, 'Dunrovin'; he planted the place with shrubs and today the little house is barely visible from the lake. Harry and his wife had seven years

Harry and Cynthia Rice aboard the *St Clair* on the occasion in 1954 when the potential of the river was 'sold' to the Tanaiste, William Norton

together exploring and charting the lake before she died. In the days when Vincent and I used to visit him, he had just remarried. It was here that the plans were laid to found the Inland Waterways Association of Ireland to protect the heritage of Ireland's waterways and, in particular, the Shannon Navigation. I well remember Harry and Vincent disputing hotly about how the campaign should be run, both talking at once and neither listening to the other, whilst his wife, Cynthia, and I retired to the kitchen and smiled at their childish behaviour. They were the best of friends for all their anger with each other and they both felt passionately that Ireland's waterways must be saved. Sometimes Sean MacBride would join the discussions and there was a constant stream of other visitors. How many people, as they steam past there now, realise that if it had not been for the association launched from this little house, they might not have a navigation to sail on today? Harry's niece Rosemary and her husband Norman Furlong have made a home for themselves next door to Dunrovin but they look out on a very different scene today with boats coming and going all the time. I sometimes wonder what Harry and Vincent would have made of it all if they had lived to see the results of their efforts, and whether they would have approved of the way their beloved Shannon has been developed.

There was a ferry in the old days from Coosan Point to the Killinure headland where the quarry was opened in the 1840s to provide additional stone for the Athlone works. The *Illustrated London News* for 8 March 1845 recorded an accident here when the ferry boat capsized throwing the occupants, nine men and two women, into the water. Despite efforts to save them, made by people who witnessed the accident, including Lord Castlemaine, eight of the men were drowned; one of the women 'owed her escape to a bag of bran which was fastened to her back and kept her afloat'.

Looking at a chart or map of the Inner Lakes gives a very misleading impression of the place. Most of the islands are surrounded by reedbeds which make them merge into each other, just as they do in the Carnadoe Waters, creating a similar world of natural beauty alive with birds and fish. Coosan Lough, which some say is a corruption of 'Coursing Lough', is entered through a natural cut, known locally as 'Levinge's Cut'. Standing at the head of this lough is Creaghduff House where Walter Levinge lived until his death a few years ago. He knew and loved every inch of Lough Ree and spent many hours sailing its waters. He was a skilled boat builder and he built many of the Shannon One Design (SOD) fleet which are still racing on the lakes today. Walter also made for himself a larger sailing boat to take his wife, Marian, and his three daughters out for the day picnicking on the lake. He himself was no mean sailor and he was so successful in the boat he built for himself, the *Maime*, No. 34, that it is said that Bertie Waller bought the boat from him to prevent him winning outright the most coveted of all the SOD awards, the Belle Isle Plate. Bertie had presented this salver and had stipulated that it had to be won three times in succession by the same owner and boat; this feat was at last achieved in 1986 by Alf Delany's No. 37 (which had been built by Walter Levinge in 1922) but he very sportingly represented it straight away to be raced for under the same conditions. Walter was equally successful in the new boat he built for himself, the No. 58, and he was a familiar figure sitting in the stern of this boat, wearing his trilby hat and quietly puffing his pipe. I remember seeing him capsize one day, an

97

unusual occurrence, and he emerged unruffled, still wearing his hat and with the pipe still alight. The tradition of building Shannon One Designs is still being carried on in the Inner Lakes today with great skill by Peter Quigley at Killinure Point. The experts can be heard disputing whether a 'Furey' or a 'Quigley' boat is the best but, as Jimmie Furey quietly points out, it is really the skill of the helmsman which matters.

Walter's father, R. D. Levinge, published a little booklet many years earlier called *A Sportsman's and Tourist Guide to the Shannon*. In it he described the river from Loop Head to Lough Allen. These were the days before the hydro electric scheme put paid to the salmon fishing. His words would make the modern fisherman wince: 'As regards fishing, it is again quite free. Salmon to be got under the weirs or other shallow parts of the river; trout, pike and perch, large and very plentiful on the lakes.' He told a number of stories and the one I like best concerned his friend, a magistrate, who was hearing a case in Eyrecourt in which two women were disputing the ownership of a duck. Not knowing which one to believe, he instructed a policeman to take the duck out and release it on the street and come back to report to the court to which house it went.

In the south east corner of Coosan Lough the oddly named Gibraltar Island, surrounded by dense reed beds, creates a strange little back channel which is a completely sheltered secret mooring place. Levinge's Cut is also a popular mooring with on one side Cnocknamuck Island, connected with the mainland by a causeway, and on the other side Friar's Island. I am told that this island is also connected to the mainland by a causeway in the south east corner, across which the friars used to go in penal times to make their way to the Irish quarter of Athlone to say mass in defiance of the law. I believe there are remnants of this mass path to be found today but little remains of the friars' settlement on the island except a featureless ruin heavily covered in bushes and undergrowth at the east end of the island.

Temple Island is not, as you might expect, so named because of an ancient connection with druidic times but because it was owned by Robert Temple, who was the Commodore of the Killinure Yacht Club and the owner of the yacht *Louisa* which had left its mark on the shoal at the entrance to Galey Bay. The club lasted only a few years from 1831 to about 1836 and during that time used the Commodore's island as its headquarters. It appears to have been a breakaway group from the Athlone Yacht Club and it is suggested by Billy English, who wrote a short history of the present Lough Ree Yacht Club, that the rift was on political grounds between the landed gentry and some of the officers of the Athlone garrison.

The Killinure Yacht Club of the 1830s was run on very authoritarian lines with printed regulations which make amusing reading today. Regulation five stated:

The members are always to appear on board their boats in the blue uniform (on the days mentioned in the first regulation) viz: Blue Jacket with appropriate Buttons, Waistcoat White Cashmere with the Club Buttons, Trousers Blue, White or Chequered, as the member may think proper to wear. A fine of 2s 6d to be levied for the breaking of this Regulation.

Regulation nine covered behaviour when cruising in company:

Members will dine together with their friends in the mess tent at 6 o'clock each day when the club are out on a cruise, and breakfast at 9 o'clock precisely in the mess tent as agreed. Wine not allowed at mess, but the best spirits to be provided by the Purser. When the fleet is to return home after dinner, one glass of grog only allowed. Any member disobeying this order will be fined 'Five Shillings', which shall be demanded by the Secretary on the fleet coming to their moorings.

It is not surprising that when the principal officers died, the surviving members sought to amalgamate with the original less autocratic club. Visiting Temple Island recently I found it easy to imagine how it must have looked in those days. The yachts would have anchored off and the gentlemen would have been rowed ashore by their paid hands to the little landing pier on the east side of the island where there was provision for a flagstaff. A path, much overgrown today, led to a building which looked out to the west.

Leaving the Inner Lakes past Peter Quigley's yard and heading down-stream, the present site of the Lough Ree Yacht Club is at Ballyglass on the east shore just where the lake begins to narrow before entering the next stretch of river down through Athlone town. Yacht racing on Lough Ree would seem to date back at least to the 1730s according to an advertisement quoted by G. T. Stokes: 'A buck hunt was announced for every evening of the week, a Regatta, a ball and other diversions every evening for a week from Monday 28 July to Saturday 31, 1731.' Documentary evidence to support the claim that the Lough Ree Yacht Club, known as the Athlone Yacht Club in its early days, was founded in 1770 is no longer in existence, but it is strongly supported by hearsay; this would make it the second oldest in the world. In the 1850s it was referred to in the local newspaper as the 'Lough Ree Club', but it was not until 1895 that a meeting was held at which it was formally decided to establish the club to be known as the 'Lough Ree Yacht Club', which 'shall consist of gentlemen desirous of encouraging yachting, match sailing and boating on Lough Ree'.

The Athlone Yacht Club had used Ballyglass as a rendezvous from at least the 1830s, and possibly earlier, in addition to holding regattas at other places like Galey Bay. The regattas in those days were popular events attended by large crowds of local people and there were rowing races as well as races for the sailing boats. A young man called John Keegan, who came from nearby Moate to Athlone to get employment with the Ordnance Survey, recorded visiting the regatta in his diary published in 1837:

Ballyglass Hill lies between Ballykeeran and the Shannon. It is here that the tents are pitched and the people assemble annually to witness the regatta on Lough Ree. Thornley and I went there in August, and a pleasant day we had, although we got wet to the skin in crossing from the Westmeath to the Roscommon side, where the regatta was held this year.

It was probably not the first time, and certainly not the last, that being on the weather shore with the prevailing westerlies was to cause problems for the organising committee.

In 1853 the week-long regatta was postponed from August till September due to Queen Victoria's visit to Ireland and the event was reported in the *Westmeath Independent*:

On 7th September, the evening previous to the regatta, a large muster of yachts appeared at the rendezvous (Athlone), including several from Lough Derg and a number belonging to the 62nd Regiment. The aquatic gentlemen were most sumptuously entertained by the Lough Ree Club at Madam De Ruyter's Railway Hotel, where every delicacy of the season was provided and wines of the choicest vintage... at an early hour all the yachts got under weigh for Carberry Island (Ballyglass). Here the scene was most striking and picturesque; on the shore might be seen a vast extent of canvas tents.... Looking towards the lake might be seen an assemblage of craft, some 200 in number, from the turf cot to the majestic steamer, all cruising about on the broad expanse of the Shannon.

By the turn of the century the larger yachts were on the decline, as we saw in Bulfin's account of the Galey Bay event, and the open centreboard boat was becoming more popular. These were built to different designs and R. D. Levinge, Walter's father, wrote to the secretary as early as 1902 complaining about the fact that people were building further 'queer-shaped things' in their efforts to design a faster boat. Finally, a positive step was taken when the secretary of the North Shannon Yacht Club, Robert Devenish, suggested that the Shannon clubs should get together to adopt a one design class. A meeting was held in Athlone in 1920 at which it was decided to ask Morgan Giles to design an 18 foot open centreboard boat. Thus was born the Shannon One Design, which as already mentioned Walter Levinge was to build so successfully for many years and which is now being built with such skill by Peter Quigley and Jimmie Furey. She is a beautiful boat, gaffrigged with a large single sail, which is crewed by three people, the helmsman, a sheethand, who trims the sail, and a third hand who operates the centre-board and acts as ballast. It is still a very popular class today, delighting third and fourth generation sailors with its lively performance and its exciting antics off the wind; its long boom makes gybing in a fresh wind a manoeuvre not to be undertaken by the fainthearted.

Opposite Ballyglass is the Hill of Berries, a hill surmounted by a clump of trees, which is a prominent landmark from the lake. It has nothing to do with 'berries' but is the townland of the Barrys: Barrybeg and Barrymore. When John Weaving was preparing the charts for the *Shell Guide to the Shannon* some years ago, he conceived the idea that drawings of the shore, representing the visual appearance of the places when approaching from the lake, would be helpful to the visitor. He drew these, similar to the drawings to be found on Admiralty charts. He is an accomplished artist, the drawings were beautifully done, but unfortunately, the firm advising on the layout of the new guide wanted to present a modern image and John's drawings were considered old-fashioned. They took his little pen and ink sketches and turned them into silhouettes which removed all the detail from them. The result was that the Hill of Berries with its clump of trees became a

Lough Ree Yacht Club during a regatta in the 1920s

flat-topped mountain and it was always known as 'Table Mountain' by us after this.

Ballyglass has seen many assorted fleets off its shores over the years and I have happy memories of races sailed in the SODs and friendships made there. Not least of these memories is that of being taken by Vincent 'to inspect the Cross', the cross erected in 1950 on Ballyglass Hill to mark the Marian Year, on that first visit to Lough Ree Yacht Club with the Goodbodys in the *Phoenix* all those years ago. It was there looking out over the lake on a beautiful evening that we realised our short acquaintance had grown into something deeper. I have not been able in this single chapter to do justice to this lake and its many stories and delightful moorings. I hope that some day someone will take up where Billy English left off and devote a book to the Lake of the Kings.

Our Shannon One Design *Gaviotta* at Lough Ree Yacht Club in 1951

The *Blue Peter*, one of the original 18ft boats sailing past the Lough Derg Yacht Club in the early 1900s.

The Lough Ree Yacht Club during regatta week in 1986

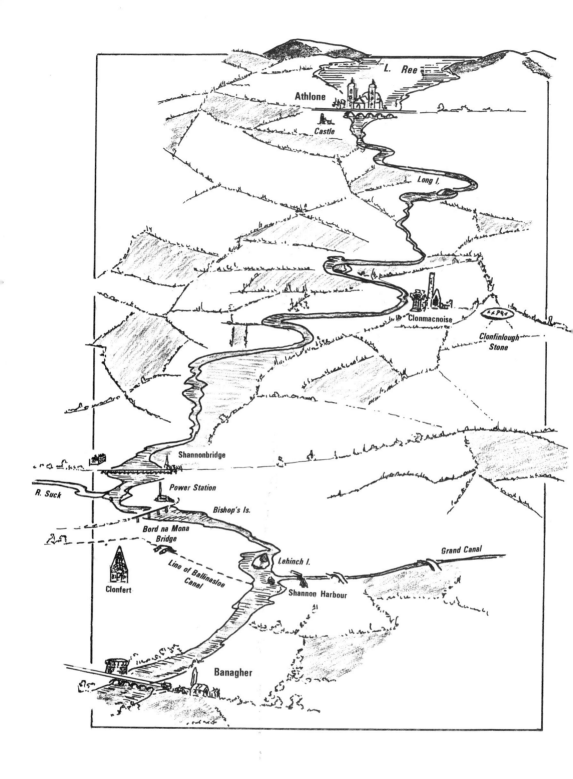

L. Ree

Athlone

Castle

Long I.

Clonmacnoise

Clonfinlough
Stone

Shannonbridge

R. Suck

Power Station

Bishop's Is.

Bord na Mona
Bridge

Grand Canal

Line of Ballinasloe
Canal

Lehinch I.

Clonfert

Shannon Harbour

Banagher

Chapter Six

SOLDIERS, SAINTS AND SCHOLARS
Athlone to Shannonbridge

ONE OF the things which make it difficult to accept the early Irish legends is the more fanciful aspects of some of them. You will remember that Queen Maeve stole the bull from Ulster which then fought a battle to the death with her husband's bull. Well, the story goes on to say that Maeve's bull lifted up his rival on his great horns and bore him off around the country shaking him to pieces as he went and that the places where the dismembered joints fell still bear these names today, Athlone being named after the loin which was deposited there. The Rev. Paul Walsh in his book *The Placenames of Co. Westmeath* quoted this story but also offered another legendary explanation. He described how the beautiful Estiu, wife of Nar, fell in love with Buide and he and his foster brother, Luan, used to visit her in the form of birds, lulling everyone to sleep with the magic of their song so that the lovers could enjoy each other's company. Nar discovered their secret and with one cast shot Buide and Luan as they flew away. Estiu died of grief by the shores of the Shannon at a place called Moystown, near where Shannon Harbour is today. The wounded Luan managed to reach a ford upstream but there he died and the ford become known as the Ford of Luan or Athlone.

I have heard yet another version, that Luan lived in the first century and kept a hostelry beside the ford which was a favourite haunt of travellers. Today, an equally well-known innkeeper, Sean Fitzsimons, keeps a hostelry, Sean's Bar, here, which is the haunt of modern river voyagers and many a piece of helpful advice has been given to visitors by Sean about the river which he knows and loves so well — he is a worthy successor to the ancient Luan. Another legend says that there is a fathomless hole, the Polaphibroch or Piper's Hole, somewhere between the railway and the town bridge where one of the O'Conors, a piper, fell in when he was being rowed across the river and that everyone falling in at this fateful spot is drawn under and into the depths.

Because of its location, Athlone has played an important role in history down the ages and this is well recorded in the journals of the Old Athlone Society by Harman Murtagh, who has made a lifelong study of the town's history. Athlone presents its most attractive face to the waterborne traveller and this is the aspect of the town which interests me and on which I will dwell. Brian Boru is said to have made a causeway here in the year 1000 and it is recorded that Turlough O'Connor erected a bridge here in 1129 with a fort on the Connacht side to protect it. The Normans maintained a bridge here with a motte-and-bailey castle and parts of the present castle date back to this period. The annals record that in 1272 the town was burned and the bridge broken down and there is evidence that there was only a ferry here in the early fourteenth century. Norman supremecy had waned and it is probable that no effort was made to rebuild a bridge here until 1566 when Sir Henry Sydney, Elizabeth's deputy in Ireland, wrote: 'I gave order for the making of the bridge of Athlone, which I finished a piece found serviceable; I am sure durable it is, and I think memorable.' Prophetic words, because this bridge was to be the scene of a brave resistance by the Jacobite forces in 1691 when Sergeant Custume with a small band of men held it against repeated attacks. Eventually, the Williamite forces managed to ford the river just below the bridge and stormed the castle.

The navigation works have of course completely altered the river here today but it seems that in those early days it would have been comparatively easy to ford the river. For example, the annals record that in 1252 there was 'great heat and drought in the summer of this year, so that people used to cross the Sinuinn without wetting their feet'. There is also a puzzling entry for the year 1586: 'The stream of the Sionainn turned back to Lochrigh; and it was twenty four hours in that order, in the presence of all who were in Ath-Luain'. I am told that when hurricane Debbie hit this country in recent years the water was blown upstream over the weir and that places at the south end of Lough Ree dried out when the waters of the lake were blown northwards; it is possible that it was an event such as this which is described in the annals. As recently as 1765 *Faulkner's Dublin Journal* reported: 'This hath been the driest season ever known in this kingdom in so much that the bed of that fine river the Shannon was dry at Athlone Bridge'.

The Elizabethan bridge had ten arches and there were three mills built on it: Jones's mill at the east end, Bracken's mill (referred to later as Steele's mill) in the middle of the bridge, where there was a small island, and Dawson's mill (later Mullin's mill) at the western end. The maximum use was therefore being made of the water power, but these mills and numerous eel weirs greatly impeded the flow of water causing flooding upstream around Lough Ree in winter. By the 1830s, when Rhodes was carrying out his survey for the Shannon Commission, this bridge had become very congested and he described it as follows:

The present old bridge is most inconvenient, and extremely narrow, not exceeding fourteen feet in breadth of roadway, without footpaths, and the confined passage is very much obstructed on market days, by persons attending for the purchase of meal and flour at the three mills which have been erected in the river course and open on to the bridge. Owing to these inconveniences, accidents are of frequent occurrence, and occasionally, after fairs or market days, the general passage for carriages and carts is altogether interrupted for a considerable time, by large droves of cattle.

Athlone in the 1840s

Leitch Ritchie described Athlone in the late 1830s in his book *Ireland Picturesque and Romantic* as an 'irregularly built, confused, huddled, but withal substantial looking town'. He found that the bridge was virtually impassable on a fair day: 'The peasants flocked over, as they usually do, like a herd of bullocks, but with this difference, that they, unlike cattle, had neither dogs nor men to direct and control them.' He remarked that even the police appeared to have to fight their way across like everyone else. His description of the condition of the streets was far from complimentary but maybe he did not feel too kindly disposed towards this place because he had been attacked there; he surmised that his attackers probably thought he was a gentleman from the garrison. Ritchie went by road from Athlone to Shannon Harbour where he boarded the steamer for Killaloe, changing into a larger boat at Portumna for the crossing of Lough Derg but, as with so many of these accounts of travel by water, he adds little to our knowledge of the river at that time. Both Henry Inglis and Isaac Weld had also criticised the bridge at Athlone in the 1830s, Weld saying it was 'not merely a discredit to the town alone, but a positive stigma upon the nation'.

The navigation at this time by-passed this stretch of river and was carried in a canal, one and a quater miles long, to the west of the town. Work had commenced on this canal in 1757, two years after the commencement of the works further downstream. *Faulkner's Journal* for 23 July 1757 records that: 'Mr Omer arrived in Athlone on Thursday and appointed a spot for erecting a lock on, where contrary to expectations there was a fine foundation. There are thirteen gangs at work of twenty-five men each which makes in the whole 325 men on the canal.'

Omer had to overcome a fall of a little over 4 feet at Athlone and he constructed a large lock, 120 feet by 19 feet, about one third of the way up the canal. He widened out the canal to form a harbour adjacent to the main street of the town and upstream of this he put in a single pair of gates, to act as floodgates, which could be closed off when the river was in flood to protect the lock. It is hard to understand why he did not put the gates at the upper end of the canal as is usual with river navigations. They do not appear to have been used much; by 1802 when John Brownrigg surveyed the canal for the Directors General of Inland Navigation, the body responsible for the waterways at that time, he was told that they had never worked satisfactorily. The result was that the floodwaters poured through the canal damaging the banks and the lock. This problem was made worse by the use of the canal banks by the military for watering cattle and Brownrigg said that he saw a horse and cart drive into the canal through one breach and come out from another.

It will be remembered that Omer's professional expertise was later shown to be questionable and although the canal had been operational in the 1780s, the deficiencies soon became apparent. The original suggestion that the ground chosen for the lock would make a bad foundation proved accurate, the walls became warped and leant inwards 'in a remarkable manner' and by the early 1800s the lockgates needed replacing. The Grand Canal Company, which was completing its canal to the Shannon at this time, became most concerned about the state of the Shannon works; there was little point in making a canal from Dublin to the Shannon if the river itself was not navigable. After a protracted, bitter and, at this interval in time, amusing series of negotiations between the company and the Directors General, the canal company took over the restoration of the middle Shannon and Omer's lock had to be completely taken down and rebuilt.

The high ground to the west of the canal, known as Gallows Hill for obvious reasons, attracted the military authorities as a strategic place to build defences in the Napoleonic wars when the threat of a French invasion from the west became a distinct possibility. Five batteries were erected on the hill, and the area, now a housing estate, is still known as The Batteries. The canal acted as a second line of defence with three more batteries between it and the river, while the castle guarding the bridge was strengthened; battery No. 8 was dismantled by the Grand Canal Company when working on the canal, and never rebuilt.

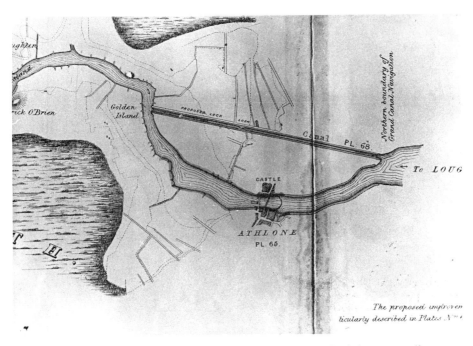

Athlone: Thomas Rhodes's plan showing the old canal which he originally intended to enlarge; he subsequently decided to make the channel in the river

When Rhodes came to survey the river in the 1830s for the Shannon Commission, he first of all recommended enlarging this canal and re-siting the new lock but, subsequently, it was decided to abandon the canal alto-gether and use the river channel. The principal reason for this change was the fact that the bridge across the river had to be replaced, and an inspection of the bed while making preparations for the new bridge had shown that creating a channel here would be a more practical scheme.

It is possible to walk along the old canal today but it is not a pretty sight in places where it has been used for dumping rubbish. The lock was sited just opposite to the entrance gate to the Shamrock Lodge Hotel and the canal and lock have been filled in here and a small park created. The old canal bridge has been replaced but upstream of the harbour under the small modern bridge into the housing estate, the recesses for the guard lock gates can be seen.

The Shannon Commissioners' new bridge across the river was sited slightly upstream; a buttress of the old bridge remains on the east side indi-cating the old location and the main road at that time passed to the south of the castle and is still called Main Street today. The supports for the arches of the new bridge were constructed inside caissons and an opening span was

Athlone: the gate recess for the guard lock on the old canal

made on the west side using the same design as the other opening bridges. The new bridge was opened to the public in November 1844, the mill owners were compensated and the old bridge was demolished.

In the meantime, a giant coffer dam was constructed for the building of the new lock, using eight pile drivers and 35,000 cubic feet of timber. The work was carried out under the supervision of John Davis who had recently returned from Pesth in Hungary where he had been engaged in the erection of the coffer dams for a suspension bridge across the Danube. At the same time as the lock was being built, work commenced on driving in the piles for the new weir wall which stretched across from the lock to the east side of the river. The clearing of the river bed was undertaken by a stream dredger but progress was very slow because of the hard nature of the rock.

The lock was completed by 1849 but enormous difficulties were encountered not only in the construction of the weir which was constantly being undermined by the flow of water but also in the deepening of the river bed, and so it was decided to try to lay dry the entire river bed by building a dam across the river upstream of the town at the narrowest place, where there had been a ford, and by diverting the water down the old canal. This

110

was obviously a rather risky undertaking and it was anticipated that it would not be possible to hold back the waters for any length of time. It was decided to carry out the operation in July when the river would normally be at its lowest levels and arrangements were carefully made to make the maximum use of the time. Word was spread through the surrounding countryside, which was still suffering from the effects of famine, that a large number of men would be needed and the *Westmeath Independent* reported on 30 June: 'Some thousands of poor creatures crowded into the town . . . many of the starving creatures having travelled a long distance with the hope of being engaged.'

The intention was to achieve three things while the river was dry: the weir would be completed, the excavation of the river bed would be finished and the abutments of the old bridge and eel weirs would be removed. The *Westmeath Independent* confirms that work continued through the months of July and August with up to 1,500 men employed at times in the river bed. On 14 July it was reported: 'All is activity and bustle. The spectacle of nearly one thousand men engaged in excavating the bed of the river which is completely dry, and which as far as the eye can reach is filled with workmen and horses, miners and engineers etc. is a novelty not often met with.' I have sometimes stood on the bridge and tried to conjure up this great scene. The lock had been completed by this time and in order to let off pockets of water which had lodged in places, they opened all the gates. All this time the water was building up on the other side of the temporary dam and, eventually, it burst through and the water rushed down the river. There was no report of lives being lost so there must have been enough warning to get the men out. However, the lock gates were not closed in time and William Forsyth, one of the engineers, recorded later that he was summoned from Dublin to try to get the gates closed 'and with a good deal of difficulty we got them shut at last'. Curiously, there is no report of this mishap in the local paper, which simply stated on 1 September: 'Yesterday a great portion of the river was turned into its natural channel and in a few days we expect to find the navigation open to traffic.'

There must have been moments, however, when all the effort seemed worthwhile. On 8 September 1849 the *Westmeath Independent* reported:

The appearance on Thursday of one of the City of Dublin Steam Navigation Company's large vessels, the *Lady Lansdowne*, on the Upper Shannon was a novelty which came unexpectedly upon the inhabitants of Athlone. As she steamed up our noble river, a large number of spectators congregated on the bridge and quays and by hearty cheers welcomed this, the first attempt to open the navigation for vessels of

Athlone in the early 1900s

any burden above Shannonbridge.... We are happy to learn that in future the company's steamer will ply regularly between Limerick and Athlone with passengers and freight.

Within ten years this steamer service was to find itself in fierce competition with the railways and before long it had lost the struggle for survival.

It was here in Athlone that a great deal of the overspending on the original estimate had occurred which was to lead to curtailing the work upstream; nearly twenty per cent of the total expenditure of £584,806 was spent here. Certainly the Athlone works are impressive with the fine stone quays, the bridge, the lock and the weir, monuments to the engineers who built them. The weir helped to maintain a constant level in Lough Ree and the deepening of the channel and the removal of obstructions enabled floodwaters to pass

Athlone: the weir, showing the sluices fitted to the open weir, in the 1880s

more freely through this stretch of river. Sluice gates added to the weir in the 1880s further improved control of the levels upstream in the lake but did not solve the problem of flooding downstream. In time of flood it is quite common to see the water at the same level above and below the weir with the river below the town overflowing its banks to form a vast lake as far as the eye can see.

In the 1950s a new battle of Athlone Bridge took place. This time the protagonists were Harry Rice, supported by the newly formed IWAI, against the local authority who wanted to replace the opening bridge with a fixed structure. This required an amendment to the Shannon Navigation Act and, while the headroom under Athlone bridge was reasonably good and, in fact, the bridge had not actually worked for many years, the association felt it was important to fight the permanent fixing of any of the bridges, as a matter of principle, because, as we have already noted, some of those upstream also needed replacing and they were considerably lower.

The battle was won by a clever scheme instigated by Harry's great friend and ally, Sean MacBride, who invited William Norton, the Tanaiste in the coalition government at that time, and T. C. Courtney, chairman of CIE, for a trip on the river in the *St Clair*, owned by Harry's daughter Betty and her husband, John Williams. The potential of the river was 'sold' to them and Mr Norton encouraged CIE to put two passenger launches on the river which required a minimum headroom of 14 feet. The IWAI recognised that this clearance was sufficient to preserve the navigation and agreed that the bridge at Athlone be replaced by a fixed structure on condition that the lower bridges must have opening spans. This meant that sailing boats would no longer be able to navigate the river without the masts being lowered but the association felt that this was a concession which had to be made in view of the small number of sailing boats on the river at that time. There had been allusions at local authority meetings to 'yachts owned by the privileged few' and it was suggested that public money should not be spent to keep navigation open with full headroom for these boats. In retrospect, the decision to do away with the opening bridges was a pity because of the large numbers of sailing boats on the river today but at the time the association was fighting for the very survival of the navigation and was well pleased with the concession gained.

Harry Rice died in May 1964, four months after my husband Vincent, but they had succeeded in setting up a strong association and, despite the severe blow of losing its two founding members, the IWAI continued to work actively for the preservation and maintenance of the waterways. In 1973 the Athlone Branch of the IWAI constructed a boat slip, to be called the Harry Rice Memorial Slip, at the Jolly Mariner Marina just north of Athlone, which

113

The *Coill an Eo*, the Board of Works maintenance boat, with the old maintenance boat alongside on which Denis Madigan worked

was owned at that time by Syd Shine, and a stone memorial was erected which was unveiled, fittingly, by his friend, Sean MacBride.

There is another memorial in Athlone, a tablet in the wall below the lock which was erected by the Athlone Branch in memory of the late Denis Madigan. Denis had been skipper of the Board of Works repair boat for many years, a role that was carried on for a time by one of his sons, and had always been a good friend to people on the river. He was one of the Shannon's best known characters and his work was much more than just a job to him.

The river had many characters in the old days and I think the best tribute I can pay to them is to reproduce in full the following poem which is signed W. Doyle, Drumshanbo, and which was given to Vincent many years ago by the late Andy Killeen, who was the ESB engineer responsible for the Shannon river:

> Down somewhere in Limerick near the old Treaty Stone
> Where Irishmen valiantly fought for their own
> And won proud 'Conditions', our land would have served
> Alas! those conditions were never observed.
> I found myself placed in a fine spacious hall
> With pictures, historic, hung round on the wall
> There Sarsfield on horseback with gleaming sword drawn

And Danny Mann drowning the Cailin Bawn
And brave Colonel Grace and the martyred Wolfe Tone
And a group of jig dancers in old Garryowen.
A long line of Shannon men entered the hall
Lock keepers, sluice keepers, boatmen and all
Each dressed in his best with cuffs, collar and tie
And looking quite big when no bigger was nigh.
I saw Conlon and Leslie, Big Tom and McGarry
And Inspector Bourke from old Tarmonbarry
Shouldice and Madigan, Collins and Crowe
And a good many more whom I did not know.
On my right an ex-peeler with language bombastic
On 'tother another with visage fantastic,
But why criticise them? Sure I must agree
They tendered a right hearty welcome to me.
I got a great welcome by skipper Joe Mack
Who forced me to draughts of Three Star Cognac
The next who came to me was Pat Considine
Who made me to drink a large goblet of wine
I'd a piggin of porter brought to me by Farrell
That Daniel O'Mara drew fresh from the barrell
I had whiskey from Shouldice and rum from McGee
Matt Reddin says 'Now you'll have something from me'.
I was drunk as a lord when some one in the throng
Says 'Bard of Lough Allen please give us a song'.
So proud of my title, I loosened my coat
I coughed and recoughed for to ready my throat
The veins on my forehead began for to swell
And my eyes turned up like a frog in a well
I looked at the pictures that hung in the hall
And Sarsfield was chasing them round on the wall.
'Now boys you'll excuse me to sing (hic) I'm not able'
Then fell like a bag of sand under the table
My old corporation with liquor well stored
A high situation down under the board.
Now soon on the scene came my old time friend Hewitt
Saying 'Why do you let him lie there like a brute?'
Then he with three more took me off on a stretcher
When someone says 'Close boys, here comes Mr Fletcher'.
In one minute more, to my horrid surprise
He was conning me hard with his two pair of eyes

Saying 'What lubber is this? He's drunk I suppose
Ha! Tis Doyle from Lough Allen, I'd know his big nose
He left without leave and he'll pay for the roast
He'll hear from me sure by tomorrow night's post'.
Then he grabbed at my hair for to turn my head
But the hair was not there and he scratched me instead.
I awoke from my dream, 'twas a mouse 'pon my soul
Was trying to climb up my smooth greasy poll
I jumped to right angles, my mind in a maze
I thought for an instant the room was ablaze
'Twas the dawning of morn that peeped through my screen
So I rose and I wrote the whole thing to Killeen.

Some people say that the middle Shannon from Athlone to Portumna is the least attractive part of the river and I must admit it can be bleak on a wet and windy day but, for me, as it winds its way south in great curves, it is at its most majestic. Its reed-lined banks and marshy meadows are full of interest. Often you will be accompanied by a heron, patrolling his territory, flying ahead of the boat and then landing and remaining motionless, pretending that he is not there. There are usually all sorts of interesting birds in the meadows to be identified, including the curlew with its mournful cry, one of the species which move inland in the summer.

The multiplicity of markers may seem unnecessary but if the river is in flood they are essential and are carefully located to prevent boats ending up in a field. We have a favourite mooring place in behind the little island at the head of Long Island. The early navigation passed down the west side of Long Island; this was an artificial canal, creating the island, but the Shannon Commissioners changed the navigation back to the river. It is not possible to pass through the old channel today because there is a causeway across about halfway down. At the south end of Long Island is the Three County Pile, marking a rocky stretch of river and, as its name denotes, this is the meeting place of counties Westmeath, Roscommon and Offaly.

The Dean of Rochester published a book in 1892 entitled *A Little Tour in Ireland*. It had been written many years earlier when he was an undergraduate and is a lighthearted account which he had not tried to alter because 'gaiety becomes an undergraduate as much as gaiters a dean'. He travelled with his friend down the Shannon by steamer but paid more attention to the ladies on board than the scenery. He did remark on the 'quaint looking tumuli' of hay studding the fields, 'too large for haycocks and too small for stacks' and the beacons 'of an original pattern'. His travelling companion suggested that the round towers of Ireland were 'most probably lighthouses, which had come ashore at night for a spree, and had forgotten the way back again'.

What were Ciaran's thoughts as he sailed down the river in the sixth century in search of a place to found a new settlement? The river cannot have looked so very different then. What prompted him to abandon his paradise on Hare Island to seek out the windswept site on the esker ridge by the banks of the river? We are told that he died on 23 January 544, seven months after he had come there at the early age of thirty-three but his settlement was destined to grow into a great monastic city famed far and wide through Europe. It seems that, like St Diarmuid, he continued to keep a watchful eye on his foundation because the story is told that three hundred years after his death, in 844 when the king of Cashel had twice plundered the termon lands of Clonmacnoise, St Ciaran pursued him and thrust at him with his crozier giving him a wound from which he later died.

Approaching Clonmacnoise the round tower is visible for some time as the river winds its way towards it. I always picture Mervyn Wall's Fursey crouching behind the stone wall, his magic rope slung over his shoulder, looking out apprehensively for fathers Crustaceous, Furiosus and Placidus. It was not until quite recently that I discovered there actually was a St Fursey, who was a disciple of St Brendan.

P. W. Joyce in his *Social History of Ancient Ireland* gave an interesting account of life in one of these monastic settlements and there is also a fascinating description in Kathleen Hughes and Ann Hamlin's book *Celtic Monasticism, The Modern Traveler to the Early Irish Church* which was published in 1981. They make the point that the people living in these settlements were not the misfits of society, the naturally humble and retiring, but were in fact the social élite. There is a long and detailed legend told about Ciaran choosing the site for his new settlement and how he was marking out the land with a staff when Diarmuid MacCerbhaill, an exiled prince, came by. Ciaran asked him to hold the staff while he drove it into the ground and grateful for Diarmuid's help, he promised him that one day he would be king, a promise that was later fulfilled. It is more likely, however, that he would have been granted the land by the local lord or king; it was customary for the land for a foundation to be made available in this way and usually some members of these families joined the monastery in one of the leading roles. It would seem to be a bleak spot today but at that time it represented a strategic place with traffic moving north and south along the river and east and west along the esker ridge. In the larger communities, like Clonmacnoise, there would have been a considerable number of people involved; it is recorded that in 1179 during an attack one hundred and five houses were burned. There was usually a bishop, priests, abbot, steward, monks, lay monks, who

117

often had wives, and various craftsmen such as stonemasons and metal workers; a patronage of these arts was one of the features of the foundations and the fine stone crosses and finds of jewellery and other objects are evidence of this.

Investigations by archaeologists have shown that these communities were largely self-supporting. Oats, barley and a little wheat were grown, the corn was ground and made into loaves and gruel was made from the meal, water and butter. Cattle were grazed in the surrounding area in peaceful times and brought inside the stockade when the settlement was under attack. The cows provided milk, butter and cheese and the community also kept pigs; fresh and salted pork were an important part of the meat diet. They kept bees for honey and fowl for eggs and also made full use of natural resources such as fish, berries and nuts. Greens and root crops were also grown; the agricultural work would have been shared but much of it was probably carried out by the lay brothers, who, like Fursey, 'possessed the virtue of Holy simplicity in such a degree that he was considered unfit for any work other than paring edible roots in the monastery kitchen'. Sheep were kept for their wool which was dyed and woven to make into habits. Wood was important as a fuel and for constructing buildings; also for making furniture and equipment.

The monks lived in small huts, and prayer and the saying of masses was an important part of their day. They were also involved in teaching and in copying, illuminating and composing manuscripts. The local people would not have been allowed to take much part in the religious activities; they had to be content to leave their salvation in the hands of the monks who did the praying for them, almost inaudibly and in Latin. The people did come seeking medical advice and would have been given herbal remedies. Hospitality was always offered to travellers; it was the custom to give three nights free lodging in the guest house or hospice and the guest would be offered a bath, with hot bricks being used to heat the water in the tub.

I have seen references to the fact that there was a bridge here at one time and there are certainly two places where there used to be fords in the river, one just opposite the Norman castle and the other upstream beyond the second bend where it is still rocky and narrow today. The castle was erected in 1214 by John de Gray, bishop of Norwich, and it was later blown up leaving it with one corner perched precariously ever since.

The Clonmacnoise which we see today, however, does not belong to the period of early monastic settlement for it was not until the ninth century that stone began to replace wood in buildings and the ruined churches we see here date from the ninth, tenth, eleventh and twelfth centuries. There is an excellent colour coded plan of the place which makes it easy to date each of the ruins and there are leaflets which point out the interesting features. Like other monastic settlements, Clonmacnoise suffered many attacks from the Vikings and sometimes from the Irish themselves. For a time it was a great centre of learning and when the Church was reorganised along diocesan lines in the twelfth century, Clonmacnoise was chosen as the centre of a see with a cathedral and bishop. It declined in importance and by the late fifteenth and early sixteenth century it was without an effective resident bishop because of the poverty of the see; in 1516 the cathedral was reported to be roofless and ruinous.

In 1552 the place was sacked and looted by English soldiers from Athlone and it never recovered fully from this attack. The story goes that the soldiers stole the great bell and, loading it into a boat, pushed off from the shore, but they began to quarrel as to who should have it and in the ensuing fight they killed each other, the boat capsized and the bell sank to the bottom of the river. This part of the river ran red with blood for many a year and some say that at night you can hear the tones of the bell tolling beneath the waters.

The Church must have retained some presence here for a time because it is recorded that in the 1640s Cardinal Rinuccini, the papal nuncio in Ireland, was rowed by the McCoghlans up the river from Raghra (later Shannonbridge) to Athlone and on the way he stopped at Clonmacnoise to take breakfast with the bishop. It was to lie deserted for several centuries apart from the annual pattern, and when we first used to visit the place it had an unkempt appearance; in many ways it was easier to capture the atmosphere of the past then. Today the grass is well kept, there is a large car-park, a tourist information centre and a constant stream of visitors.

Guided tours are arranged and Harry Rice would smile if he could hear the young ladies who act as guides interpreting the figures on the Cross of the Scriptures with such conviction. He spent many hours carefully drawing it and putting his own interpretation on the carvings. These differed from the ideas of schoolmaster Molloy, who lived beside the site and acted as unofficial guide. The Molloys had lived there over several generations acting as guides and providing accommodation to the many distinguished scholars who came to see the place. If you do manage to get a quiet moment in front of the great Cross, before reading the modern interpretations, it is interesting to try to work out for yourself what you think Turcan, the ancient sculptor, was portraying. Who knows, your guess could be right.

Many people have written interesting accounts of visits to Clonmacnoise over the years. In 1779 Gabriel Beranger, who had been appointed by the Hibernian Antiquarian Society to draw and make plans of monastic sites in Connacht, wrote a letter about his visit to Clonmacnoise:

We have been at Clonmacnoise full of hopes of finding great antiquities,

119

but were mistaken and found nothing equal to our Expectations except the Two round Towers, who undoubtedly are like those of their kind of unknown creation... The doors of the Seven Churches particularly of the Cathedral are carved and somewhat in the taste of the Abbey of Cong. The other doors are round and plastered to make them even, the plaster is another sign of modern work as in the old Buildings it is all destroyed by time, in Harris's translation of Ware, they are pretty well represented, also the Crosses which since that time are much wore, children throwing stones at them and the figures blunted.

The annual pattern held here appears to have led to such excesses that it was eventually abandoned. Thomas Cromwell in a book describing his 'Excursions' through Ireland, published in 1820, said that some three to four thousand people used to attend:

They continue here for two days; and so often do these meetings end in quarrels, (from the effects of which many are confined to their beds for weeks afterward) that some respectable inhabitants have thought their abolition would be every way desirable.

Caesar Otway came here in 1839, transported by river from Athlone by the vicar of St Mary's on the day following the annual pattern. He compared the stark landscape of the river with the Thames:

Clonmacnoise: an early engraving by Bartlett

Here no trade, except that carried on by one steam-barge, no timber, no smiling lawns, no cultivation — the solitary hopelessness of the bog is all around, and nothing interrupts the silence of the waste but the wild pipe of the curlew, as it whistles over the morass, or the shriek of the heron, as it rises lazily from the sedgy bank, and complains aloud against our unwonted interruption of its solitary speculations. If ever there was a picture of grim and hideous repose, it is the flow of the Shannon from Athlone to Clonmacnoise. We met but one specimen of way-faring on this great navigable river — as we rowed down with the slow stream but against the strong south west wind — a large boat met us half way, it bore down on us, urged along by a square sail composed for the nonce of blankets and quilts, the coverings of yesterday's tents and was freighted with drunken publicans, 'Canponibus atque malignis', belonging to the town of Athlone, who had gone on a whiskey venture to the patron of Clonmacnoise, and were now returning drunk with the draining of jars and kegs of spirits, that they had nearly emptied for sale on the previous day, which found horrible and peculiar desecration as falling on the one dedicated to Kieran . . . many a tent was still standing, many were still keeping up the deep carouse that had continued all through the Sabbath night.

In a book written by the Rev. Canon Monahan, PP of Cloghan in 1886, on the history of the diocese of Ardagh and Clonmacnoise, there is an interesting account of a pilgrimage to Clonmacnoise by the Historical & Antiquarian Society of Dublin. They travelled by train to Athlone and then down river in the steamer *Ida*. On arrival we are told: 'they were greeted by the cheers of a vast multitude numbering about 8,000 persons, who anxiously awaited their coming'. The assembled multitude were addressed by the Reverend Canon in stirring words. Pointing to the Norman castle he declared:

Look around and what do you behold? Yonder on that green fort, the remains of a castle built by the English, under De Lacy in 1214, and now leaning over and presenting a pile of high masses of dangerously inclining stonework. Perhaps in its present tumbling shape it is emblematic of their bad laws and worse administration, together with the civil influences on which they rested so many gloomy years, but now tottering and falling fast, let us hope, to rise no more. (cheers)

He concluded with the rousing words:

I pity the Irishman whose patriotism is not increased by reading the brave deeds of his ancestors on the plains of Clontarf or the hills of Aughrim, and whose piety does not become more fervent and practical by a visit to the ruins of Clonmacnoise.

Canon Monahan had an interesting map of the area in his book in which he indicated the field behind the enclosure as the site of the ancient city with a gateway leading into the churches. He showed another ruined church on the east wall named 'Temple Aspick', just north of it were the ruins of the arch-deacon's house and in the north east corner the ruins of the hospice. Marking the causeway leading across to the Nun's church, which he called 'Dervorgilla's Nunnery', he marked 'The cairn of the Three Crosses' on the left hand side of the path and, facing it, 'The Grave of St Kieran's Housemaid'! The three crosses marked the graves of three criminals who were refused burial within the enclosure; this went back a long way in time because there is a reference in the *Annals of the Four Masters* for the year 1026 which states: 'The Causeway from the garden of the Abbess to the cairn of the three crosses in Clonmacnoise was made by Breasal Conaille (the Abbot)'. In more recent times three new crosses were put up to replace the old ones which had long since disappeared but a well-known local historian remarked: 'I think they are terrible things! One has mercifully fallen down. May the rest soon follow.'

For some reason most visitors to Clonmacnoise never traverse the cause-way to the Nun's church which is a pity because I think it is the most inter-esting of all the ruins. The women as usual were banished to the outskirts of the monastic settlement and this little church was built in the tenth century. It suffered the usual fate of pillage and destruction and then, in 1166, it was restored by Dervorgilla. Now, as every Irish schoolchild knows, she was the wicked woman who was responsible for bringing the Normans over here and so initiating our eight hundred years of foreign occupation. Consumed with remorse, she restored this church and sought solace here at Clonmacnoise but the church and adjoining nunnery were destroyed by fire a few years later in 1188. The Romanesque doorway and chancel arch were partly restored in 1865 by the Rev James Graves with financial help from the Royal Society of Antiquaries of Ireland. Most nineteenth-century restoration is looked upon with horror by modern archaeologists but this is considered to be an example of enlightened work and the carving is exquisite. Set apart from the busy scene, this is a place of peace and because, unlike Turcan who asked future generations to pray for him in his inscription on his high cross, Dervorgilla was not able to do so, maybe we should spare her a thought as there is little doubt that the Normans would have found another excuse to invade Ireland.

It has been suggested that the area around Clonmacnoise should be declared a Heritage Zone. The scheme would involve compensating the farmers to encourage them to continue with traditional farming methods and thus preserve the ecology of the area. This would be in line with current EEC policy which recognises that it is no longer sensible to encourage increased productivity at the expense of the environment, adding further to existing mountains of surplus food supplies. Apart from the monastic settlement there are a number of other interesting features in the vicinity. To the south at Clerhaun is the limestone quarry where some of the stone for the Athlone works was obtained. In the bend of the river there is a fine example of callows rich in distinctive flora and a wintering refuge for many wildfowl and waders; to the west, Mongan bog is a raised bog of international scientific importance and to the south of the bog is Lough Fin where there is a calcareous fen with an unusually wide variety of plants with nearby the Clonfinlough stone.

In all the times I had been to Clonmacnoise I had never found time to visit the Clonfinlough stone. Recently finding myself there with a car I decided to set off to look for it. It was a full three mile drive from the river along the Athlone road and up a side road to the church at Clonfinlough and so it would be quite a walk from the river. I found it easily because it is well signposted and a path had been made around the church to the field in which the stone lies. I had seen a drawing of it in Harry Rice's book but it was not at all as I expected. It is a large boulder, about 10 feet by 8 feet, sitting in the middle of a sloping field and the markings on it are quite difficult to make out. These markings are similar to those found on stones in north west Spain which are said to date back to the Bronze Age. There are some crosses and circles, bisected by a perpendicular line with a small knob on the top; Peter Harbison suggests that the latter, which some people say represent men with arms akimbo, are, in fact, just carved circles with the lines through them made by natural erosion. Because of the controversy which surrounds it, it is well worth seeing and, like the Cross of the Scriptures, you can reach your own conclusions about interpretation.

The bridge at Shannonbridge is one of the few early Shannon bridges to have survived the Shannon Commissioners' works in the 1840s. In 1759 Henry L'Estrange and William Talbot were granted £2,000 by the Irish parliament to build a bridge here at Raghra, as it was called then. A parliamentary committee later reported that the work had been completed and that considerably more than the grant had been expended. They built well; some underpinning was carried out in the 1840s but, today the sixteen arch bridge still stands with a navigation span on the east shore.

In the eighteenth century, when Omer was making the river navigable, he had to overcome a fall of only 1 foot here and so he made a short canal on the east side by dredging out a channel and building a bank to separate it from the rest of the river; he made the canal wider near the bridge to form a small harbour. He did not think it was necessary to make a lock because of the small fall and so he put in a flash lock or single pair of gates and he built another of his attractive two storey lockhouses above the canal. This is a particularly fine example of one of his houses, built in cut stone, and it is good to see that it survived the recent widening of the approaches to the bridge, although it is a pity that it is not occupied or used for some purpose.

The Grand Canal Company made a conventional lock here in the early 1800s but Rhodes decided to remove the canal and lock and deepen the channel in the 1840s. He did this by removing the embankment and lock and carrying out extensive dredging but he left the landward side of the old canal and the original wall is still there today with the recesses for the old lock under the bridge and the original harbour area with steps. Rhodes put in another of his turning bridges here and, thanks to an enlightened local authority decision, this old bridge was carefully moved to a prepared site on the quay when the opening span, which had been strengthened for many years by a temporary bailey bridge, was being replaced by a fixed structure recently. I believe they had their problems trying to lift out the sections and nearly lost bridge and crane into the river but they persevered and this was a very worthy action because all the other turning bridges had been dismantled and this was the last one.

The fortifications erected to frustrate Napoleon's plans to invade Ireland from the west still dominate the river at Shannonbridge. It was the defection of a French general, General Dumouriez, which was largely responsible for the adoption of the coastal and Shannon defences in Ireland. He was fully aware of the activities of Irishmen in Paris, who were attempting to persuade

Shannonbridge

Napoleon to send a large expedition to Ireland, and he prepared a detailed 'Military Memorandum' for the British Government in 1808 suggesting the steps to be taken to defend Ireland. However, Napoleon had many sources of information in Ireland to supply him with details of the defences and his preliminary plans for the invasion included boats for fording the Shannon to avoid the heavily defended river crossings.

The Shannonbridge defences provide a unique example of artillery fortifications of this period and it is a pity that they are not more accessible to visitors. I tried to bring some people to see the main redoubt and we were faced by a locked gate and waist-high wet grass. It is essential to be able to get right into this area to appreciate the design. The inner courtyard had accommodation opening off it and the central apartment has a little structure called a caponier which protrudes out into the dry moat. From it, the musket men could pick off any of the enemy who might succeed in gaining access to the moat. Climbing up on the wall of this central redoubt, you can observe the four traversing rails for the guns, probably 24-pounder canon with a range of over a mile. These commanded the approaches from Ballinasloe and the west, looking out over the glacis, which was an artificial slope extending out about 200 yards with the dry moat separating it from the redoubt.

The main road runs through the military enclosure and until a few years ago it passed through an arched gateway in a wall connecting the redoubt and the blockhouse, but these had to be removed to cater for modern traffic. The blockhouse is the large building looking out on the river. In it there was further barrack accommodation with a heavily protected powder magazine and three more guns mounted on the roof covering the southern flank; a corresponding small-arms battery protected the northern flank. In addition,

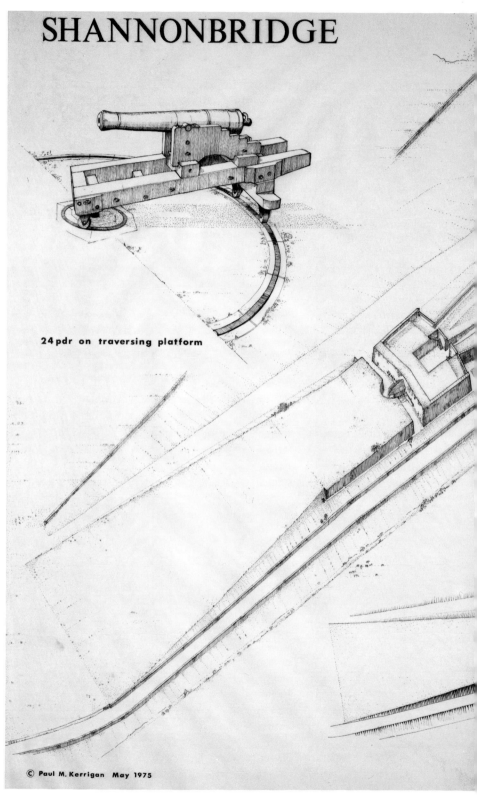

SHANNONBRIDGE

24 pdr on traversing platform

© Paul M. Kerrigan May 1975

Shannonbridge: an asymmetrical drawing of the fortifications

1 Glacis	6 Small-arms battery	11 Battery no. 2
2 Caponnière	7 Guardroom	a,b,c,d traversing rails
3 Redoubt	8 Barrack	for redoubt guns
4 Road gate	9 Ditch with palisade	e, f, g traversing rails
5 North gate	10 Site of battery no.1	for barrack guns

50 0   100 feet

N

11

on the east side of the river there was another powder magazine, some defences protecting the bridge and another battery a little way downstream, with a further gun emplacement on the island just to the north of the bridge. It is easy for us now to question the necessity for all these elaborate defences, the Shannonbridge fortifications alone cost about £30,000, but the obvious state of preparedness of the military authorities in Ireland must have acted as a strong deterrent to any would-be invaders.

Shannonbridge has always been a place where Shannon sailors like 'to stop to buy milk' and it is a popular venue for IWAI rallies. Killeens at the top of the town has seen some memorable evenings. I expect there are still one or two people around who can remember one such evening many years ago when Colonel Hooker, one of the Shannon's most distinguished sailing race officers, clad in kilt, performed the sword dance for the assembled company. For many years we used to moor down in the cut below the bridge to get away from the clatter of the 'temporary' bailey bridge but now the new bridge is in place and all is at peace. The Board of Works have made a new extension to the old quay wall which is rather low and tends to disappear when the water is high in the river. The bank moorings in the cut are still attractive for those of us who are anti-social.

One of the early Shannon guides in the 1960s bore a warning about the River Suck which said: 'This river has a dangerous shoal a short distance from its confluence', and it is still off-limits to hire boats. Douglas loved exploring and when he fitted an echo sounder on *Harklow,* he decided he would try out his new toy by going up the Suck gently until the water began to shoal. We continued on for several miles without encountering any shallows and so we decided we would return with a stronger crew and see just how far up we could get. It was still early in the season when we returned, the water was fairly high and we went up gently for more than 4 miles until we reached a place where there was a ford with very little water over it but with a gap on the south side. The boat was bowhauled through the gap in case she grounded and damaged her propellor and, once over this obstruction, we continued on for quite a distance until the river became very wide with an island in the middle. The channels on either side of the island were sounded out from the dinghy and found to be too shallow for *Harklow* but we continued on in the dinghy and discovered that once over these shallows there was deep water again until Ballinasloe was in sight. We found to our amazement that it would be a very simple matter to make the river navigable to within a short distance of this town, all that would be required would be one lock at the island and a little dredging at the ford.

The Grand Canal Company minute books had revealed that a scheme to make the Suck navigable was put before the Directors General of Inland

Navigation in the early 1800s at the time when the company was carrying out the reconstruction of the locks on the middle Shannon. The company pointed out that it was a good opportunity to make the Suck navigable while the men and materials were on hand; the cost of the scheme was £15,000 or £26,000 if a towpath was included. When financial support was not forthcoming, the plan was dropped but in 1817 the company once again looked into the question of extending the navigation to Ballinasloe because this town was an important market centre for the west and a considerable amount of goods found their way from there to the Grand Canal at Shannon Harbour. This time the directors opted for making a canal to Ballinasloe instead of opening up the Suck which would have meant the additional expense of making towpaths which they considered would be essential not only along the Suck but also along the Shannon from Shannon Harbour to the confluence, a distance of over four miles.

Ironically, by the time the Ballinasloe Canal was completed, with the help of a government loan, the first steamers had arrived on the river making it no longer necessary to have towpaths. If they had known this was going to happen it would have made the River Suck scheme the much less expensive option. From our point of view today it was a great pity they opted for the canal because it has now been abandoned whereas the river navigation would have survived. Since we visited the river, a new railway bridge has been erected by Bord na Mona for conveying turf from this vast area of bog to the power station which is located on the east bank of the Shannon, a short distance from the confluence. I am told that there is reasonable headroom under this bridge but there is a notice on it which states in English and German: 'Danger — Beware of rocks, shallow water and submarine boats'. So if you do go up there, keep a sharp look-out for periscopes.

A similar Bord na Mona railway bridge was built some years ago across the main river beside the power station, just south of the confluence with the Suck, and this is a favourite spot for fishermen because of the warm water being discharged from the cooling system. A short distance downstream of this bridge there is a group of small islands, called Bishop's Islands, which were part of the Bishop of Clonfert's lands. The Shannon Commissioners' drawings show a short canal here which was subsequently abandoned by them when they dredged the river channel. Some day I must see if I can find this old canal because this is the nearest place on the river to Clonfert Cathedral and it would be a useful place to moor the boat. We usually anchor here and row ashore to walk the 1½ miles to the cathedral. About halfway there, the road crosses a bridge over a narrow gauge turf railway. This railway runs in the bed of the former Ballinasloe Canal but there is little indication that it was a canal except for the faintly discernible towpath;

further west where the next bridge spanned the canal the railway track passes through the old lock chamber. I remember mooring *Hark* at the first bridge to visit Clonfert before the canal was closed. Harry Rice also recorded that he visited Clonfert by water and he chatted with an old man there. The conversation turned, as it sometimes does, to the depredations of Cromwell, who is attributed with knocking down a great number more castles that he actually did. The old man turned to Harry and remarked in all seriousness: 'Ah, Cromwell. Yes. I remember him well.' We Irish have long memories.

St Brendan returned from his voyaging around the world and founded a monastic settlement here at Clonfert in the sixth century. As you would expect nothing remains of this early settlement but the saint is said to be buried here beneath a flat slab beside the little cathedral. Because of its importance, Clonfert was chosen as the centre of a diocese when the Church was reorganised in the twelfth century and the façade of the cathedral dates back to this time. You need to take time to stand in front of the magnificent doorway and examine the wide variety of carving. It is interesting that the jambs are sloped slightly inwards, a survival from the time when this was architecturally necessary to support heavy lintels. This is made more noticeable by the insertion in the fifteenth century of another order in the arch which is in a vertical position and greatly spoils the effect. The triangular pediment surmounting the doorways is without equal, every inch was used by the sculptor's tool. The chancel of the church is said to be thirteenth-century with a fifteenth-century chancel arch decorated with angels and a strange mermaid-type figure who seems to be holding a mirror in her hand which is thought to have some association with the sailor saint. There is a ruined Romanesque south transept and the friary-type bell tower would have been added at the same time as the Gothic north transept, which has now been removed.

The IWAI held an ecumenical service here in 1985 to celebrate the 1500th anniversary of the sailor saint's birth. During the service the Catholic Bishop Cassidy referred to the fact that the little cathedral, which was packed with people of all persuasions, pre-dated the unhappy divisions in the Church. I am sure it gave St Brendan much pleasure to see the Shannon 'Boat People' bringing people together again to worship here. How times have changed since a previous Catholic Bishop of Clonfert wrote of the cathedral:

It has passed, however, from Catholic hands, and will, doubtless, soon be abandoned by the Protestants too, for the few persons who attend divine worship in the old Cathedral of St Brendan can hardly be called a congregation.

I hope the day is not too far distant when our people will come to worship together in these old churches which are so much part of our heritage.

In the old days the bishop walked through the graveyard and, passing through a gateway, he walked up a fine yew walk to his palace. This yew walk, known as the Friar's Walk, had side passages, creating the impression of a vast cruciform cathedral; one of the side aisles is now gone but it is still impressive. The last and rather unlikely occupant of the palace was Oswald Mosley who came to live in Ireland in 1946 because his fascist activities had made him unpopular in England. It is a sad and dejected sight today. About one mile up the Eyrecourt road stands the local Catholic church and inside it there is an interesting fourteenth century wooden statue of the Madonna and Child. It is said to have been found hidden in a tree and is greatly venerated by the local people.

Just below the confluence with the River Blackwater stand the ruins of Derryholmes House. There was an extensive ford here and the early sailing course zigzagged up through it. The Shannon Commissioners set about removing the shallows and even today there are signs of the extensive works of excavation which they had to carry out. Where possible they usually tried to remove shoals with the dredgers without laying dry the area. When large rocks were encountered a diver was sent down to pass chains around them and sometimes they were blasted underwater to reduce them to more manageable proportions:

by means of boring holes into them, with long jumpers worked by men in barges moored immediately over them; the holes being bored from two to three feet in depth, tin canisters of powder, with patent fuze attached, were inserted and fired, which succeeded in many instances in breaking the rock into fragments. Canvas bags of powder, tarred, were tried, which produced a better effect in blasting than the tin canisters. The fragments were raised in some instances by the pentagraph shears, and by means of Lewis bolts and chains, worked by crab winches.

Where the shoal was very extensive, 'stanks' were formed by erecting coffer dams and the area was unwatered by steam pumps. The men worked in two shifts, from 2 am until noon and from noon till 10 pm to remove the rock but often the water burst through and the operation had to be repeated.

Just upstream of the entrance to the Grand Canal there is an island called Lehinch. On another of Douglas's explorations, we tried to pass up the west side of this island and, in fact, succeeded in doing so, but we spent the best part of a day getting the boat off a shallow en route. During this operation a local farmer came over and told us that we should not be there. I thanked him politely and explained that my husband liked exploring. I think he thought that we were quite mad, and if anyone else is mad enough to try to do the same, I suggest that he watch out at the upper end of the channel just before coming back out into the main river.

The river is wide and exposed where the Grand Canal enters and, when the company constructed the Ballinasloe Canal, the directors were faced with the problem of how to get the boats and the towing horses across the river. They decided to construct a wooden bridge just wide enough to accommodate a horse. A large number of piles were driven into the river bed to carry the walkway and two opening spans were made, one in the middle of the river and the other close to Bulloch Island on the east side, where a quay was made; it is possible to get a good idea of what the bridge looked like because a small portion of it remains linking Bulloch Island with the shore. Crossing the river in bad weather must have been a hair-raising experience: the horses were walked across the bridge, towing the boat along, and it is recorded in the minutes of the company that on occasions the passengers opted to cross on foot instead of remaining in the boats.

By the time the Shannon Commissioners came along in the 1830s, the bridge was in a pretty precarious state and there were reports of the new steamers having difficulty passing through the opening spans, causing further damage. The commissioners decided it would be best to remove the bridge completely and they made ready a chain-operated ferry for bringing the horses across. The canal company objected strongly about the lack of consultation and the usual long and bitter correspondence ensued. The commissioners expressed surprise at the attitude of the canal directors:

Instead of the language of remonstrance, the Commissioners might have expected an expression of acknowledgement for the promptitude which induced them to prepare beforehand for the evil day when the superstructure of the wooden bridge at Shannon Harbour might be seen floating down the river, and all communication with the two canals suddenly and totally cut off, and to guard against such a state of things, they have prepared the ferry-boat.

The directors of the canal company felt a certain amount of resentment about the Shannon Commissioners taking over the middle Shannon because the company had spent a considerable amount more than it had received by way of grant in restoring the old navigation and now stood to lose the tolls. In the end the bridge was taken down and the company was awarded a derisory £5 compensation for the loss of the entire middle Shannon. The ferry remained in operation until after 1911 when engines were fitted in the canal boats: remnants of the old winches were still visible when I looked for them some years ago.

A delightfully quiet mooring can still be found in the entrance to the Ballinasloe Canal. The lock here, one of the deepest on the whole canal system, was named Fanning's Lock; Nicholas Fanning was the chairman of the canal company when the canal was under construction and was one of a group of business men who engineered a *coup d'état* in 1810 which deposed many of the old guard at 'the largest meeting of Proprietors that ever assembled'. Fanning was an energetic chairman and even went to London to further the cause of the company in the Westminster parliament. Some of the difficulties of making this journey are expressed in a letter he sent to his fellow directors:

I am heartily tired of this place, and wish I was safely landed in old Ireland again. I had a very unpleasant passage coming over, three whole days at sea, it blew a hurricane, and our supply of coals ran short on the second day, so much for the rascally establishment of the steamers.

Climbing up and looking out along the line of the old canal from the top of the lock, it is hard to envisage that this was ever a canal. It was not abandoned until 1961 and it is remarkable how quickly the bog has swallowed it up. It had not been an easy stretch of canal to make because of the boggy terrain and in the years following its opening in 1828 there were problems with the embankments. These difficulties were added to by the un-settled state of the country in the 1820s and 1830s and some of the breaches were caused deliberately by gangs trying to create employment.

It is a pity to pass by here without visiting Shannon Harbour itself; we usually moor below the 36th lock and it is only a short walk from there along the towpath. It is some indication that the Shannon Commissioners' works did bring about a partial improvement in the flooding problems of the river when we consider that a report recorded in the minutes of the Grand Canal Company in December 1833 stated that the water was within 2 inches of the top of this 36th lock and that there was 4 feet of water on the road from the harbour to Banagher, two thirds of the inhabitants of the village had to leave their homes and 'there was much loss, misery and distress here and at Banagher'.

Much has been written about Shannon Harbour elsewhere. For me, it is one of the places along our waterways which most evokes the past. I can picture Richard Griffith arriving there in the 1790s to inspect the place where the canal was to enter the Shannon. He was a member of the board of the canal company, a 'gentleman engineer', who volunteered to keep a watchful eye on the works on behalf of his fellow directors. He remarked to them: 'You have terminated your canal in a wild and unfrequented situation to which it is useless to open a navigation unless you provide shelter at the same time for men and merchandize.' The last bridge on the canal at Shannon Harbour is named Griffith Bridge in recognition of the interest he took in the works.

When we first visited the place in the 1950s, it was a quiet spot with only an occasional private boat berthed here. A canal boat would arrive and there would be a bustle of activity while the goods were transhipped into the larger Shannon boats. At other times the canal boat men would lock their boat down into the river and continue along the Shannon themselves, the characteristic noise of the Bolinder diesel echoing out over the bog. It is easy to conjure up the scene here in the mid-nineteenth century as Father Mathew, standing on the steps of the canal company hotel, administered the pledge to the assembled emigrants who were setting off in a spirit of hope to escape from the despair of their famine and trouble torn country. Today, particularly at weekends, the harbour is once again a hive of activity with many people keeping their boats here, but the ghosts of the past will always hover over the place for me.

The chain operated ferry for the horses across the Shannon to the Ballinasloe Canal near Shannon Harbour

Shannon Harbour in the 1950s

Shannon Harbour during an annual Canal Boat Rally in the 1970s

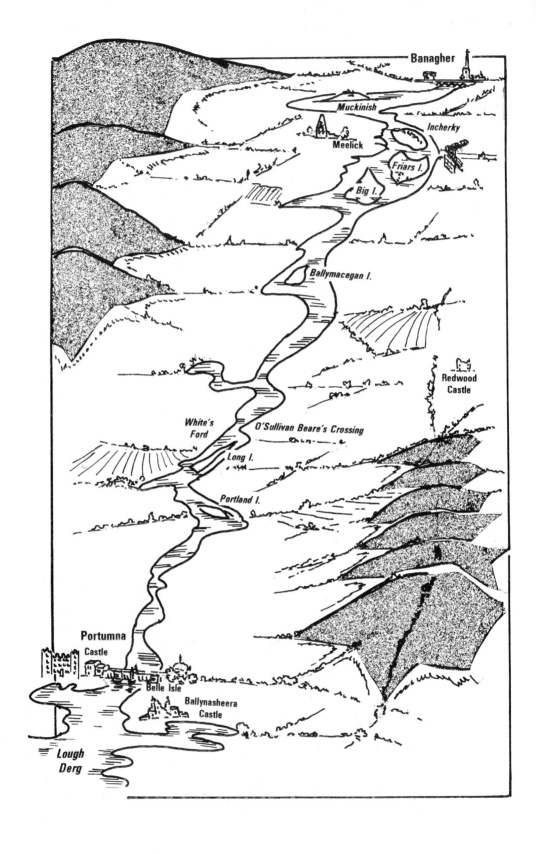

Banagher

Muckinish

Incherky

Meelick

Friars I.

Big I.

Ballymacegan I.

Redwood
Castle

White's
Ford

O'Sullivan Beare's Crossing

Long I.

Portland I.

Portumna
Castle

Belle Isle

Ballynasheera
Castle

Lough
Derg

Chapter Seven

THAT BATES BANAGHER
Banagher to Portumna

THE FIRST thing that every visitor to Banagher should do is to go up the town and buy a copy of the excellent guide book published in 1985 by a local historian, Valentine Trodd. According to him there is evidence that Roderick O'Connor built a 'spacious bridge of eighteen arches' across the river here in 1049. This was replaced by a medieval bridge of 27 arches 'of divers architectural form, each different from its fellow' which stood for 500 years. In the seventeenth century a 17-arch bridge was built and there is an early engraving showing this structure which spanned the river about 50 feet downstream of the present bridge; there were extensive mill buildings below it at

Banagher: an engraving of the old bridge from Thomas Cromwell's *Excursions*

137

the east end, with a mill pond between the bridge and the mill.

In the 1750s Thomas Omer arrived to inspect the place to plan his navigation works. He decided to by-pass the bridge because of the extensive shallows in the river and construct a short canal on the west side. To overcome the 3-foot fall, he put in a single set of gates which proved very unsatisfactory, requiring a great number of men to pull the boats through against the stream. He made a harbour on the canal near the bridge and built another of his lockhouses here; this is one of the last of his houses which is still occupied today. The Grand Canal Company installed a conventional lock here in the early 1800s but they did not alter the bridge over the canal, which was the cause of considerable headroom problems when the river was high, particularly for the new steamers.

This was the position when Rhodes arrived here in the course of his survey for the Shannon Commission. At first he planned to enlarge the canal, remove the lock completely and fit a swivel bridge but, when he came to examine the bridge over the main river, he found that it would not be practical to try to underpin it because it was 'built of rubble masonry of a very inferior description'. Once he had decided that a new bridge would have to be built, it was more practical to abandon the canal and make a navigable channel up the main river. In fact, they experienced enormous difficulty in deepening the river, encountering great blocks of limestone rock weighing from 11 to 20 tons; coffer dams had to be erected to enable the rock to be blasted and the water broke through the dams on several occasions.

One of the people who had given evidence before the Select Committee set up to examine the Shannon Navigation in 1834 was a gentleman called Thomas Steele. He laid before the committee details of his diving bell and his invention of a system of holding conversations with the person in the bell and artificial submarine illumination. He had written a pamphlet in 1828 in which he said that the details of his diving bell had been published by the *London Philosophical Magazine and Journal* two years earlier. The title of his pamphlet reveals that he was also interested in politics: *Practical Suggestions on the Improvement of the Navigation of the Shannon between Limerick and the Atlantic with some Remarks intended to create a doubt of the fairness of not keeping faith with the Irish Roman Catholics after they had been lured into a surrender of Limerick* [then principal fortress] *by a Treaty.* I could find no reference to the use of his diving bell on the Shannon works but they were certainly already in use at this time. John Rennie had recommended the use of a 'new diving bell' on the Howth harbour works in 1814; it was operated by two men 'to whom half a pint of spirits and a crust of bread was allowed every tide after returning from the condensed air'.

The new bridge was completed and opened to the public on 12 August

THIS BRIDGE
WAS ERECTED BY
THE COMMISSIONERS FOR THE IMPROVEMENT OF THE NAVIGATION
OF THE
RIVER SHANNON
UNDER THE ACT 2ND & 3RD VICT.C.61
HIS EXCELLENCY
THE RIGHT HON.BLE THOMAS PHILIP EARL DE GREY.K.C
LORD LIEUTENANT
THE FIRST STONE WAS LAID 21 AUG 1841
THE BRIDGE WAS FINISHED 12 AUG 1843
THOMAS RHODES ENGINEER   WM MACKENZIE CONTRACTOR
COUNTY GALWAY v KINGS COUNTY

The bridge plate on Banagher Bridge

1843 with great pomp and ceremony and then the engineer, Harry Jones, of the Corps of Royal Engineers, was faced with the problem of how to get rid of the old bridge. He decided to blow it up and the event is described in the Shannon Commissioners' report for that year:

A charge of 50lbs of powder was placed in one of the piers of the old bridge, which when exploded, succeeded perfectly as to the effect desired; it was then decided to destroy the remaining portions by simul-

Banagher: a drawing by the contractor, William Mackenzie, of the opening of the Shannon Commissioners' bridge on 12 August 1843

Banagher: the MacCoghlan castle, known as Cromwell's castle, which was adapted as part of the fortifications during the Napoleonic wars

taneous explosions; every alternate pier was then charged as above and fired; the effect was admirable: the entire length (550ft) of the old bridge was gently thrown up, and fell a mass of rubbish.

An eye witness's report would seem to suggest that it was not quite as successful as this report implies, he said that parts of two piers remained standing.

It is still possible to find the abutment of the old bridge near the castle on the west side of the river and, although much of the old canal has been filled in, the lock is still there and the low road bridge, while the lockhouse and other buildings give a good idea of what the harbour area must have looked like. Most of the old mill buildings had to be removed by the commissioners and a new tail race was made which ran around the back of the buildings. The maltings have been owned by the Waller family since 1880 and were previously owned by the Harton family. It was from here that Otway Waller set out in his 4½ ton yacht *Imogen* to sail singlehanded to the Canary Islands in the days before radios and modern equipment had made this a routine trip in small yachts. On the way he perfected a system of using twin spinnakers to steer the boat off the wind, a forerunner of the modern self-steering gear.

The fortifications erected here to prevent the French from crossing the Shannon are nearly as extensive, but less impressive, than those at Shannonbridge. The old castle by the bridge, which is known as Cromwell's Castle, had been erected many years earlier by the MacCoghlans to guard the bridge. This castle was strengthened and a gun was mounted on the roof. Nearby a martello tower was built with another traversing gun on its roof. It always seems strange to see a martello tower so far inland because we usually associate them with sea defences. A strongly fortified barracks with a further three guns guarded the east end of the bridge; the walls of it are still there in line with where the old bridge used to span the river. In addition, a five-sided battery, surrounded by a moat, was erected a short distance downstream on the east bank. This was known as Fort Eliza and it had a strong central building which was the magazine and four guns looking out over the river. It is barely noticeable from the river and difficult to approach by water but it is well worth a visit and is only a short walk from the town down the first turn on the right.

I like Banagher, it has many pleasant memories. I remember going to the pictures here in the 1950s in the local cinema which has long since closed. There was always a great deal of audience participation at the cinema in the country in those days and it was also not unknown to find yourself scratching during the performance. The railway and the station are now gone; the station was removed when the new marina was under construction. The 18-mile railway ran between Banagher and Clara on the GS&WR (Great Southern and Western Railway) but it never crossed the Shannon. The railway reached here in 1884 and, for a time, the passenger service linked with a steamer service on the river, making it possible to do a round trip from Dublin, returning by train from Killaloe. The passenger rail service ceased in 1947 but freight trains continued until the 1960s and I

Banagher: the *Countess of Cadogan*, one of the Shannon Development Company's steamers, passing through the bridge in the early 1900s

Banagher: the dispute on the bridge when Rory O'Hanlon was trying to have the bridge opened in 1951

remember seeing a fleet of dragon yachts arriving here by rail in the 1950s. They were a great sight coming across the bog sitting up in open wagons. This expedition was organised by Rory O'Hanlon who, not content with his voyage up the river in the previous year, was anxious to see keel boats racing again on Lough Derg. It was quite a feat trundling the boats from the station to the quay where they were craned into the water. Christy Mahoney, the boat builder from Dun Laoghaire, was brought down to direct operations and, when the boats were all successfully floating in the river, there was a monumental party. Christy, and an undisclosed number of other people, ended up in the bridal suite in the Shannon Hotel, which was reputed to have the largest four poster bed in Ireland.

In the previous year the bridgekeeper had received a mysterious telegram which read: 'Delay the bride till Thursday.' This, in fact, had been a message from Rory to warn him that he had been delayed and had nothing to do with a local wedding! There followed great scenes on the bridge as the bridgekeeper remonstrated with Rory claiming that if he opened the bridge it might not shut again, while his wife was complaining loudly that he must not be made to open it because he had a bad heart and the local garda sergeant, in on the act, was none too happy about the prospect of the long queues of cars which would form if the bridge could not be closed. Eventually Rory relented and agreed to take out his mast and re-step it, and everyone parted good friends.

Today, Banagher is a busy town with a large marina and, armed with Mr Trodd's booklet, there is much to be seen: there is the house that Anthony Trollope lived in at the top of the town when he took up the position of Deputy Postal Surveyor, and the ruins of Cuba Court, where you might even see the pale ghost of Charlotte Brontë, who spent her honeymoon here with her husband, Arthur Bell Nicholls, just nine months before her death. Here in Cuba Court the Royal Free Charter School of Banagher, which had been founded in 1628, flourished for some years and numbered amongst its pupils some well-known names, such as William Wilde and William Bulfin. Charlotte's husband was to return to Banagher and he lived out the remainder of his life in Hill House, which is still there today. He married his cousin, Mary Anna Bell, and it is said that when he died she placed a picture of his beloved Charlotte on his breast. Four adjoining graves in St Rynagh's churchyard and the fine Resurrection window in the church are a reminder of this family.

According to tradition, a high cross once stood in the market square beside 'a crystal clear spring'. The shaft of this cross was later discovered by a local historian, Thomas Cooke, lying in the nearby cemetery of the old church of St Rynagh, which had been the site of an ancient abbey. Cooke 'rescued' it and brought it to his home in Birr. One panel of the shaft depicted an ecclesiastical figure on a horse and below it a deer caught in a trap. Cooke surmised that the cross commemorated Bishop William O'Duffy, who according to the annals had died from a fall from his horse in 1297; the significance of the deer, he said, was that the name 'Duffy' means 'a red deer' in Irish. Subsequently, the shaft was brought to Clonmacnoise by the Rev. Mr Graves because he said that it was of much earlier origin and that it belonged to the Clonmacnoise school of artisans. It finally ended up in the National Museum, where it is today. This is just another example of the enormous pleasure these old crosses have given to scholars over the centuries, as each one interpreted the figures carved on them, only to be contradicted by others.

Before leaving Banagher I will risk the anger of its people by disputing that the expression 'that bates Banagher' is associated with this place. Oswell Blakeston in his exploration of Ulster *Thank You Now* says that the expression 'That bates Banagher and Banagher bates the band' related to the village of Banagher, near Dungiven, in Co Londonderry. Not only that, but he explains how the expression arose. Beneath the tomb of one of the O'Heney family in Banagher Old Church can be found sand which, according to legend, has magic properties. If it is thrown at you by a member of the O'Heney family it 'beats the band' bringing you good fortune, thrown at a race horse it ensures that he will win his race, and sprinkled on a witness in a law case, it ensures that he will tell the truth. So, until some Offaly man comes up with a better story, this is the one I am sticking to.

The river takes on a new urgency as it leaves Banagher. Gone are the low lying fields, the cattle drinking at its banks, the slow lazy river twisting and turning this way and that. The flow of the river increases, confined in narrow channels and divided by many islands. It is this stretch of river between Banagher and Meelick that is responsible in a large degree for the Shannon floods; the fall of the river between these places is about 2 feet per mile whereas the fall between Athlone and Banagher is only about 1 inch per mile. At Counsellor's Ford south of Inishee Island the great waters of the river are forced through a narrow channel less than 500 feet wide.

Here in the past there had been eel weirs built on the old ford with just a narrow navigation channel close to the east shore. Rhodes had said in the 1830s that these weirs should be removed and the river widened at this place. Hubert Moore, who lived here in Shannon Grove, was paid compensation for the removal of his weirs but the Shannon Commissioners did warn in their final report that further excavation would be desirable both here and in a number of other places if flooding was to be alleviated. We have already seen that it was part of the Shannon Commissioners' brief to relieve flooding as well as to provide navigation and there is no doubt that the 1840 works did help but the many inquiries which were to follow the serious flooding in the 1860s proved beyond doubt that escalating costs had forced cut-backs in the original plans.

As Harold Wilson once remarked: 'Royal Commissions take Minutes and waste Years' and, certainly in the 1860s there were endless parliamentary investigations about the flooding problem and pages of minutes of evidence recorded. From these it emerged that the commissioners had raised the weirs above the authorised levels to reduce the need for excavation: for example, the upper sill of Meelick lock was found to be 6 inches higher than it should have been. It was suggested that the natural level of Lough Ree was 4 feet lower and that holding it at a much higher level was causing too much pressure of water downstream. The fact that the waters of the Shannon are further augumented by those of the River Suck below Shannonbridge adds to the problem and the inquiries pointed to certain places which needed further excavation: at Bishop's Islands, Derryholmes, Shannon Harbour, Banagher, Shannon Grove and at Keelogue, upstream of Meelick weir.

A Memorial from the gentry and landowners in the Banagher area took exception to the statement in the 11th report of the Shannon Commissioners that a considerable portion of land had been reclaimed by the works which had previously been covered for nine months of the year.

They said that this was 'totally unfounded and shamefully incorrect'. When the Board of Works representative said that he was not 'aware of having left undone anything that could legally or justifiably have been done to relieve the lands', they replied: 'The Jesuitical, evasive statements of the Commissioners of Public Works cannot be regarded as a satisfactory answer.' And so it went on. When there were further bad floods in 1866, a new Memorial was prepared consisting of seventeen points. The eleventh read:

Your memorialists humbly submit, that besides an immense damage caused to private property, there is also a serious public evil resulting from these works; they exhibit striking evidence of the ignorance and negligence with which Government works are designed and executed in this country; they impress the public with the idea that everything done by the Government officers is badly done: they are an outrage on common sense, and a disgrace to the engineering knowledge of the age.

Hard words, but it must be remembered that they were spoken by people who were critical of the drainage aspect of the works; there were some who spoke up at the inquiries about the benefit from nutrients deposited on the fields by the flood water. And let us not forget that we are still enjoying today the navigation works of these engineers who were accused of being 'a disgrace to the engineering knowledge of the age'.

It is when there is prolonged flooding because of bad weather that it becomes a live issue. The alleviation of Shannon flooding has been a plank in the platform of more than one political party over the years and there have been further surveys carried out and reports published including one by an American expert, Louis E. Rydell, in the 1950s in which he made the oft-quoted comment: 'no simple or obvious solution has heretofore been found nor has the writer now found one'. Following serious flooding in 1985 and 1986, the Athlone Branch of the IWAI asked John Weaving for his views and he remarked that anyone who had travelled upstream in a laden boat in flood conditions would realise that the flooding was due to the natural restrictions in the river channel. He listed the places where this occurred which were the same as those mentioned above which had emerged at the earlier inquiries but he added a number of other stretches further upstream, above Shannon-bridge and near Clonmacnoise. He maintained that the weirs, sited on wide stretches of the river, can handle any volume of water which reaches them and that increasing the section of the river where the channel is confined and clearing the back passages behind some of the islands would go a long way towards alleviating the flooding between Meelick and Athlone without harming the ecology of the river. It was stated in the Dáil recently that the Board of Works is not authorised to carry out piecemeal dredging to relieve flooding and that this work could be undertaken only as part of a comprehensive drainage scheme for the entire river. I find this difficult to comprehend; if the limited dredging suggested by John Weaving could bring about some improvement it is hard to see why it cannot be undertaken.

The second house tucked in behind Inishee Island is called Shannon Lodge and William Waller, who owned the maltings in Banagher, lived here. He was a keen sailing man and, back in the early 1900s, he was on his way home from church in Banagher in a small sailing boat with his daughter and another man, James Willington, when the boat capsized. William and his daughter were drowned but the other man survived and he explained that William had given the helm to his daughter while he was lighting his pipe when they were hit by a sudden squall. It was a ballasted centreboard boat which immediately sank to the bottom. When it was recovered it was found that the mainsheet was wound around the girl's wrist and her father was caught in the rigging with his clasp knife still clutched in his hand with which he must have been trying to cut her loose. Such an accident could not have

Meelick: Thomas Rhodes's plan showing the early navigation via the Cloonaheenogue Canal with the Hamilton lock and the proposed new canal; a further channel was subsequently opened between the canals to alleviate flooding

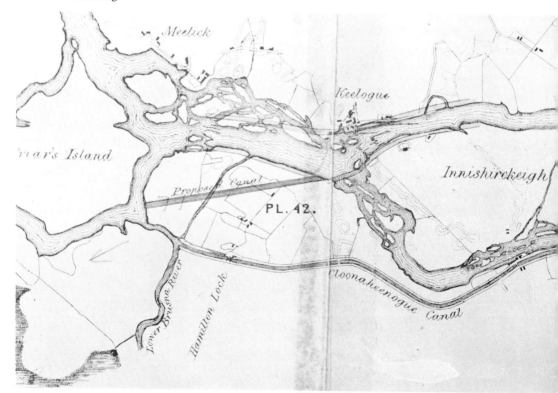

Meelick: the original lockhouse built by Thomas Omer in 1755; the porch was added later and the date is engraved over the original door

Meelick: the old Hamilton lock, the site of the very first lock on the river built by Thomas Omer in 1755 and subsequently rebuilt by the Grand Canal Company in the early 1800s

happened at a worse place as the water swirls through here like a fast receding tide.

The old Shannon navigation passed east of Muckinish Island and ran down into the Cloonaheenogue Canal. It was 1¾ miles long with floodgates at the upper end and a lock at the lower end; it was spanned by three accommodation bridges giving access to the island it created. It opened out into the Little Brosna, a short distance from its confluence with the main river, and thus by-passed the two main areas of rapids at Keelogue and Meelick. This had been the first navigation work undertaken by Thomas Omer in 1755. He had to overcome a fall of 7 ft 3 in., considerably more than anywhere else on the river, and so he had to build a conventional lock here. He had obviously not designed his little lockhouses at this stage because the house he built here was of a much simpler design; it has been added to since then but it still bears the date over the door inside the porch. Like so much of his work, the lock soon began to give trouble and, when John Brownrigg surveyed the river in 1801, he reported that it was in such bad repair that the boatmen were forced to drag their boats up the rapids instead of using the canal because the lock could not be operated:

the timbers of the upper gates are in their place shut and fixed, the swing beams gone, the sluices broken, and demolished, the sheeting rotten and sticking in pieces, the gates stopped with sods and bundles of potato stalks to retain some water in the upper level of the canal.

This lock had to be completely rebuilt in the early 1800s by the Grand Canal Company and was then named Hamilton Lock as a gesture of goodwill to the Directors General of Inland Navigation whose chairman was Sir Sackville Hamilton and with whom an agreement had at last been reached concerning payment for the works carried out on the middle Shannon.

When Rhodes came along in the 1830s to survey the river for the Shannon Commission, Meelick was one of the most difficult places to tackle. He decided to abandon the old canal completely and to construct a new canal with a large lock to by-pass the Meelick rapids. He made a U-shaped weir at the head of the canal and above this weir he had to carry out considerable excavation to remove the Keelogue rapids.

Arriving by boat at Meelick, it is very difficult to follow all this without a map. It is possible to walk across from Rhodes's new lock, which was named Victoria Lock, to the old canal. On the way you will cross a wide channel which was made many years later as a result of the flood inquiries to try to reduce the quantity of water passing over the weir. The McGarry family, who have been lockkeepers at Meelick for many years, opted to live in the old lockhouse at Hamilton Lock because there was no road acces to the new lock. The late Stephen McGarry, father of the present lockkeeper, was another of our friends in the old days. He knew the river well and loved to talk about the boats and people. Somehow we did not seem to be in such a hurry in those days and there was always time to stop for a chat as the great lock filled quietly. It was Stephen who pointed out to me the little cut stone plinth beside the lock which was put there in 1897 to carry the Union Jack for the visit of the Duke and Duchess of York who were lending their royal patronage to the inauguration of the new steamer service.

Because of the two fording places, this was a place of importance from early times. When the Keelogue shallows were being excavated in the 1840s many interesting items were uncovered. There is a list of items presented by the Shannon Commissioners to the museum of the Royal Irish Academy in the second volume of their proceedings: ornaments, druids' rings, pieces of deer horn and weapons. Close to the surface they found weapons such as matchlock guns, lower down there were swords, battleaxes and spearheads made of iron, beneath these were bronze swords and spears and still lower down some stone hatchets from prehistoric days.

There appears to have been a Christian settlement here by the twelfth

Meelick: one of the Shannon Commissioners' bollards at the Victoria lock

149

Meelick: one of the Shannon Commissioners' casings for the winding gear at the Victoria lock

century. The following interesting reference to Meelick is made in the *Annals of the Four Masters* for the year 1203:

A hosting by William Burk, accompanied by the foreigners of Mumha and Midhe, into Connacht, when he erected a castle at Milec ... and the place where the castle was erected was round the great church of the place, which was lined round with earth and stones to the pinnacles; and they devastated the west of Connacht, both church and territory ... great famine in all Erinn generally in this year, so that the clergy used to eat meat in Lent.

It is recorded that the castle was levelled in the same year but it must have been rebuilt a number of times because there are references to a castle at Meelick being burned down in 1316 and accounts of it being attacked in Elizabethan times.

This early church and castle were at the present village of Meelick; a Franciscan abbey was founded there in the fifteenth century and the

Franciscans remained until the nineteenth century. Mooring at the new quay above the weir on the west shore, it is only a short walk around the road to this site. The medieval church is still in use today. The walls, west doorway, the two aisle arches in the south wall and another arch beside the altar, which originally led to a south transept, are said to be part of the original church and the other ruins nearby would have been part of the domestic buildings of the abbey.

The little island just off the shore is called Cromwell's Island, which suggests that there was a fort here guarding the rapids and this might even have been the site of the original castle. Early maps show that there were earthwork defences on this island and on the larger island to the south, Moran's Island, in the late eighteenth century before the military authorities decided to strengthen the defences here in the days of the Napoleonic scare. I have never been on either of these islands to look for signs of the defences; they would probably have to be approached by dinghy from downstream.

There were also probably early defences guarding the Keelogue shallows further upstream where the new quay is today; the finds of the Shannon Commissioners are proof of battles fought here. It was obviously considered an important strategic crossing place judging by the elaborate defences erected here to forestall the possible French invasion in the early 1800s. These defences were on Incherky Island looking out over the Keelogue shallows and they are well worth inspecting. I was fortunate enough to visit them with Paul Kerrigan who, as I have mentioned before, has made a life-long study of the military architecture of this period.

We rowed across to Incherky from the new quay above the weir making sure to keep ourselves well clear of the pull from the sluices because all the

Meelick: a drawing of the Keelogue Battery

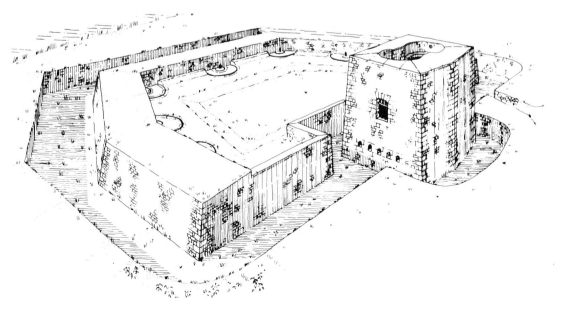

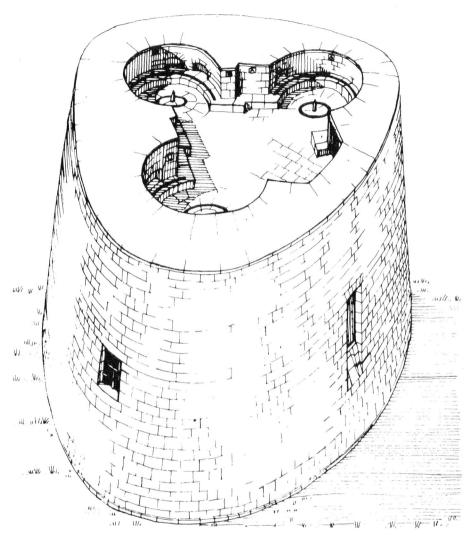

Meelick: the gun emplacements

gates were open. Paul said that there had been earlier earthwork defences here and we found evidence of this at the northern end of the island, but for the later works they chose a location a little downstream directly opposite the shallows. It was a very strong stone battery similar in some ways to Fort Eliza in Banagher but larger and more elaborate. It was six-sided, surrounded by a moat and there were seven guns mounted on traversing platforms around its walls giving very good coverage of the river crossing.

152

Access to the battery was across a drawbridge on the side away from the river into a strong blockhouse built on the lines of the martello towers but rectangular in shape. This would have provided accommodation for the garrison and have housed the magazine. There were two further guns mounted on the roof and the rails and some of the fittings are still intact.

Moving the boat down to Victoria Lock, we set out to inspect the martello tower on the island to the west of the canal. This was erected to command the Meelick rapids and, of course, when it was built the new canal was not there and this was part of the mainland with just the old canal acting as a defensive moat to the east. I had been to see the tower on a previous occasion and so this time we took the precaution of bringing the ship's ladder with us, which we carry aboard as a gangway. It had two uses, it helped us to get across a deep ditch on the way to the tower without getting our feet wet and it also made it easier to gain access to the tower through the raised doorway.

Paul was delighted with the tower which is a very large one and is one of the few cam-shaped towers erected in Ireland, although he said that this design was used in England on the Essex and Suffolk coasts. The roof of the building is supported by a large mushroom-shaped central pillar, making it very strong, and there were mountings for three guns on the roof. He thought that these would probably have been one 24-pounder and two howitzers which fired explosive shells. Because of its isolated position this tower seems to have suffered less from interference over the years. The iron

Meelick fortifications: the Martello tower on the island

pivots, tracks and ring bolts were all in perfect condition and the original iron-sheeted door of the tower was still in position. It was easy to imagine the officer with his 32 privates who were stationed here in 1811 keeping a careful watch for the first signs of the French. I am told that the Irish army garrisoned some of the Meelick defences in the 1940s.

There is an embankment stretching all the way from Meelick to Portumna on the west side of the river with pumping stations at intervals. This was erected in more recent years to keep the low lying land on this side of the river free from inundation. I believe you can walk along it all the way and it would be a fine walk for those who like to observe river life. The new ESB high voltage power lines cross the river about halfway to Portumna, cutting an unsightly line across the country with their ugly pylons. Further downstream at the tip of Long Island an older set of power lines crosses the river at what was formerly White's Ford.

This was the place where O'Sullivan Beare crossed the river on his epic march to Leitrim on a cold December day in 1602. Peter Somerville Large, in his fascinating book *From Bantry Bay to Leitrim*, recounted how he himself walked the route taken by the Irish chief as he tried to bring a group of his people north to link up with Hugh O'Neill in Ulster. The author was relying on the graphic account of the march which has survived, written by Philip O'Sullivan, who was twelve years old at the time and was one of only thirty-five of the one thousand who had originally set out to make it to Leitrim.

They had been harassed all the way from Co. Cork and on their arrival at Portumna, had found it impossible to cross the river because the ferries were closely guarded. Making their way up the east shore of the river cautiously because they were aware of the presence of the Queen's Sheriff, MacEgan, in nearby Redwood Castle, they reached White's Ford. There they camped and slaughtered some of their horses, which provided them with much needed meat to eat and skins to construct makeshift boats. It took two days to make a 26 foot curragh, using eleven skins; the skills involved in making these craft would have been well known to these Bantry men. One group favoured making a coracle-shaped boat, using a single skin, and so one of these was made as well. For some reason MacEgan did not attack although he must have been aware of the presence of such a large group so near his castle. They eventually started to ferry the people across, but the river, swollen by winter floods, was very wide, stretching out over the low lying land to the west, where it is now protected by the embankment. The overloaded coracle sank on the first crossing and its occupants were drowned, and the currach's trips backwards and forwards were slow and hazardous. MacEgan chose to attack when some of the people were already on the far shore. Possibly he wanted to let the group become divided. There was considerable slaughter on both sides

154

and MacEgan himself was killed. Peter Somerville Large was told by a local man that the field here is still known as the field of the horses. Passing this peaceful spot today, it is hard to visualise the scene but it is just one more example of the many stories this great river could tell.

The channels behind Long and Portland Islands used to be navigable and we have been through them in *Harklow* but they have become heavily silted with turf dust from the bog workings and are probably too shallow now. Portland House built by the Stoney family is on the east shore downstream of Portland Island. When Butler Stoney died in the late 1920s he left his house to the Bird's Nest, a Protestant society for orphans but before they could take possession the house was burned down and it was suggested that it was no accident; there had been a rumour circulating in the neighbourhood that the house was to be used to proselytise Roman Catholic orphans. A hotel has now been built adjoining the old house.

Halfway between here and Portumna bridge there used to be a little island which is now almost submerged and is marked by a black marker in a clump of rushes. This was called Herring Island and it is just another of those rather baffling names you come across on the river. Joyce's *Irish Place Names* states that there are a number of names inland in Ireland which contain the Irish word for herring in them because traditionally showers of herrings fell there, 'raised from the sea and borne inland by violent whirlwinds'!

The river is not particularly fast flowing as it approaches Portumna but for some reason I always get a strong sensation of travelling down hill here. The two sides of the river contrast sharply. To the west the land stretches away into the distance beyond the embankment while to the east there are more trees and cultivation and the land rises to a small hill overlooking the bridge at Portumna.

When John Cowan was writing his *Description of the River Shannon* in 1795 he said that there was a ferry at Portumna but that there were remains of an old bridge of which 'whole arches survive' on the island in the middle of the river and on the Tipperary side. I cannot find any information about this early bridge or when it was replaced by the ferries. When Henry Cromwell, Oliver's son, was granted the confiscated lands of the Clanricards in the 1650s, he is said to have intended to replace the ferry with a bridge but the restoration of the monarchy cut short his stay at Portumna. It was the famous bridge builder, Lemuel Cox, whose services were sought in 1796. The bridge at Portumna was the same design as his others at Derry and Waterford, a timber structure, built in two sections, using Hayes's Island in the middle of the river and with a drawbridge close to the west of the island. Administered as a toll bridge by commissioners, whose registrar was aptly named Mr Shrewbridge, there was frequent trouble with the drawbridge and

Portumna: the tollgate from the old bridge with its pedestrian turnstile which is now used at the entrance to the quay

Portumna: the old bridge in 1910 which was replaced by the present bridge one year later

boats were often held up. Then in 1814 the western end of the bridge was carried away in a flood, the company received a loan from the government to repair it and the well-known engineer, Alexander Nimmo, supervised the work. The loan had been issued on the security of the tolls but when it could not be repaid, a receiver was appointed and the bridge was allowed to fall into a ruinous state.

Fortunately, the Shannon Commissioners came along and replaced it in the 1840s. They built another wooden bridge, with the roadway carried in a metal casing; as this was no longer a toll bridge, the gate and turnstile were moved to the entrance to the quay where they still remain today. By 1907 this bridge was reported to be in a bad state of repair and, when two men fell over the low parapet and were drowned, it was suggested at the inquest that the sides should be raised to 5 feet and sheeted, even though it was considered that 'owing to the rotten condition of the whole structure, a good gale would blow the bridge over altogether'. This incident led to a public inquiry at which it was said that the state the bridge was 'in the highest degree alarming' and, eventually, in 1911 the present structure was erected with the opening span on the west side.

Sean Butler, the bridgekeeper lives in the house on Hayes's Island. I

Portumna: Sean Butler, the Bridgekeeper

remember him telling us in the 1960s that his wages were £10 per week with an additional payment of 5s per opening on Sundays. It was hard work winding open the bridge, especially when there was a strong wind. He had been promised a motor to operate the bridge and year after year went by and still there was no motor. 'Sure, it's coming down by wheelbarrow,' he said. After that we would ask him each year if the wheelbarrow had arrived and, eventually, it did arrive; today he sits in his little cabin and presses buttons.

Some years ago I wrote to my friend Kevin Murray of the Irish Railway Records Society (IRRS) and asked him for the real story of Portumna's Stolen Railway. He replied sending me the details I was looking for and added: 'The Stolen Railway certainly deserves a book to itself. One of the IRRS members had accumulated a lot of notes about the line, but they were stolen too, with his bicycle, and he lost heart after that.'

The Parsonstown & Portumna Bridge Railway Company was the brainchild of the Marquis of Clanricard of Portumna Castle. Some people wanted to continue the line across the Shannon to the west but the GS&WR had made a deal with the MGWR (Midland and Great Western Railway) that they would not cross the river and the marquis was quite content to have a twelve-mile long line from Birr, on the main line of the GS&WR, terminating at the bridge and connecting with the steamer service. Work began in 1863 but was plagued by problems, the most pressing being a shortage of money. There were a number of law suits involving disputes about road crossings and actions by contractors looking for payment and, had it not been for Clanricard's financial support, the whole thing would have been abandoned. Eventually, five years later, the line was completed but it was not a commercial success and in 1871, the company was put in the hands of a receiver. The Commissioners of Public Works had lent money to the company and were the principal creditors and so they organised to have the line patrolled until 1883 when even they abandoned further interest. Immediately, the smaller creditors decided they would move in and try to mitigate their losses. Rails, sleepers and everything movable disappeared and it is said that the entire railway station at Portumna, the only one on the line, vanished in one night. The iron bridge across the Brosna nearly went as well but the police surprised the man with a crane who had begun to remove the girders. You will find it very hard to trace any sign of the railway today at Portumna.

One of Bunny Goodbody's many stories with which he delights his listeners on the Sunday Miscellany programme on Radio Eireann is the story of the great duel on the ice at Portumna. The incident took place in the early nineteenth century when duelling was illegal but still very prevalent. A Galway squire named McDonagh, whose forbears had been dispossessed of their land by Cromwellian settlers and who was therefore no lover of the establishment, was very fond of picking rows with both the landed gentry and the gentlemen of the garrison. He was known to have a hair trigger on his pistols and was greatly feared by his opponents — with good cause. He challenged a Tipperary landowner called Bodkin to a duel and it was agreed to fight the duel on the River Shannon at Portumna which was frozen over at the time; they considered that duelling on water was outside the law. McDonagh felled his opponent but there were a great number of Bodkin's supporters present and they moved in to lynch the victor. McDonagh leapt on his horse and set out across the ice to the Connacht shore while his followers kept the crowd at bay by skipping pistol balls across the ice at them. Halfway across the river, the ice gave way and man and horse had to swim to the far shore, which they did successfully. In those days the king's writ did not extend very far into Connacht and so once back in his home territory he was safe from retribution both from Bodkin's faction and the Crown. Lever, in his novel *Charles O'Malley*, draws on this episode but his hero escapes off down the lake and eludes his pursuers by taking a short cut in his boat inside the Goat's Road shoal.

No account of the Shannon would be complete without a mention of the late Bertie Waller. He was the son of William Waller who had been drowned near Banagher but this did not seem to affect his love of sailing and 'messing about in boats'. I can still picture Bertie standing up in the stern of his SOD,

Portumna: Belle Isle in the 1840s from a drawing by William Stokes

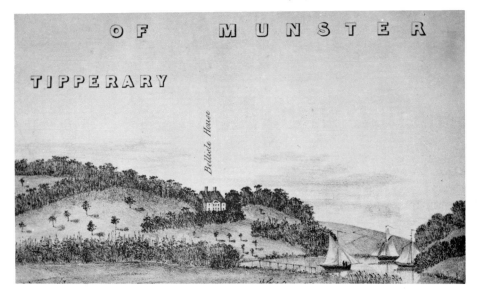

159

aptly named *The Dipper*, with the tiller between his legs, waving his cloth cap in the air with exuberance as she ran at great speed before the wind, rolling both gunwales under. For some years he lived in Belle Isle, the beautiful house on the east shore just downstream of Portumna bridge which had been built by Lord Avonmore. Sir Henry Seagrave, who died while attempting to break the world water speed record, also lived here. In the lord's day this had been the venue for an annual yacht racing event, and Bertie continued this tradition keeping open house for his many boating friends. He had an extraordinary capacity for making boating hard work. He had bought the *Tigh-na-Mara* in England after the 1914-18 war; it had been an experimental lifeboat designed about 1917 to float off with the passengers if the mother ship was torpedoed. I never heard whether she had actually been put to the test and she had already been converted into a houseboat when Bertie bought her. Boarding up her windows, he and his wife, Marjorie, sailed her across to Ireland in very bad weather. She had many adventures on the Shannon because her engine was very unreliable; his 'man', Johnnie, was the only person who knew how to operate her. His butler, James, was also brought boating with them and adapted well to 'butling' on the boat.

Bertie could be very contentious on occasions. He was towing a long string of boats down the river between regattas and one of the lockkeepers said that he was allowed only one boat in tow toll free. Bertie promptly detached his tow and locked the boats through one at a time, deciding that if he had to pay for the boats then the lockkeeper would have to work for his money. I saw him arrive at Portumna one evening in the *Tigh-na-Mara* and loud

Meelick: Victoria lock with a group of boats including Bertie Waller's *Tigh na Mara* travelling between regattas in the 1950s

arguments could be heard echoing across the water as she came through the bridge. Marjorie wanted to have a bath and did not want people looking in through the porthole so she wanted to moor up the river. The younger members of the crew wanted to tie up at the quay. Bertie, typically, deciding to please nobody, rounded up the boat and drove her hard on to Hayes's Island. The rest of the evening was spent trying to get her off again with large numbers of people pushing on the telegraph pole which he carried on deck for that purpose. I never heard whether Marjorie got her bath.

In the grounds of Belle Isle, out towards Derry Point, near the entrance to Lough Derg, are the ruins of Ballynasheera Castle. I have never visited it because it did not look very imposing from the river but an interesting article by Conrad Cairns in a recent issue of *The Irish Sword* has shown me how wrong I was. He refers to it as Ireton's or Derrymacegan Castle and says that it is mentioned in the Civil Survey for Tipperary in 1654 as 'standing but scarce finished, lately built at the commonwealth's charge'. Cromwell's artillery was to make castle building a useless form of defence and so this would have been one of the last castles still surviving to have been built in Ireland. It is apparently of a unique design with two circular turrets at opposite corners which have projecting spurs. There are numerous spike-holes for musketeers enabling them to command all the ground around the castle walls from the turrets and spurs. General Ireton is reputed to have lodged here in 1651 and launched an attack against Ulick the 5th earl of Clanricard of Portumna Castle, who was a royalist. Ireton forced him to surrender and his lands were confiscated, which led, as already mentioned, to the short sojourn of Henry Cromwell in this district.

It is only in recent years, with the opening of the new harbour, that we have really begun to explore the old Clanricard estate; it is now administered by the Forest & Wildlife Service and Portumna Castle has been partially restored by the Board of Works. Like Rockingham on Lough Key, Portumna Castle Forest Park embraces all the many facets that places on the Shannon have to offer. There are a number of local guide books about the castle but what is needed is a good comprehensive guidebook which would deal with both the rich history of the place and the fascinating flora and fauna to be found here.

The architecture of the old castle is particularly interesting. It was built by the 4th earl of Clanricard in about 1618 at a cost of £10,000. The Clanricards were descendants of the Burkes or de Burghs, a Norman family who had been granted extensive estates in Connacht in the twelfth century and who, in time, wielded great power, becoming one of the Norman families who became 'more Irish than the Irish themselves'. Harman Murtagh has carried out a detailed investigation of the Burke family and he presented a

Portumna: the old castle. *Lawrence*

paper on the subject to the Munster Historical Society in the 1950s. A local historian, Michael MacMahon has also written a most interesting booklet about this family: *Portumna Castle and Its Lords* and Maurice Craig has also written about the castle in the Gatherum series. The first earl, known as Ulick the Beheader, because of his summary treatment of his captives, had availed of Henry VIII's policy of surrender and re-grant and, thereafter, the family had undergone a process of re-anglicisation and loyalty to the crown, although they refused to conform to the established Church for some generations.

By the time of Richard, the 4th earl, the family was very powerful and, as President of Connacht, Richard had distinguished himself in battle and had succeeded in obtaining written confirmation of title to his vast estates which up to that time had been held in the King's name. Having married a wealthy wife he decided to have a castle built at Portumna and the design is quite unique because it represents a transitional style between the fortified tower house, which had been the norm up to this time because of the disturbed state of the country, and the country mansion which was already popular in England; at the same time he built a house for himself near London and it was here that he spent most of his remaining years. The tower house castles usually had bawns or defended enclosures around them and Portumna had two of these fortified enclosures with the entrance covered by flanking towers and with a most attractive classical gateway separating the bawns. The house itself, which was classical in style, broke away from the vertical style of the tower house with the accommodation arranged horizontally, but it also had defensive features: projecting angle towers with musket loops, small inaccessible windows and only two entrances to the building. The front door was protected by a machicolation, an opening in the parapet above, through which the defenders could drop things on intruders, and the door itself was fortified by an iron grille; the chain holes for operating this grille have been confused with pistol loops. The house was very strongly built with thick outer walls that had a slight batter and two massive interior walls, which supported the roof, forming a spinal corridor on the long axis with staircases at either end. As already mentioned, the castle was put to the test in the confederacy wars and fell to the parliamentarians, leaving Henry Cromwell the task of repairing the damage caused in the siege before the Clanricards again took possession.

During the eighteenth century some major alterations were made: the long gallery, which ran the length of the house on the first floor looking out over the lake, was divided up into a number of apartments and the Gothic main gateway, which is attributed to Robert Adam, was added. There is a very vivid description of the castle and its furnishings at this time in the diary kept by Louisa Beaufort when she travelled around Ireland in 1807-10. She described entering the capacious hall where 'over a large fireplace is a stately chimney piece of black marble and a piece of sculpture above it of three figures nearly as large as life representing Faith, Hope and Charity, these and the decorations reach almost the top of this lofty Hall — there are other emblems and family banners placed there ...' Descriptions of other rooms follow: 'the ceiling of the drawing room is done with the richest stucco, the freize broad and handsome. The border of the carpet made to match it ...' John Bernard Trotter visited the castle in 1817 in the course of his *Walk Through Ireland* and it would seem from his comments that the alterations had not been completed at that time:

The castle is very grand, and highly interesting. The great hall, staircase, and the state drawing-room, are very handsome; and a long room,
in the highest story, is calculated for a fine library. It is in an unfinished
state.... There are several family pictures, and a great deal of ancient
furniture, which give a venerable air to many of the rooms.

Then, tragically, in 1826 the castle, with all its historic contents, was destroyed by fire.

The family lived for some time in the adjacent farm buildings down near

Portumna: the 'new' castle. *Lawrence*

the lake and in 1864 the famous Cork architects, Deane and Woodward, designed a new house for them. This house was built about one mile to the south looking out over the lake but by this time the Clanricards had become absentee landlords and although the new castle was furnished it was never actually occupied before it, too, was destroyed by fire in the 1920s. The Clanricard title had died with the fifteenth earl, Marquess Clanricard, in 1916. He had been one of the most unpopular landlords in the country, living in his London club most of the time and expecting his agents to collect the rent or evict the tenants; in the 1880s he owned over 56,000 acres in County Galway, which earned him about £24,000 per annum. Stories about him are legion but the best known was his callous remark when he heard that his agent had been murdered by his angry tenants: 'They needn't think they can intimidate me by shooting my agent.' On his death the estate passed through his sister to the Lascelles family.

There seems to be some confusion about the date of the fire at the new castle. I was told that it was just prior to a visit by Henry Lascelles and his wife Princess Mary, daughter of King George V, but that visit took place in 1928. It was suggested that it had been started maliciously but this was never proved and a function was held there on the previous night when Archie Moeran, who was agent for the estate at the time, had arranged for the Lough Derg Yacht Club members to use it. Lord Harewood did consider the idea of restoring the original castle to a plan drawn by the architect John Bilson but he decided instead to sell the entire estate to the Land Commission in 1948 for the small sum of £12,000.

Because of its architectural importance it was decided to carry out a partial restoration of the old castle in order to preserve what was left. The last time I was there the restoration work had made good progress but had been suspended, probably because of the scarcity of public funds. The garden of the inner court had been laid out with rose beds and an enthusiastic young local man had carried out research into the original layout of the flower beds and the types of roses that might have been growing there so that a faithful reproduction could be carried out. Most accounts of visits to Portumna Castle include the discovery of the tablet beneath the little rounded window facing out towards the lake; it must have been found nearby and affixed to this gazebo which would have been part of the later alterations to the castle. It commemorates a faithful dog which died in 1797:

> Who with a beauteous form possessed
> Those qualities which are esteemed
> most valuable in the human species
> Fidelity and Gratitude
> And Dying April 20th 1797, aged 11 years
> Was interred near this place.
> Alas poor Fury. She was a dog.
> Take her for All in All
> Eye shall not look upon her like again.

Down near the harbour beside the farm buildings, are the ruins of a Dominican Friary. The main church replaced an earlier Cistercian chapel in 1426; the north and south walls with their narrow pointed windows are thought to be part of the original thirteenth-century church. The Dominican church must have looked very well with its fine traceried four light east window and another similar one in the south transept, there is also an unusual quatrefoil window in the sacristy to the north of the chancel with a rather baffling upside-down head at the bottom of the sacristy doorway. There are interesting ruins of the domestic buildings with the refectory at the north west end. Most of the cloisters were re-erected in 1954; it was well done, at least to my unpractised eye, and gives a good impression of what it all must have looked like.

It is possible that the reason why the 4th earl had chosen Portumna on the edge of his estates to build his castle was because this attractive site became available with the dissolution of the friary. The 8th earl had conformed to the established Church and re-roofed the chancel of the friary church, using it as a family chapel. Louisa Beaufort includes a delightful account of attending worship here in her diary. The thirteenth earl had just died and his young son had succeeded to the title:

A small door in a wall led us immediately into the ruins of a large Abbey — the choir of which is roofed, and fitted up as a Church — the East window in good preservation — the Tracery handsome, there is a small gallery opposite to it in which a few soldiers sat, the church is small — but full large enough for the congregation — it is fitted up very plain, and has a gloomy light, we were shown into Lord Clanricarde's seat, in which sat Lady Catherine, the eldest daughter, about ten years old, rather pretty, the little Lord, not more than five, a sweet lively looking boy, and a large lady dressed in a black satin pelice who I afterwards learned was the Swiss governess — I expressed my surprise (for she chatted very freely) to see the children particularly the little lady at Church! She said it was an odd thing, for my Lady had her Chaplain at the Castle — the Curate, Mr Travers told us it was the late Lord's dying request to his Lady to bring the children up to be Protestants, and she religiously observes his directions.

We had set out from the harbour on one occasion to look for the remains of the other house. It was a very pleasant walk of about a mile through the woods. It was then that we discovered that the ruins had been completely removed and the area made into a car park for the forest park; I subsequently read that the stones from the house had been used to build the new church in the town in the 1960s. It is strange to think of this enormous house finished and lying empty for years.

The car park was the start of a Nature Trail and so we collected leaflets and set off around the twenty four 'stops'. It must be one of the most interesting nature trails in the country and we were fascinated by the rutting stands of the fallow deer where each autumn the master buck strips the bark off the trees in time honoured fashion. The trail takes you past a number of turloughs, or dry lakes, and everywhere there are signs of the occupants of these woods, pine martens, foxes, badgers and all sorts of birds; we even glimpsed an owl sleeping away the day. We regretted that we had not brought binoculars because there is a fine observation tower down at the lake's edge and a bewildering array of birds to be seen on the little islands in the rocky bays; this whole area of the lake is a nature reserve. Lough Derg stretches away to the south invitingly.

Portumna Castle: the inner gateway of the bawn, an early example of classical architecture. (Lawrence)

Portumna: the ruined church of the Dominican Friary

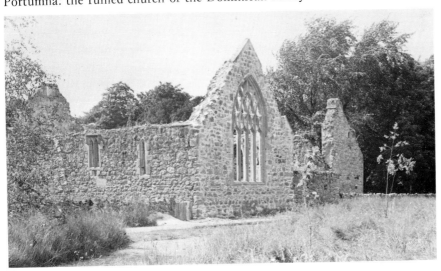

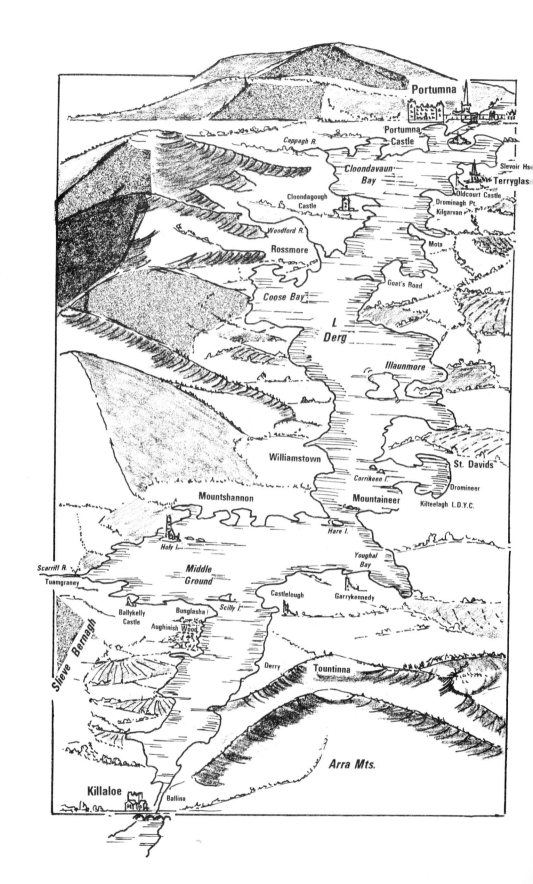

Chapter Eight

THE LAKE OF THE BLOODY EYE
Lough Derg

I HAVE voyaged on Lough Derg at all hours of the day and night, in storm and in flat calm and it has given me some of my most unforgettable and some of my worst moments. The lake seems to express the spirit of Sinann freed again from the constraints of the river after her long journey from the Cuilcagh hills far to the north. Why the Lake of the Bloody Eye? Well, it was so named by a chieftan long ago, Eochy, king of south Connacht and Thomond, who had only one eye, having lost the other in battle. One day he was visited by the famous harpist, Ahirny, who went about the country composing songs in honour of the famous. It was the custom to reward the bard with gifts when he was leaving and Eochy made the rash promise to give him anything he desired. The malicious Ahirny, who had taken a dislike to the old king, asked him for his remaining eye. The king had to keep his promise and so he plucked out his eye and handed it over. He was led down to the shore of the lake by his attendants and there he washed the gaping socket. To their surprise they noticed that the waters had turned red and the king proclaimed that the Lake of the Bloody Eye should be the name of the lake for evermore.

From that time, when the blood cleared from the lake until about twenty years ago the waters of this lake remained clear. Now, in two decades we have managed to bring it to the brink of ecological disaster. I can trace records in the log of *Harklow* as recently as 1963 when we were still filling our drinking water tank from the lake. Today, there are places where we hesitate even to swim. Situated at the lower end of this great river basin, Lough Derg receives all the agricultural and domestic pollutants which have entered its waters together with increasing quantities of turf deposits. In warm, still weather, dense clouds of green algae float to the surface and the fresh water mussels in shallow water on the bottom all lie open and lifeless. I have watched it worsen year by year. We in Ireland had a unique opportunity to benefit from the mistakes of other countries and keep our waters clean instead of waiting for them to die before launching costly rescue operations. Maybe there is a greater degree of urgency being shown at government level now and people are becoming more aware of their environment, but I fear that this generation have a great deal to answer for in neglecting our heritage of clean water.

Terryglass is tucked away in the corner of a little bay sheltered from all except northerly and north westerly winds which tend to send a swell into the harbour. The little community of Terryglass has done a great deal to make the most of its lakeside position and the pride the people have taken in their village brought them the well deserved major award in Bord Failte's Tidy Towns competition in 1983; particularly impressive is the way they have tidied up and grassed over the old graveyard.

Terryglass was formerly an important monastic centre known for its asceticism, a trait no longer practised by the villagers today with two friendly public houses catering for the visitor. The community was founded by St Colm in the sixth century and it is even suggested that St Patrick had visited here a century earlier and baptised people. When I mentioned this to one of our modern historians he replied that he discounted many of the 'wanderings' of the saint 'as moonshine concocted to justify the claims by Armagh of ecclesiastical hegemony over the rest of Ireland'! St Patrick, like Oliver Cromwell, would need to have been a very active man to have traversed all the ground he is credited with covering in Ireland. Terryglass was a famous centre of the reform movement in the late eighth century; it survived several Viking attacks but suffered a serious fire in 1162 after which it ceased to receive further mention.

There is little to be seen here now. Two walls of a fifteenth century Norman parish church remain, with a west doorway formed by a single stone lintel. The Church of Ireland church had not been used for many years and had been allowed to decay but it has now been renovated and is used as a craft centre. The Catholic church on the hill nearby, which is such a prominent landmark from the lake, is also built on part of the original monastic settlement but only fragmentary remains have been found here.

The fine Norman castle of Oldcourt is approached from Terryglass village. It dates from the late thirteenth or early fourteenth century when the de Burghs, from whom the Clanricards were descended, had crossed the Shannon and extended their sway into Connacht. The experts say that they are more likely to have been the builders than the Butlers of Ormond. It always reminds me of the square sandcastles we used to make on the beach as children, carefully inverting our buckets to make the tower in each corner. It belongs to a later stage in Norman castle construction in Ireland: the motte and bailey castle gave way to castles like Rindoon with strong central keeps surrounded by defensive walls and then came this typically Irish type without a defensive wall, a strong keep fortified by round towers at each corner and with buildings of wood inside. Waterway travellers will notice its similarity to Carlow Castle but Oldcourt has a strangely truncated appearance and it obviously was meant to be several storeys higher. Opinion seems divided as

Cloondagough Castle

to whether the castle suffered damage or whether, in fact, the upper part was ever built; one puzzling feature is that access to the tower in the north east corner is by outside steps. I remember sitting on its walls watching boats sailing out on the lake and thinking that its former occupants must have looked out on a very similar scene but they may have had more cause to fear the approaching boats.

There is a long fetch out of Cloondavaun Bay when there is a westerly wind and, because *Harklow* rolls so badly in a cross-sea, we usually tack down this part of the lake if it is rough, standing across to Cloondagough Castle before altering course under the shelter of the land to clear Drominagh Point. Because of this, I had often been able to see the castle at close quarters and we had noticed that there was some work being carried out on it but had never gone ashore to have a closer look. Eventually, I did manage to visit the place with my brother-in-law, Alf Delany and his wife, Pat. Standing in quite close before dropping the anchor, we were surprised to find a very large rocky outcrop on the shore in front of the castle almost like a natural slipway, where we landed and pulled up the dinghy. The castle is a good example of the tower houses which were built from the fifteenth until well into the seventeenth century as fortified houses; a number of these castles are to be found around the lake.

We squeezed through a gap in the boarding across the entrance, ignoring a warning to people to keep out because the building was dangerous; the castle appeared to be in good repair but there was a large crack down one wall. We were able to climb the spiral staircase to the upper floors and discovered that it had been re-roofed. I subsequently learned that this had been done by an Irish American but that he had not stayed long enough to complete the restoration.

Walking out to the nearby road, we looked at the houses there and decided that altogether it was a very pleasant and peaceful spot. I was most interested, therefore, some time later to read about this place in some articles, given to me by Reggie Redmond, written by a correspondent calling himself 'Induction Valve', which appeared in a journal called *The Motor News* in 1906. The author had made a trip on the river in an early motorboat and he happened to visit Cloondagough while a Clanricard eviction was in progress. The castle had been garrisoned by the local people who succeeded in holding the authorities at bay for a long time. Finally, at break of day, a flotilla had crossed the lake and stormed the castle before the occupants were awake; Bunny Goodbody's version of this story is that the people were so delighted with their success in thwarting the eviction that they held a celebration party and when the authorities returned they were all helplessly drunk. The correspondent described his visit:

Close by is the house of the celebrated Dr Tully, who earned his medical degree by a speech which he delivered, and in which he declared that he had a pill which was good for the landlords, and an emetic which, when administered to landgrabbers, always made them throw up. Dr Tully's house was fortified with earthworks to prevent the walls being battered in, and the defenders, armed with forked branches, pitchforks, hot irons, eggs, hot water etc., were all on the upper storey or loft. I photographed them inside and afterwards took a group outside. The man with the beard and poker in the group is Dr Tully. Tuohy's house was fortified in a different way. Trees were cut and fixed in the ground inside, so as to support the upper floor; then the knocking down of the wall did not dislodge those in the loft.

Cloondagough Castle: the group who resisted eviction by Clanricard's agent

This must have been one of the last eviction battles fought in Ireland.

We brought the *Harklow* up the Cappagh river in the north west corner of Cloondavaun Bay on a Christmas cruise one year when the water was about 2 feet over normal summer level. There was about 7 feet on the bar at the entrance and we went up the river about a mile and a half to where it is joined by the Ballyshrule river. It was a bleak and lonely spot. We continued up the river in the dinghy and found a small Christmas tree which we brought back and tied to the mast. It was an enjoyable expedition; there is something special about these winter trips, the reeds have all died back, the trees are bare, everywhere takes on a different appearance and, best of all, you have the entire world to yourself.

There are a number of fine houses visible from the lake which came through the troubled times unscathed. Slevoir House on the east shore of Terryglass Bay was the family seat of the Monsells and then the Hickeys. On the point across from Cloondagough Castle is Drominagh House, formerly called Castle Biggs, which was the home of Dr W. Biggs, and later the Esmonde family, whose son, Eugene, was awarded the DSO during the 1939-45 war for the part played in the sinking of the *Bismark*; he sighted her and succeeded in damaging her steering, making her an easy prey. He later was awarded a posthumous VC for the daring attack of his squadron on part of the German fleet which had slipped out of Brest into the English Channel and was trying to break through into the North Sea. Down on the lakeshore there was an O'Kennedy castle commanding this narrow part of the lake and nearby is Gurthalougha House which is now a popular hotel with its own private mooring facilities.

Kilgarvan is on the east shore behind a group of islands. These are called Fool's Islands on the old admiralty chart (surveyors Beechey and Wolfe charted this lake as well) but they seem to have become Foot's Islands on recent charts. I always assumed that there was a slip of the pen somewhere and that Fool's Islands made more sense because they are surrounded by rocks and only a fool would try to approach them but I recently learnt that there was a family called Foot who lived in this area so it looks as if the admiralty chart was in error. Kilgarvan used to be a collection depot for barley for the maltings in Banagher but the original Inland Steam Navigation Company's quay was at Mota in the next bay to the south; there is a modern amenity area at Mota now.

Visible from the lake between Kilgarvan and Mota is Waterloo Lodge. This probably started out as a small farmhouse in the early nineteenth century but it was bought from the Rev. Roberts and converted into a fishing lodge by Richard Lloyd Vaughan DL who lived near Roscrea. He leased it for a while to a man named St Leger, who was a member of the Grand Jury in Nenagh which found a True Bill against the two McCormick brothers, who were accused of murdering a land agent called Ellis. It was said that they were convicted on perjured evidence and, on the day of their execution, their widowed mother cursed by name each and every member of the Grand Jury, saying that they would die violent deaths like her two innocent sons. A violent

Waterloo Lodge

thunderstorm broke out over Nenagh during the execution, adding weight to the widow's curse. St Leger, deranged in mind from worry and alcohol, took his own life in the hallway of Waterloo Lodge; his aim was none too good and instead of shooting himself in the head he hit his jugular vein making it a messy affair. All efforts to remove the bloodstains from the floor and wall were to no avail.

When Lloyd Vaughan died in the 1930s, he left the lodge to his nephew Captain McIvor and on his death, his sister sold the house to Bunny Goodbody (who, if you have not guessed it already, is responsible for this tale). She felt it her duty to warn Bunny about the stain and it was agreed that he should be allowed to pass a night in the house before signing the papers to establish whether St Leger's spirit was at rest. Bunny slept the sleep of the just and the sale went through. He and his family lived there for eight untroubled years but two of their more psychic guests passed uneasy nights there. The stains continued to resist all efforts to remove them; Bunny even tried painting the wall but the stain reappeared. The present owners, George and Hilary Henry, are carrying out extensive renovations to the house and, in the course of the alterations, they have removed the stone floor from the hall, including the offending stone. Beneath it they uncovered a weeping red sandstone. Hilary Henry is philosophical about their 'ghost', perhaps he has been laid to rest?

The widow's curse also fell on another member of that Grand Jury called Cambie who was drowned together with his wife, son and daughter. They had set out in a sailing boat to return to Castle Cambie on the east shore behind Illaunmore, a house that is now called Castletown, and they struck the rock off Gortmore Point which is now marked by a black buoy. Some local people working in the fields saw the upturned boat drifting ashore and were astonished to find the boatman, still alive, but very drunk, trapped under the seat.

Although there are no facilities at Rossmore, it is one of my favourite places on Lough Derg; maybe this is just because fewer boats put in here due to that very lack of facilities. In the past, boats of up to twenty tons went up the Woodford river to Rossmore Bridge, serving the mills there and the nearby town of Woodford. There were plans to improve the navigation and build a quay but these did not materialise. Some years ago we took *Harklow* up the river in the spring when the water was high. There was the usual bar across the entrance with a dog's leg approach but once over the bar the water was quite deep. We went up the river some distance until it widened out into a pool in which we turned. We tied up to the bank and were welcomed by the farmer who gave us some warm milk straight from the cow. Since then John Weaving has dredged a channel into the river making it accessible at all times.

Up this river you pass through high reeds into an isolated world; once one of our visitors caught a trout here. Although we carry fishing rods aboard, we rarely seem to do any fishing, there always seems to be so many other things to do. I always used to dread the shout of triumph when one of the children caught a fish, the cry quickly turned to one of panic when they found that the fish had to be killed and this was a job I did not relish. And then there were the hours spent unravelling endless fishing lines and the occasional painful operation of removing hooks from various parts of the anatomy. Douglas had two young nephews aboard at one time and they caught a rudd; these are a golden coloured fish with red fins. The boys were anxious to eat their catch and Douglas, unsure about this, asked the advice of one of the lockkeepers. He took one look at the two boys, who bore that distinctive appearance of English public schoolboys, and said: 'I dunno. The English eats some queer things'! You can usually be sure that the fellow sitting on the bank with a large umbrella, all the paraphernalia, a keep net for his catch and a little book for entering up the weights of his catch before returning them to the river, is from the other side of the water, or an Angler Saxon. The Irish fisherman is usually a far less organised being.

The Goat's Road extends out into the lake from the east shore at its narrowest point. Before the hydro electric works in the 1920s the lake was about one foot lower and Goat Island, with the line of rocks stretching out to it, was more obvious. It is useful to know that you have about one foot to spare over the readings on the admiralty chart. The Goat's Road was one of the first places to be marked with a beacon in the early 1800s but this beacon was demolished recently because it was causing confusion with the black buoy outside it; some boats tried passing between them, which brought them over the outer end of the shallow. Two other hazards were considered so dangerous that they were marked in these early years, the Benjamin shoal, further south, and the Deer Rock, down near the southern end of the lake. At first they erected beacons and then they began to use buoys to mark other dangerous shoals. These sometimes caused problems; one early report stated that the Split Island buoy was adrift because the chain had broken: 'notwithstanding all the caution that was used, some British Iron had been introduced in the Chains'.

The busts on the Benjamin and Horse Island beacons were put up there in 1961. A boating party set out from Dromineer aboard the Tottenham's canal boat the *Venus* one night during regatta week. The boat was laid up against the beacons, and the busts, which had been removed from the Tottenham family home in Wicklow, were cemented into position. They have survived many winters since then and must have puzzled many a visitor passing by boat.

The Benjamin Beacon in 1979 when the level of the lake dropped revealing the shoal

The names given to the islands and shoals on the Shannon lakes have always fascinated me. Most of them go back so far in time that their origins have become obscured; I have never discovered who 'Benjamin' was. The Corrikeen Islands to the south of the Benjamin shoal are spelt 'Carrigeen' and 'Quoirgies' on earlier charts. Maybe it just meant 'little rocks' in Irish and the little rocks grew into small islands. The name Coose Bay is taken from the river which discharges into it. The word means 'stepping stone' in Irish and there are a number of fords on the river. Not all the names are so easily unravelled and I had better desist before I incur the censure of the experts.

We always treat the area in behind Illaunmore with great respect, having had a number of close encounters with shoals there; the surveyors seem to have missed a few rocks here which we have managed to discover. Vincent always said you had to keep the windows of Annagh Castle, which is up on the hill over Luska, open when coming in here but the ruin is so overgrown with ivy that this is no longer easy. The Tiernans who used to live on Illaunmore, like the islanders of Lough Ree, relied on eel fishing to supplement

177

SHANNON NAVIGATION,

Act 2nd & 3rd Vic., cap. 61.

The Commissioners of Public Works hereby call attention to the following

EXTRACT FROM SECTION XXXVIII., 2nd & 3rd VIC., CAP. 61:---

"And be it enacted, That it shall not be lawful for any Person whomsoever, from and after the passing of this Act, to fish upon or from any of the Weirs or any Dams or other Work or Works which shall be erected by the said Commissioners, without the Consent of the said Commissioners, which Consent shall be signified by Warrant, and shall continue in force for Three Years and not for any longer Period."

Persons offending against this are liable to a fine not exceeding **TEN POUNDS.**

BY ORDER,

H. WILLIAMS,

Secretary.

Office of the Board of Public Works,
Dublin, 1st July, 1907.

200—W.S.No.1711—7.07—216. PRINTED FOR HIS MAJESTY'S STATIONERY OFFICE BY BROWNE & NOLAN, LTD., NASSAU STREET, DUBLIN.

An interesting notice issued by the Shannon Navigation authority

their income. One of them was interviewed on Radio Eireann recently and he told how one day he decided to go to Billingsgate to find out what happened to his eels there. He had never been further than Nenagh before but found his way there and discovered that the middle man was reaping a very large profit so he did a deal with the merchants to supply them direct in future. All this ended when the ESB took over the fishing rights of the river. They even tried to introduce licences for coarse fishing but all the notice boards arrived mysteriously in the front gardens of the local police stations and no more was heard of this.

Across the lake on the west shore is Williamstown which was an important Inland Steam Company station at one time. In the late 1820s the company had made the harbour here by joining one end of Cow Island with the mainland. Beside the harbour a hotel was built which became a popular base for fishermen. A notice under the heading 'Fashionable Intelligence' in the *Nenagh Guardian* for 1 August 1838 records:

Arrivals at Williamstown Hotel this week: the Countess of Clanricarde and suite, Lord Viscount Avonmore, the Hon. W. Yelverton, the Hon. Misses Yelverton, William Osborne Esq. and Captain Bailey. The above party left Williamstown on Wednesday morning, delighted with the beautiful scenery of the lake, and highly pleased at the accommodation of the Hotel.

W. F. Wakeman in his little guide book *Three Days on the Shannon* published by Hodges & Smith and printed in 1852 by M. H. Gill of Dublin (great great grandfather of Michael Gill of Gill & Macmillan, the publishers of this book) described the scene as the steamer lay off the shore in order to land passengers:

We now approach Williamstown, a little fishing station upon the Galway side of the lake; the steam is shut off, and a boat from the shore comes alongside. Here, reader, if you be an angler, we would advise you to stay. The little tender will convey you to an hotel where you will have all attention paid to your wants; and if you seek for sport, there is no place upon the Shannon where better angling can be had. The trout are numerous, of great size and take freely. The salmon fishing is also excellent, and pike upwards of 40 lbs in weight have been killed in the neighbourhood. Boats, tackle, and, if necessary, attendants may be hired at the hotel.

Like the earlier description of fishing on Lough Ree, this description will upset the modern fisherman. Shannon fishing has been sacrificed in the cause of progress to make electricity.

Williamstown was the scene of a remarkable escapade about 1919 which is related in a book called *In the Gloaming - Chronicles of the Holles Street Club* by John Herman Rice. A group of friends had set out for a trip on the Shannon taking the train from Dublin to Banagher. On their arrival they discovered that they had missed the steamer and so they hired two rowing boats and followed her downstream eventually arriving in Portumna. The steamer was standing at the quay with steam up awaiting the arrival of an excursion party and just as the two large wagonettes were crossing the bridge, the group from Dublin hijacked the boat, and locked the crew below. Once down the lake they released the men who took their abduction in good part, 'numerous bottles made their appearance all over the deck and song after song lost itself across the pleasant waters'. When they were off Williamstown, the hijackers were put ashore and the steamer set off to return to Portumna. The group split up to evade detection but some of them were arrested and brought before the court in Feakle. However, they obviously knew some 'friends in court' because telegrams were dispatched to Dublin and the learned judge let the defendants off with a £20 fine.

When the steamers ceased to trade, the hotel was closed and became the private residence of General Cooper. He had made his money in trade, a matter he would not have been too keen to dwell upon. On one occasion he was entertaining some of his sailing friends and they all retired to their yachts for the night. The following morning he was disconcerted by the unconcealed mirth of the people on the boats moored around his steam yacht the *Vixen* and eventually he discovered that written across the side of his boat in large letters was the legend: 'Buy Cooper's Sheep Dip'. The culprit was known to be Traherne Holmes, a prankster, whose jokes often had a malevolent streak, and of whom more anon.

The *Vixen* was a sister ship of the *Phoenix* but she was constructed of ordinary steel plates, not Lowmoor iron. She was involved in a sadder incident in Williamstown harbour in 1920 when this part of the country was under martial law. The *Phoenix* was commandeered in Killaloe by the Auxiliaries and she proceeded up the lake to Williamstown where they had learnt that three men on the run were in hiding. The men were captured, the *Vixen* was scuttled and together with the caretaker of Williamstown House they were brought back to Killaloe by steamer. The rest of this story is best told in the words of a local ballad:

> They tied them up both hands and feet,
> With thongs they could not break,
> They brought them down to Killaloe,
> By steamer on the lake.
> Without clergy, judge or jury

180

On the bridge that night shot down
And the blood flows with the Shannon
Convenient to the town.

A plaque on the bridge at Killaloe marks the spot where they were shot. The *Vixen* was later purchased for £5 by Bertie Waller who raised her and sold her for considerably more to the Perrys of Belmont who used her on many a fishing trip until she finally succumbed. Ireland's gold medal Olympic hurdler, Robert Tisdall, who lived across the lake at Hazlepoint, had helped Bertie to raise her, diving down and shutting the portholes.

These were troubled times on the lake; in 1922 the *Eclipse* was hijacked and brought to Mountshannon where her cargo of flour was distributed to the people of the area. Williamstown House was set on fire and never rebuilt but the outhouses have now been converted into holiday apartments by Shannon Castle Line who have developed the harbour as a hire boat base.

Around the corner from the old harbour, the Board of Works have made a new harbour. The experts shake their heads about this harbour and it has proved very open to a swell in easterly winds. There are no amenities here and the nearest shops and pubs are over two miles away at Whitegate. I always used to smile at the petrol pump outside the pub in the village which until recently was simply labelled 'The Best', and the notice outside a house on the road to Mountshannon which read 'Warm Meals'.

And so we are back in Dromineer Bay from which I had set out all those years ago on a voyage which was to have such an influence on my life. I had found my first trip on Lough Derg after Vincent's death a very emotional experience but I have discovered that it is not wise to cut yourself off from places where you have been happy. It is foolish to shut out these memories because that is all that you have left of people you have loved.

Dromineer Bay has long been the centre of sailing on the lake which was well established by the 1830s; regattas were held also at a number of other venues with hospitality provided by the various gentlemen who lived in these places; the local people derived pleasure from these events as well. The *Nenagh Guardian* reported in 1861: 'In the evening a large party of ladies and gentlemen were entertained at St David's by Captain and Mrs Holmes, where, when it got dark, there was a brilliant display of fireworks, and dancing was kept up till a late hour.'

Over the years many different keelboats were based on the lake but the fleets at any one time were not very large. Amongst the best known were Captain Holmes's 15-ton *Corsair*, Robert Harvey's *Achilla*, the *Knockrockery*, owned by William Minchin and Traherne Holmes, H. Jackson's *Seadrift* and Lord Dunally's *Countess*. William Waller of Prior

181

The 'Midge' McGrath, *Corsair's* boatman

Park built his own boat the *Surprise* in 1875 in the grounds of his house, using the ingenious method of digging a hole in the ground as a mould; the hole is still there today. When she was finished she had to be manhandled four miles to the lake.

A poem written by one of the paid hands in those days gives a good idea of the atmosphere of the time:

> The yachtsmen from Portumna they watched the glorious view
> And the best upon the Shannon from Athlone to Killaloe
> To see the *Countess* sailing most pleasant to their mind
> The *Corsair* taking in the waves and she lay far behind.
> Now the crew of the *Countess* I mean to let you know
> Was headed by Captain Smithwick and the Honourable Mr Coe
> The first mate of the vessel William Collins was his name
> And the second mate James Gleeson from Youghal too he came
> Some say Johnny McGrath, the old Midge, is the best man on the lake
> But Collins is a better man, five hundred pounds I'd stake,
> For he is both young and active his business to get through
> He can climb his mast in any blast and set his foresail too.
> Now to conclude and finish, the racing was all over
> The *Corsair* she was well beat, what she never was before
> Long life to Captain Smithwick, the *Countess* steered with skill
> The race she run, the cup she won and brought it to Youghal again.
> When the Captain and his *Countess* appeared in Youghal Bay
> They were highly saluted by the cheers from Youghal Quay
> And the shores built so united that the people did admire
> And in honour to the Captain they lit a large bonfire.

Like their counterparts on Lough Ree, the yachtsmen observed a certain amount of formality. 'Evolution signals' had to be obeyed when the boats were proceeding 'in squadron'. Detailed instructions were issued, for example:

When a signal is made from the officer in command to perform any evolution it must not be obeyed, but merely acknowledged until the Pilot Jack, or the Ensign at his gaff end is hauled down. . . . Any yacht that cannot understand an Evolutionary signal should hoist Flag N. etc.

There were occasional visitors from the north Shannon and Lough Ree. In the 1870s William Potts brought the *Audax* down river to participate in regattas on a number of occasions. She drew 8 feet and went aground several times in the river and her mast became entangled in the telegraph wires at

A page from the log of W. R. Potts's *Audax* dated 22-23 August 1874, the day they caught the topsail yard in the telegraph wires

Banagher. The log of these trips, illustrated with drawings, is most entertaining. The racing was keen and there appears to have been much the same sort of nocturnal activity which is enjoyed at regattas today. For example, the entry for Saturday 22 August 1875 in Portumna reads:

Before turning in last night heard a frightful row, and a female voice shouting 'Never steered up her before' and 'Shall we anchor?' We concluded the nautical lady was making her way somewhere in the dark, and was not in a very good temper at being out so late in a flat calm.

In 1883 it was decided to formalise the club and draw up rules. Records exist from this date; at that time the club was based at Kilteelagh on the south side of the bay; it did not move into the present premises until it amalgamated with the Lough Derg Boat Club in 1922. The official records do not, however, tell the full story behind all the events which affected the club and one of these concerns the Holmes family of St David's.

When Arthur Young visited Ireland in 1777 he stayed with Peter Holmes at Johnstown which was some distance from the lake, behind Urra wood. He recorded that at that time Mr Holmes was building a new house for himself down by the lake where 'the face of the country gives every circumstance of beauty'. This was St David's on the north shore of the bay, still one of the most attractive houses on the Shannon. In the course of time Captain Bassett Holmes, already mentioned above, became one of the early commodores of the club.

On Thursday 2 September 1894 three yachts competed for the Lough Derg Challenge Cup on the second day of the annual regatta. It was a calm day and the *Seadrift* gave up after the first round. The committee stopped the race after the second round and awarded the race to Robert Harvey's *Achilla*

Dromineer about the turn of the century: the Boat Club before the amalgamation with the Lough Derg Yacht Club. (*Lawrence*)

on handicap. Traherne Holmes and W. R. Minchin the owners of the other boat, the *Knockrockery*, lodged a protest claiming that Mr Harvey's paid hand had steered the boat for part of the course, which was against the rules. Harvey lodged a counter protest that the other boat had failed 'to display an ensign conspicuously in the main rigging' when lodging the protest. The committee took the line of least resistance and declared the race null and void but a case was stated to the Yacht Racing Association under whose rules the race had been sailed. The YRA awarded the race to the *Knockrockery* on the grounds that the committee should have disqualified the other boat for the infringement of the rules regardless of how the protest was lodged. Dixon Kemp, secretary of the YRA, subsequently wrote an account of the affair in *The Field* in which he said that the protest had been disputed because no ensign had been displayed and 'it was not made in time'. Captain Minchin wrote to the secretary of the Lough Derg Yacht Club (LDYC), who happened to be Robert Harvey, asking him to contradict the erroneous statement that the protest had not been made in time but he decided to send this letter to Traherne with a note which said: 'If you disapprove of the enclosed going to Bob Harvey, Esq., burn it, if not, please close it and send it on. You ought to write too, only let him down easy!' Whether deliberately or not, Traherne sent on Minchin's letter to Harvey but also enclosed the covering note that had been addressed to him. Harvey promptly asked for an apology for the insult implied by both gentlemen.

Dixon Kemp subsequently admitted that he had added the words 'it was not made in time' in error and apologised to Harvey 'for the annoyance my inadvertance had caused', but by this time one thing had borrowed another and there had been further exchanges of letters in one of which Holmes had praised Harvey for 'the gentlemanly and courteous manner with which you gave up the cup', adding by way of postscript: 'Veni, Vidi, Vici. I hope your bees are doing well. Bad weather for making honey.' In the end Holmes resigned and established his own yacht club at St David's which he called the Lough Derg Corinthian Yacht Club.

Thus a minor affair had been blown up out of all proportion. There was correspondence in the local newspaper attempting to heal the breach but this seems to have made things worse. One letter read:

Why not settle the great dispute (on the one side) controversy, and decide this matter by having midnight naval manoeuvres between the rival fleets, the survivors to have the grilled bones afterwards on Cormorant Island?
Yours truly
Bumboat

This was followed by a note from the editor which read: 'The above controversy has been sufficiently ventilated, so the correspondence must now cease.'

At one stage there was an incident with a top hat in the North Tipperary Club in Nenagh when Holmes was alleged to have used the hat for a purpose for which it was not intended. The two yacht clubs operated in opposition for a number of years and it was not until after Holmes's death that sanity prevailed and the Corinthian members were elected *en bloc* to the LDYC in 1908 bringing with them their 18-ft centreboard boats which were to be the forerunners of the SODs.

Robert Harvey lived in Kilteelagh and wrote a book entitled *The Shannon and its Lakes* in 1896. In the light of the above, the following remark in his book is amusing:

One object in writing this, is that many kindly strangers may, in the pursuit of an enchanting form of recreation, add to their too scant knowledge of this beautiful and unhappy country, and its pure sport-loving people.

There might, in fact, have been a deeper reason behind the split and there was obviously a clash of personalities even before the incident of the protest. In a 'Comment' written by Archie Moeran for a Memoir of the Lough Derg Yacht Club in 1956, Archie, who was then well over eighty years old and a greatly respected member of the sailing community, wrote:

my experience of the 'turmoil and fighting' goes back further than anyone else alive. The founding of the Corinthinian Yacht Club on Lough Derg, as I remember well, was directly due to Traherne Holmes. It started at Portumna one day when the original club was holding a regatta there, and when the very intemperate language of a certain flag officer, shouted across the bay so that all heard, was so much resented by most of the yacht owners there that they refused to sail their boats in the following races, and the regatta fizzled out. Then next year, Holmes got the discontented yacht owners together and founded the Corinthian Yacht Club, which flourished exceedingly.

By all accounts Traherne Holmes was quite a character; stories about him are legion and he became a legendary figure. It is said that one day in a light flukey wind *Corsair*, using all the well-known tricks, was trying to overtake the *Countess* when, finally, Traherne stripped off and slipped over the side, resurfacing beside the *Countess* which was being steered by Lady Dunally. She 'took a weakness' at the sight of a naked man and let go the tiller allowing the *Corsair* to slip by. Traherne reboarded his boat and went on to win the race despite a protest from the Dunallys. On another occasion he was sailing home with his hand, Mick Donlon, and he asked him to go below to fetch something. When he returned to the deck, his skipper was gone and although he searched the waters around, he could find no trace of him. Eventually, he returned to St David's to announce the sad tidings and further searches were made. That evening the search party put into Garrykennedy only to find Traherne in the local pub having spent the day there drinking. On another occasion he is reputed to have jumped on the gunwale of a boat full of ladies at a regatta plunging them into the water, crinolines, parasols and all. Arriving late for church one day, he turned the key in the door and went away, locking the vicar and congregation in the church for many hours until someone heard their cries for help. I am quoting these stories from memory, having heard them related many times, but I hope that one day Posie Goodbody (née Holmes) will put them all down for posterity.

Since those days the club went through some lean years during the two world wars and keelboat racing died out; Con Jackson's *Vanja*, which coincidentally Douglas was to buy some time later to race in Dublin Bay, was the last keelboat to leave the lake in 1956. Today the club is prospering, with a large and active SOD fleet and with interest in keelboat racing reviving. These waters could tell great tales of races lost and won. It is a safer sport today with lifejackets and buoyancy in all centreboard boats obligatory. Instead of those great running starts with the boats finishing around Goose Island, Olympic courses are sailed but, I venture to suggest, there are few places in the world where the old traditions of sporting behaviour are better preserved although, dare I add, ignorance of the racing rules is not unknown.

People like the late Edgar Waller have left their mark; for him it was taking part that was important, not winning at all costs. He loved to sail the '53', which had sailed so many hard races and had become such a flexible boat that, as Vincent used to say: 'She would turn around and look at you.' Edgar had a wonderful philosophy of life. I remember once hearing him discussing the after life and he said in his inimitable way with his tendency to drop his final 'g': 'Heaven will be just sailin' all day long' and then after a moment's hesitation he added: 'but the port tack will be the right tack!'

The history of the village of Dromineer goes back a long way. There is a ruined twelfth-century church in the old graveyard; according to local tradition this was to be a new foundation for a group of monks from nearby Inishcealtra which never materialised and so the church was never completed. This had been Magrath territory until it was granted with the rest of Ormond to the Butler family by King John. This area was held for them by the Cantwells and there was probably a castle here from this time. When

Butler influence waned in the fourteenth century the O'Kennedys assumed control, but the earl of Ormond reoccupied his territories at the beginning of the seventeenth century and a Thomas Cantwell was reinstated at Dromineer. Hardress Waller, Edgar's son, who has made a study of the history of the area, suggests that this Cantwell was probably the builder of the present castle. Larger than most of the Butler tower houses, it was 51 feet by 39 feet and stood four storeys high, lighted by large quadrangular windows. By the mid-seventeenth century a survey records that there were six thatched houses and fourteen cottages at Dromineer, so it was a sizable village for those times. General Ireton with his Cromwellian forces captured the castle in 1650, on the day after he had taken Nenagh. After the restoration the duke of Ormond leased the castle to a John Parker but it was subsequently dismantled in 1692 by order of the Williamite government together with most of the bigger castles in Ormond. Which all goes to show that Cromwell's role in the destruction of Dromineer castle was very slight.

Dromineer was one of the most important of the steam company's stations. Back in 1806 it was reported to the Grand Canal Company's board that 'Mr Emanuel Poe and another gentleman are building boats near the castle at Dromineer for the Shannon trade.' He had built an extensive store and a pier which is probably what is now known as the castle quay. The steam company built another store and small harbour here in 1829, and these were later absorbed into the modern harbour.

In 1838, in the era when 'paper canals' were very common, some local Nenagh people planned to make a canal from Nenagh to Dromineer using the Nenagh river for part of the way. The canal was to be over six miles long with eight locks and the cost was estimated to be £58,000. The *Nenagh Guardian* supported the scheme suggesting: 'How much better will the money be bestowed upon useful works, than given away in alms from which we can derive no profitable return.' In the following year a counter proposal was put forward to run the canal from Nenagh to Youghal Bay at a reduced figure and the Nenagh & River Shannon Canal Company was floated but the growth of the railways, with a direct link with Dublin, quickly killed the project.

The Nenagh river is now a source of pollution and mud to the lake but many years ago we had a visitor on board who was a botanist and he discovered a rare plant on its banks which caused him great delight. Mrs Holmes of St David's, who was a keen lover of nature, was able to confirm that she had noted it as well. This is just another example of the extraordinary wealth of botanical interest to be found around the lake.

There was an interesting book written in 1897 by John Bickerdyke called *Wild Sports in Ireland* in which the author described his adventures on shooting and fishing expeditions 'pages from out the history of my life spent on wild inland seas'. He assured his readers that tales of battering rams and moonlighting were misleading, adding:

The only way in which a dispute between the English sportsman and the Irish peasantry would be likely to arise, would be in connection with a raid by peasants who claimed sporting rights over some piece of mountain on which the shooting had been let.

He was using a yacht called the *Tallyhassie* and he described how he sailed her into Dromineer Bay in winter to skate on the ice which had formed around the shore. He met an old man there who told him; 'We never have such winters as in my young days. Was it in '30 or '31 that the lake was frozen right across, and we skated to Portumna and back?'

Leaving Dromineer Bay and heading down the lake, the Mountaineer buoy is on your port hand. On a very still day Vincent and I went out in the dinghy and tried to find the rock. Stabbing the water with the oar, he hit it first time about 6 ft down but then, try as we would, we could not find it again. I have always wondered about how this rock became known as 'The Mountaineer'. The steamer *Mountaineer* had arrived on the Shannon in 1826 having passed down the Grand Canal at about the same time as John Grantham's *Marquis Wellesley*. A memorial plaque in the cathedral in Killaloe attributes the introduction of steam navigation on the Shannon to John Grantham in 1825 but the records of the canal company show that neither of these boats went down the canal till 1826. There are a few references to the *Mountaineer* over the next few years with the last mention of her in March 1829. Presumably, at some time she must have struck this rock but I have never been able to find out about the incident or trace what happened to the steamer afterwards. The water is 13 feet to 20 feet deep all round the rock, maybe she lies there on the bottom or could it be that she is, in fact, the rock? The steamers must have had to battle through bad weather on occasions. Leitch Ritchie obviously made his trip down the lake in stormy conditions in the 1830s and his description evokes memories for me of passages we have made:

The clouds rushed and darkened, the waves rose and broke, and the vessel pitched and rolled; and, in short, it was a very respectable imitation of the sea in a smart breeze.

These early steamers had all ceased to operate by the 1860s and there was no service for over thirty years. In the 1890s, the Shannon Development Company inaugurated a new service: a boat left Killaloe at 8.00 a.m. and called to Dromineer by a pre-arranged signal if there were any passengers to collect. She reached Portumna at 11.20, Banagher at 1.00 p.m. to meet the Dublin train, and continued upstream to reach Athlone at 4.00 p.m. From

SHANNON LAKE STEAMERS.

TIME TABLE—16th JUNE to 30th SEPT., 1914

Daily Service each way (Sundays excepted), weather and other circumstances permitting. The Company do not accept responsibility for delays or departures from arrangements shown.

Up Service.		Down Service.	
Leave	a.m.	Leave	p.m.
Killaloe ..	7.45	Banagher ..	12.45
Dromineer ..	*9.10	Meelick	1.30
Williamstown	†9.10	Portumna ..	2.30
Rossmore ..	†9.40	Rossmore ..	†3.20
Portumna ..	10.40	Williamstown	†4.0
Meelick ..	11.45	Dromineer ..	*4.5
	p.m.	Killaloe, arr...	5.35
Banagher, arr.	12.30		

* Mon., Wed. and Fri.   † Tues. Thurs. and Sat. only.
Well-equipped Steamers. Refreshments on Board.

Special Day Trip from Dublin,

Leaving Kingsbridge Station by 9.15 a.m. train every week-day. Includes rail trip to Banagher, thence by steamer down Shannon and Lough Derg to Killaloe, and rail back to Dublin, with luncheon and tea on board steamer.
THE FINEST ONE-DAY TRIP IN IRELAND·
Inclusive Ticket, 11/- 3rd cl.; **14/6** 1st cl

THE LAKESIDE HOTEL,
Killaloe, Lough Derg.

The best centre for the Shannon Lakes. Magnificently situated, and first-class in every respect. Moderate Tariff, and cheap combined Rail and Hotel Tickets. Splendid FREE Fishing (salmon, trout, etc.). Boating, Golf, etc. For Tariff, etc., apply Manager.

The timetable for the steamers in 1914

there the boat crossed Lough Ree to connect with the train at Dromod arriving at 9.00 p.m. There was little demand for this service, however; soon there were just occasional summer services and even these ceased in 1914.

THE SHANNON DEVELOPMENT COMPANY, LTD. (26)

In Your Reply 61 / 99 *give this reference.*

In Reply to your

MEMORANDUM—From *Athlone* to *Dromineer*

6th day of *January* 1899.

Mr Burgess.

Dear Sir,

Direct steamer will call for any passenger for Killaloe. If there are none please show Red flag, and oblige

Yours truly,

J. McCormick,

Supt.

A Shannon Development Company Memo in 1899

Garrykennedy harbour was constructed in 1829 by the Steam Navigation Company for the conveyance of slate from the quarries of the Irish Mining Company on the slopes of the Arra mountains. They must have used a similar method of construction to that sometimes employed by the Board of Works today: the harbour was excavated first isolating the old castle on the outside arm of it; it is said that they used the stones from the castle to form the harbour walls. This place always reminds me of a little coastal fishing village with the 'street' running up from the harbour and its two pubs in which we were having 'come all ye' sessions before singing pubs were thought of. I remember Vincent pointing out the little cottage where the Donlons lived. They had worked the old sailing barges; the wreck of the last of them, the *Sandlark*, was in the cut beside the harbour until further moorings were developed here in recent years.

Parker Point was so named because of the Parker family, who owned this land, first occupying the tower house and then building Castlelough House which was later enlarged to the fine house it is today. Parker Point could be

Garrykennedy from a drawing in stone by Paul Gauci in 1863

said to be the Cape Horn of the Shannon because the wind tends to funnel up
from Killaloe and meet the south westerly winds from Scarriff Bay, causing a
very confused sea. In 1907 when the *Portumna* was towing eight canal boats
down the lake on a tempestuous Christmas Eve, the last four boats broke
adrift. The skipper of the towing steamer brought the first four boats ashore
just inside the point and then managed to pick up the tow ropes of the other
four. Thirty-five men spent Christmas Day here but the locals made them
welcome and maybe one or two barrels of porter might have 'gone missing in
the storm'. As the skipper of one of the boats was heard to say later: 'It was as
fine a Christmas as ever we had on the canal in those days.'

The only extant photograph of one of the sailing barges under sail

193

Garrykennedy: the hulls of the *Sandlark* and the *Aran Queen*, the last of the sailing barges

Another canal boat was not so lucky in 1945 when she foundered here in a south westerly gale while being towed down the lake by the *St James* and two of her crew were drowned. The lake is very deep here with depths of over 100 feet and she lay there until 1975 when she was raised by filling her with plastic drums instead of using the customary flotation bags. I gather that the porter she was carrying was unfortunately found to be undrinkable! We have had some bad moments here in *Harklow* when we have had engine failure in bad weather conditions and while these incidents are best forgotten, I will always remember with gratitude the people who came so willingly to our rescue on occasion, people like Ken Simmons, who was so helpful in those years when Douglas was not too well.

Mountshannon has always been one of our favourite places with a warm welcome for us in the local pub. The attractive treelined village has also had the distinction of winning the major award in the Tidy Towns contest. Now it has a deeper significance for me because I chose to lay Douglas to rest here in the little churchyard of St Caimin's church. It seemed right for him to be beside the Shannon which he loved and in a place where we had spent so many happy times together.

William Stokes, the artist who drew a beautiful set of panoramic views of Lough Derg, visited Mountshannon in 1820 while engaged in making a 'geometric survey'. He remarked of the surrounding countryside that it was 'a wild, and, generally speaking, an uncultivated tract'. Twenty years later he

Mountshannon: the old harbour. *Lawrence*

returned and found it much improved: 'not the least important and beneficial advantages enjoyed by the inhabitants of this district is having a savings bank and loan fund, well conducted under the management of Mr Reade and telling with the most wondrous advantages to the surrounding county.' He remarked on the fact that in addition to the Church of Ireland church there was 'a meeting house for Wesleyan Methodists'. A small pier was made here in 1845 principally for the landing of the rich marl dredged from the lake which was much prized as a manure. The Board of Works extended the harbour in the 1970s and today it is a busy centre with an active sailing club and a large keelboat fleet enjoying keen racing; some of these boats spend the summer months down the estuary and retreat to inland waters for the rest of the year.

I have been to Inishcealtra, or Holy Island, many times, usually anchoring off the east side but sometimes around at the north west corner if the wind

Mountshannon today, a busy sailing centre

was in the wrong quarter. Certain families enjoy burial rights on the island and there is a little pier here for the rowing boats bringing the coffins out from the mainland. A local man who lost an arm is said to have had it taken over there for burial, 'For', said he, 'what would I do in paradise wid only one arm?' Sometimes we would sail over from Mountshannon in the *Mirror* for a picnic. From a distance the round tower looks like a factory chimney; the story is that it was never completed because a witch informed the builders that she was the only one on the island who was entitled to have a conical cap.

There always seems to be something new to discover here. The monastic settlement was founded by St Caimin in the seventh century but the anchorite, MacCreiche, and St Colm of Terryglass are said to have arrived here earlier. The story of the conversation between St Caimin, his brother Guaire, king of Connacht and St Cuimmine has been told many times but I was interested to trace its source. I found that it had been related by the ancient scholar Colgan in his life of the saint and repeated by John O'Donovan in one of his letters during his ordnance survey work in the 1830s. It is too long to reproduce here but, in brief, they discussed together what each of them would choose to fill the church on the island with. Guaire said he would fill it with gold and silver which he could use to erect churches and relieve the wants of poor Christians. St Cuimmine said he would fill it with sacred books to bestow divine wisdom on his students and, finally, St Caimin said that he would fill the church with infirm people and pray that God would transfer all the infirmities to him. They each were to obtain their desire, Guaire obtained earthly riches, Cuimmine the gift of knowledge and wisdom and St Caimin, as he had wished,

always afterwards laboured through the dispensation of God, under so many and so great infirmities which he bore most patiently for the love of Christ, that his whole flesh became utterly wasted, and the nerves of his body were loosed, and his bones were hardly joined to one another, until he gave up his most pure spirit to his Saviour.

Arising from this story, the tradition grew that miraculous cures were effected on the island. After the decline of the monastic system, the thirteenth-century St Mary's church continued to be used as a medieval parish church and the island was a popular place of pilgrimage at Whitsun. However, these pilgrimages were suppressed in the nineteenth century because, like the pattern at Clonmacnoise, they led to great drunkenness and abuse. The local tradition that women who entered the little Church of the Wounded Men would not bear children led to some poor girls being duped during the pilgrimages.

Some clumsy attempts to restore some of the ruined churches in the nineteenth century have come in for criticism from modern archaeologists. John O'Donovan in his Co. Clare letters about Holy Island indulged in his usual pastime of finding fault with the pronouncements of his fellow scholars. There is an entry in the *Annals of the Four Masters* for the year 898 which states: 'Cosrach, who was usually called Traughan (i.e. the meagre), anchorite of Inis Cealtra, died.' A Dr O'Conor misinterpreted the meaning of the Irish word 'truaghan' (the meagre), as 'turaghan' (a fire tower or fire worshipper) and from this deduced that there was druidic activity on the island. O'Donovan, having pointed out his error, added unkindly: 'My only ambition is to be known to posterity as a detester of forgers, fabricators, and liars and more particularly of those who wish to make the world believe that they are possessed of knowledge of which they are entirely ignorant.' I am glad that he is no longer around to read this book.

A considerable amount of excavation was carried out here a few years ago. Although nothing dramatic seems to have been discovered, the dig was of considerable interest to the archaeologists. Items found in the vicinity of St Brigid's church showed that this had been a working area with materials such as bronze, iron and bone being used. On one occasion when we were

Holy Island: St Mary's church (*Lawrence*); the 'altar' is thought to have originally formed the base of the monument on the right

visiting the island, they had just uncovered two skeletons in a shallow grave beside the round tower; they seemed to be of very small stature. They also uncovered some old stone divisions and paved paths. The various sites were carefully restored when the excavations were finished; they took the puzzling little 'confessional' apart stone by stone to excavate under it and then restored it. It had been thought that this was an anchorite's cell where he heard confessions seated in behind the two large stones but the excavations suggested that it was more likely to have been a shrine rebuilt in the form of a wooden original. I find this little building and the old graveyard the most interesting places on the island; some of the graves date back to the eleventh and twelfth centuries.

From Holy Island the four markers on the Middle Ground shoal are clearly visible. The actual shallow is not very extensive but the markers have been laid to keep boats well away from it. Once again the lack of any sort of middle ground buoy makes this area very confusing. While visiting Holy Island I have seen many boats pass down the middle of the lake between the buoys but most of them manage to get away with their mistake.

The original steam company station was at the head of Scarriff Bay on the north shore but later, in 1829, a quay was made up the Scarriff river at Tuamgraney. The Grand Canal Company minute books record that the river was navigable in winter up to the weir at Scarriff and in summer up to the shoal at Tuamgraney. The Shannon Commissioners dredged out the river and lined the banks. They extended the navigation to Scarriff and a harbour was formed by closing off the channel on one side of the island. Scarriff was quite a busy little town in the past with monthly fairs and there is an interesting old weighbridge in the market square. Like many places west of the Shannon it suffered greatly in the famine years and Thomas Carlyle, who visited here in the late 1840s remarked: 'Scarriff itself, dim extinct-looking hungry village'.

Tuamgraney is well worth visiting. It is a pleasant walk up the lane to the village from the quay. Here there is what is probably one of the oldest churches in Ireland still in use today. A settlement was founded here in the seventh century by St Cronan and the carved head at the east gable is said to be that of the saint. The west wall of the church, with its lintelled doorway, is the oldest part of the building. The east wall is said to be twelfth century and it is thought that the south windows may have been taken from an earlier church in Killaloe. Incidentally our friend John O'Donovan says of this church: 'The present church of Tuam Greine is of no antiquity and there is nothing there by which the antiquarian can be interested'!

Passing back along the south shore of Scarriff Bay, Ballykelly Castle is on a tiny island. It is difficult to approach because of rocks and this seems to have

Derrycastle: Micháel Head's house, from a drawing in stone by Paul Gauci in 1863

made it an ideal place to try to elude the revenue men. O'Donovan said of it:

This castle was in excellent preservation until about 12 (20) years ago when it was taken possession of by some illicit distillers, who defied the assaults of several soldiers and two pieces of artillery. In 1827 it was blown up by gunpowder by order of the government to prevent those anti-Matthusian mountaineers from lessening the revenue.

There is an attractive little tree-lined bay called Bunglasha, east of Cahir Island, which is another of our favourite anchorages. The water is deep close up to the shore and there are lovely walks through Aughinish woods. We have been through the passage between the Lushings and the shore on a still day but I do not recommend it; it is both narrow and twisty.

This southern arm of the lake to Killaloe is one of the most attractive stretches on the river with the Arra mountains on one side rising to over 1500 feet and Slieve Bernagh on the west side. Lloyd Praeger explains why the river took this course, seeking the sea through a barrier of non-soluble slate when much lower ground of limestone, only 150 feet high, was all that stood between the river at Scarriff and Galway Bay. His explanation was that at one time the central plain of Ireland stood much higher, which made the route through Killaloe the easiest access to the sea. The limestone plain was gradually lowered by denudation but the river retained its original course, carving its way through the slate mountains to plunge over a rock sill at Killaloe. As we will see, when the hydro electric works were being carried out in the 1920s this natural dam was removed and a new artificial dam was made at Parteen further downstream.

There is a legend that Brian Boru tried to build a dam where the lake re-enters the river with the intention of forcing the water into Connacht to flood out his enemies. Some say that the high ground on either side of the river at the white beacon is the remains of Brian's dam. Others, less romantically inclined, attribute the land formation to the glacial age.

Passing down this last stretch of lake there is a brief glimpse of Tinerana House on the west shore. It was built by the Purdon family who had formerly lived in an older house down near the lake. The Gleeson family from Athlone purchased the property and still live there today. The late Cyril Gleeson was a well-known Shannon boating man. He owned a number of boats including a very early hydroplane motor boat. He once used it to bring Vincent up to Lough Key and back in a day but it had a very thristy engine and he said you could literally hear the petrol being sucked into it.

Opposite Tinerana was Michael Head's house, Derrycastle, which Arthur Young visited in 1779. He said that it was Mr Head's grandfather who had first discovered the benefits of dredging the shaly marl from the lake bed for use as manure. He brought men down from Dublin who had been used to raising sand from the bottom of Dublin Bay for ballast. The marl was raised and allowed to dry out for a year before spreading. Derrycastle was sub-sequently bought by William Speight of Limerick and it was part of the insurance money from the fire in this house that was used to buy the *Phoenix*. All that remains of the house is the old walled garden, but down by the lake on a little island linked to the shore by a causeway are the ruins of the original Derry Castle. John Fitzpatrick of Killaloe always said it was haunted and that it was not the place to spend the night but he did not seem to know who the unhappy spirit was. In behind the castle there is an old harbour now silted up which was built by the Inland Steam Navigation Company for shipping out slates from the quarries which still scar the slopes of Tountinna.

The Pierhead at Killaloe with the *Countess of Cadogan* and some Grand Canal Company canal boats alongside in the early 1900s. (Lawrence)

The Duke and Duchess of York "enjoying" their trip aboard the SS *Countess of Mayo* as portrayed by the *Illustrated London News* on 11 September 1897.

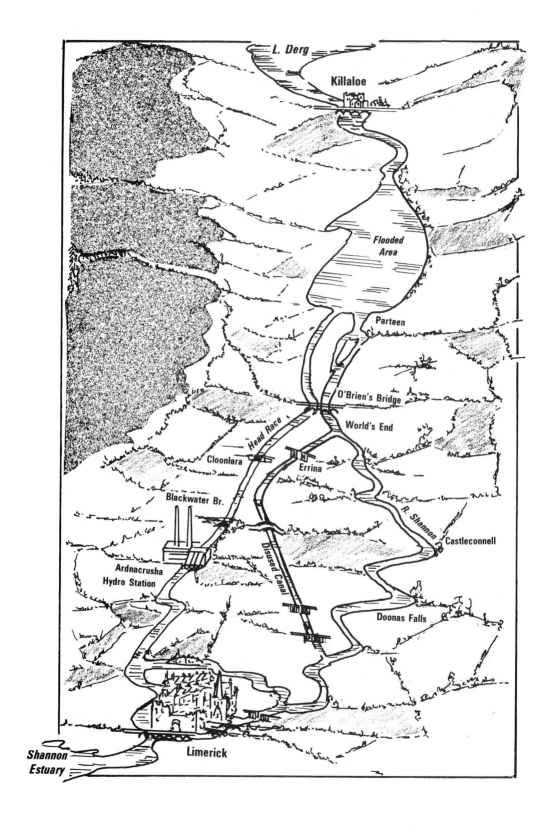

Chapter Nine

SWEEPING DOWN TO THE SEA

Killaloe to Limerick

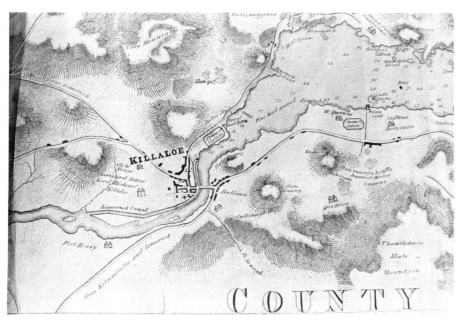

Killaloe: from a map drawn by John Grantham in 1822

PASSING in through 'Brian Boru's dam', the hill to the west is known as Beal-Borumha and was the site of an ancient ring fort guarding this old fording place; Brian probably assumed his title from the name of the fort. It was not, as some have suggested, Kincora, the palace of Brian the Great, remembered in verse by James Clarence Mangan. Once again we find O'Donovan's vitriolic pen at work: 'This is the fort which Dutton (poor man) thought was the ruin of the palace of Kincora.' We must remember, however, that O'Donovan was making these attacks in a series of letters, not intended for publication, and we must not forget his contribution to scholarship in translating many of the old annals.

Brian was born at Killaloe and the site of his palace is now thought to have been on the hill in the town where the Catholic church stands today. From here it is recorded that there was a mile-long covered passage to the fort by the river and two further covered passages leading from the banqueting hall of the palace to the kitchens. When a feast was in progress these passages were lined with servants who passed the food along a continuous chain of human hands while the empty dishes were returned along the other passage.

Brian died at Clontarf in 1014, fighting the Viking invaders, and a century later Kincora was attacked, but it was not the foreigners who were responsible for destroying it. The annals record that in 1118 'Torlagh O'Connor, at the head of a great army of the Connachtmen marched to the palace of Ceann Coradh and hurled it both stones and timber into the Shannon.' Six years later we are told that the same Torlagh 'brought a large fleet on Lough Derg and conveyed them over the cataract of Easdanainne, and plundered Hy-Connell'. So we can see that like Lough Ree, this lake has seen great fleets on it: Viking invaders in earlier centuries, intent on plundering Tuamgraney, Inishcealtra and terryglass and warlike Irish chieftains and kings trying to extend their sovereignty.

I find it hard to imagine that all this happened when I stand on the hill at Killaloe today looking up towards the peaceful lake. This had been a place of importance from very early times. St Lua founded a settlement here in the sixth century and he was followed in the next century by St Flannan who was a Dalcassian prince of the O'Brien family, an ancestor of Brian Boru. There are some monastic remains but these, of course, relate to later periods. Beside the Catholic church on the hill, there is a little ruined church which originally stood on Friar's Island, just below the bridge of Killaloe. It was moved stone by stone to its present site when the hydro electric works were being carried out because the water level was to be raised, covering the little island. This little oratory is thought to date back to the ninth or tenth century although the original nave would have had a timber roof and the chancel with the stone roof was a later addition; this style of building with the lintelled doorways is a characteristic of these early building techniques.

Down at the bottom of the hill beside St Flannan's Cathedral there is another interesting old church known as St Flannan's Oratory. It is thought to date back to the twelfth century and has a remarkable barrel-vaulted inner roof with a small loft above it and a very steep pitched outer roof. Robert Harvey said of it in 1896: 'It is considerably decayed and sadly wants the friendly assistance of the renovator' which, happily, it did subsequently receive.

Donal Mor O'Brien, king of Munster, built a cathedral here in the twelfth century, possibly replacing an earlier church. His cathedral was destroyed by the raiding Connachtmen and one fine Romanesque doorway, which has

Killaloe: St Flannan's oratory in the 1840s

been incorporated into the present cathedral just inside the main door, is all that survives of that building. The present cathedral was built at the end of the twelfth century, when Gothic architecture with pointed arches was beginning to replace the rounded Romanesque style, so both types are present. The tower is supported by the four central arches but the top 20 feet was added considerably later; the original tower had a pyramid roof. The cathedral deserves a leisurely inspection in order to observe all its interesting features and every time I go there I pray that I may be forgiven for my un-christian thoughts towards those responsible for the erection of the nineteenth-century screen. It was probably a very practical addition for the smaller congregations but it does spoil the magnificent effect of the nave and lovely chancel window.

Near the old Romanesque arch there is a unique Ogham stone which Richard Hayward said was discovered by Professor Macalister in 1916, built into the nearby wall which surrounds the old graveyard. He surmised that it formed part of an ancient cross and it is of particular interest because it has bilingual inscriptions in Ogham and runes which the experts have deciphered to read 'Thorgrim carved this cross' in Ogham script and 'A blessing upon Thirgrimr' in runic. These ancient sculpturers have managed to ensure their own immortality even though the identity of the person the cross was commemorating has often been lost. Waterway enthusiasts will want to seek out the controversial memorial to John Grantham which I have already sug-gested dates the arrival of steamers on the river incorrectly.

Killaloe, which had enjoyed such prestige in the time of the O'Briens and, in particular, in the days of Brian Boru, lost its position to nearby Limerick but it continued to be an important ecclesiastical centre and the main road from Dublin to Limerick passed through here until the eighteenth century. Crofton Croker who visited here in the 1820s paints a picture of a place in decline:

Killaloe wears a poor appearance and seems to be little frequented by strangers, as the inn, if it deserves the name, included the business of publican, linen draper, hosier and chandler under the same roof. One room was appropriated for a table d'hôte, where my companion and myself joined a noisy good humoured clerical party, none of who, could be accused of fastidiousness.

The earliest bridge was a timber one erected in 1054 but it is not clear how permanent it was because there are references to the river having to be forded at Killaloe in the fourteenth century. Eventually, a nineteen-arch structure was erected but the west end was altered when the canal was made in the early 1800s, the central spans were swept away in floods and were replaced by five larger arches in 1825 and further work was carried out in the 1840s by the Shannon Commissioners, leaving very little of the original structure.

The canal, which passes along the west side of the river at Killaloe, was part of the Limerick Navigation Company's navigation from Limerick to Killaloe. It took many years to complete and was the most difficult of all the Shannon navigation works because, although it is only about twelve miles long, there is a fall of over 100 feet, which is more than twice the fall of the entire river from Battlebridge to Killaloe. Work had begun at Limerick in 1757 but did not reach Killaloe until the end of the century and even then the completed works were far from satisfactory; as we shall see, it was left to the Directors General of Inland Navigation to take it over eventually and make it workable.

The early engineers made no attempt to construct weirs, although there had been some eel and mill weirs on the river before any of the navigation works had begun. It was not until the Shannon Commissioners came along that weirs were built, and the one at Killaloe was completed in 1842. It was constructed by making a clay dam down the middle of the river, above and below the bridge, laying dry about eight acres. Half the weir was then constructed, the shoals were removed and the work was carried out on the bridge: the bases of the original central piers had been left there when the arches were rebuilt in 1825 and four more arches needed to be replaced. The operation was then repeated for the other side of the river, giving a weir wall over 1000 feet long. The distress of the poor in the area was reported to be so bad that the commencement of these works was put forward several months to begin in May instead of later in the summer. Gangs of 380 men worked from 3 a.m. to 10 p.m. and removed 400 to 500 cubic yards per day, and the bridge was reopened to traffic on 1 December.

The weir did improve the control of the levels in Lough Derg which up to that time used to rise by as much as nearly 10 feet each winter. Like the other weirs upstream, the Killaloe weir was fitted with sluice gates in the 1880s which further improved the control of the levels in the lake. The Shannon Commissioners had removed the old wall which separated the canal from the river but then, realising that this was a mistake, they had partly rebuilt it. This had the result of throwing a greater volume of current against the incomplete part and it was reported that it took twenty men and eight horses to pull a boat from the lock to the Pierhead. This was rectified in the 1880s by constructing the present wall all the way from the lock to the island at the Pierhead.

The hydro electric works in the 1920s completely altered the navigation at Killaloe. The weir was removed and the bed of the river excavated which raised the level of the water in the stretch of river from Killaloe downstream, creating an artificial lake below the town. The old canal was abandoned, a navigation channel was made down the main river and a navigation span inserted in the bridge to allow sufficient headroom. The upper end of the old canal is still used today, providing good moorings for boats along the inside of the wall, although returning to your boat at night along the narrow wall is a good test of sobriety. The lockhouse dates back to when the canal was built but, as a glance at the roof shows, it was later enlarged. The lock gates now stand open with the levels equal above and below the town. An interesting feature of this lock chamber is the double recesses for the gates which mean

Killaloe: photographed by Mrs Shackleton in 1899 showing the weir

that the lock can be used either as a rising or falling lock. This was done by William Chapman, the well-known engineer, who had been employed at that time by the Limerick Navigation Company, because he was informed that there was some talk of lowering the level of Lough Derg about 20 feet by removing the falls at Killaloe; this would have made this little stretch of canal a summit level and the lock a rising lock but, in the event, no attempt was made to carry out such an ambitious plan.

The idea of lowering Lough Derg also came up in 1813 when William Vavasour approached the directors of the Grand Canal Company with a scheme which he said would enable the company to pay off its £200,000 debt. He asked for a payment of £1,000 before he would reveal the scheme and the board quite naturally returned his plan unopened saying that no payment could be made until they knew what the scheme was. Eventually, he agreed to accept £500 if the scheme went ahead and another £500 if it proved productive. The details of the scheme were still not revealed in the minutes but it was recorded that the envelope had been 'locked in the chairman's drawer'. Some time later the plan was once again returned to its originator because the directors had decided that it would not be advisable 'to embark in a work of such magnitude as the one suggested'; it finally was revealed that it was a similar plan to that mentioned above: to acquire the ownership of the shores of Lough Derg and then lower the lake removing the falls at Killaloe, so that the land could then be sold for a large sum.

The Limerick Packet Company had established a station in the canal just below the bridge. The passengers were transferred from the larger lake steamers to smaller boats for the journey to Limerick at the Pierhead, where the Inland Steam Navigation Company had its station at the upper end of the canal. A public notice 'to emigrants and all others travelling on the Shannon' issued in 1851 quotes the fare from Limerick to Liverpool as five shillings, including all charges by steamer, passage boat and railway.

John Forbes, a doctor who visited Ireland in 1852, boarded the steamer here at Killaloe and gave a detailed description of the trip in his *Memorandums Made in Ireland*. He described the scenes of great anguish on the quayside as the emigrants said goodbye to their families and added:

There were about twenty of these emigrants, all destined in the first place, to Liverpool by way of Dublin. The majority of them were going to the United States, but several, particularly the young women, were bound for Australia. Every one was going out on funds supplied by their friends who had preceded them to the land of exile.

Forbes went on to describe a conversation with one of the passengers:

striving the while, by an artificial and pompous mode of speaking to hide the brogue which betrayed him — that it was absurd to think of treating the Irish like civilised people; that savages must be tamed and taught before they are made the subject of legislation; that the only law-giver suited for them was another Cromwell; that, in a word, they were only fit to be treated like wild-beasts or slaves.... It is, indeed, one of the saddest and truest and most portentous things of the inveterate evils of Ireland, that she should nourish on her breast children who can so speak of a mother.

He met a Scots farmer on board who had come to Ireland with a view to settling here but 'his professional eye was shocked, beyond measure, by the wretched state of the cultivation everywhere prevalent'.

The Inland Steam Navigation Company established stores, offices and a dock at the Pierhead where the steamers had to be assembled because they were too large to pass down the Grand Canal or through the Limerick Navigation. When the steamers were withdrawn in the 1860s, as a direct result of a deal with the GS&WR, these larger boats had to be given a watery grave in Killaloe because they were too large to leave the lake.

Charles Wye Williams's contribution in consolidating and developing steam navigation on the Shannon is sometimes obscured by John Grantham's role. Williams was a lawyer, who was called to the Bar in 1812, but he became interested in developing steam transport across the Irish Sea and established the City of Dublin Steam Packet Company from which the British and Irish Steam Packet Company was to evolve which is now the state-

Killaloe with the *Lady Lansdowne* alongside from a drawing by William Stokes in the 1840s

The Paddlesteamer *Avonmore* in the 1840s

owned B&I. He saw the potential of steamers on the Shannon and bought out Grantham's Shannon Steam Packet Company with its single steamer, the *Marquis Wellesley*. He called the new company the Irish Inland Steam Navigation Company and enlarged the fleet in the years that followed; he also established services on the Limerick estuary. In 1833 he asked William Laird to build him a large paddlewheeler of 300 tons which he named the *Lady Lansdowne*. She was 135 feet long and 17 feet wide and was propelled by a 90 hp engine. Like the *Avonmore* and a number of his other steamers, she had to be shipped in sections to Killaloe for assembly.

In the 1860s when the steamer service ceased, the *Lady Lansdowne* was scuttled after her fittings, engine and paddle wheels had been removed. She was in shallow water at the river's edge in Killaloe and Vincent and I measured her from a dinghy. We found her hull was intact and some of the wooden decks were still in position. Our investigations came to the notice of a nautical historian in England called J. Foster Petree, who came over and looked at her. It transpired that she was the first iron steamer to be built on the Mersey and he organised an expedition from Liverpool University to examine her hull with a view to trying to raise her. Following an underwater inspection, they decided that the large amount of silt in her hull would make this an impractical task. They found two Cantrell & Cochrane bottles in the hull with the names 'John McEvoy' and 'John Brosnan' inside them and the date, 30 July 1867, which establishes that she was scuttled on this date. Sadly, her hull was broken up when the marina was extended in recent years and the pride of C. W. Williams's fleet is now no more. It was Williams, too, who established a marble works in the old mill on the canal below the bridge, which is now used as workshops by the ESB.

When the Shannon Development Company re-established a steamer service in the 1890s, they acquired the Lakeside Hotel. It was later commandeered by the Auxiliaries in 1920 and the late Andy Killeen, an ESB engineer, who was a great friend of ours and who was a mine of information about the river, used to point to a hollow in the ground under the trees in front of this hotel which he said was dug at the point of a gun by the caretaker as his own grave but he managed to escape the fate of occupying it.

The old steam company's dock passed into private hands for some time and finally it was purchased by the Electricity Supply Board, who still own it today. We kept the *La Vague* here for many years and Douglas berthed the *Hark* and later the *Harklow* here. John Fitzpatrick was the caretaker and we came to know him very well. He had a wonderful philosophy of life and a great contentment with his lot. The thing that gave him the greatest pleasure was to go up the lake to fish and he lived for the mayfly season each year which in those days produced some fine catches. He loved to tell the gloomy tale of how his predecessor had committed suicide by hanging himself from one of the girders of the shed. He could point to the spot where the unhappy man had laid his packet of cigarettes having smoked one before he took his own life. John suggested that he sometimes reappeared but we often spent the night aboard in the dock and never had a visitation. I remember when the first signs of the construction of a marina began across the river at the Lakeside Hotel in the 1950s, John looked across and remarked gloomily: 'The nuns will be in there in a few years, just you wait and see'. He was to prove wrong in this forecast, instead boating on the river has gone from strength to strength. Oona Quirke now presides over the dock and has been a good friend, taking great care of *Harklow* for us.

The *New Oarman's Guide* published in the 1890s says of Killaloe: 'Beware, when landing, of swarms of gamins', but today, the 'gamins' are to be seen busily engaged learning to swim at the Pierhead and large numbers of boats come and go unnoticed every day. The hydro electric works destroyed the fishing which was a big blow to tourism in the area and it has taken some time for Killaloe to recover and reap the benefit from the new wave of boating visitors.

The boat rental firms do not allow their boats to pass down below the

Killaloe: the Lakeside Hotel. *Lawrence*

bridge at Killaloe but we have been downstream to Limerick a number of times and out into the estuary. The passage through the flooded area is marked; it is important to stick to the navigation or you might run your boat up on the roof of one of the submerged cottages. Below the new lake lies the giant dam at Parteen which diverts the water down the headrace to the power station at Ardnacrusha. You pass through the Ship's Pass with its guillotine gate and into the headrace. The trip along the headrace is impressive but dull; the high embankments prevent you seeing out over them but locking down through the 100-foot double-chambered lock at Ardnacrusha is quite an experience. The chambers are concrete structures, sunk into the solid rock with vertical lift gates. There is virtually no turbulence because the water is first fed into a separate chamber from which it flows through two large pipes shaped like trumpets into the floor of the lock chamber.

It is important to check the hours when the power station will be discharging because the increased current can make the already difficult passage through Baal's Bridge in Limerick even more hazardous. The name 'Baal' was retained from the earlier bridge and indicated that it was a bridge without a parapet; engravings of it show that there were a number of houses built on it. These are tidal waters and both the headroom and depth are restricted at this fearsome bridge so, having passed down the tailrace and into the Abbey River, it is best to wait in the mouth of the old canal until the tide is right for passing through. Douglas, who tended to be impatient, found this out to his cost on the last occasion he took *Harklow* down here. He set off before the tide had come in sufficiently and, having passed under the

Limerick: a Bartlett engraving of the old Baal's Bridge

bridge safely, the boat grounded in the narrow channel between Baal's and Matthew Bridge. The power station was discharging, which was to prove his second mistake, and the current down the river was greater than the incoming tide. The boat slewed across the channel and was heeled over to an alarming degree by the force of the water so that she very nearly filled her open cockpit. Even Douglas admitted afterwards that he thought she was going to founder; however, by getting some warps ashore and around some handy telegraph poles, the boat was eventually straightened out and brought upright and she floated clear on the rising tide. Which all goes to show that this is not a place to get your sums wrong.

Ardnacrusha supplies a very small percentage of power on the national grid today but when the scheme was undertaken it was considered to be an important step towards strengthening the country's economy. A private company had been floated in 1900 called the Shannon Electric Power Syndicate; the Shannon Water & Electric Power Act was passed in the following year but it was too big an undertaking for a private concern and nothing came of it. One young engineer, Thomas MacLaughlin, had faith in the idea and he managed to interest a large German firm in investigating the potential of the scheme. He published a pamphlet setting out his plan and the opening paragraph gives some idea of economic thinking in these early years of the Irish Free State:

When considering a scheme as the Shannon Development our thoughts naturally turn to Arthur Griffith who so long preached the doctrine that political oppression has usually its origin in economic rivalry, that political freedom is mainly valuable because it makes possible successful

A contemporary postcard of the building of the headrace for the power station at Ardnacrusha in the 1920s

constructive effort and opens the way to the building up of the State on a sound economic basis, and that the real benefit of political freedom is only attained when economic freedom has been attained.

A report was published in 1925 which established that the proposals were sound and in June of that year the Dail approved the scheme despite strong opposition. The contract was given to the German firm of Siemens-Schuckert, who had backed MacLaughlin's plan, and the work was completed in five years. It was a gigantic operation; five thousand men were employed working three shifts per day but the working conditions were said to have been appalling. Efforts were made later to try to minimise the effect on the run of salmon up the river by constructing a fish lift but they were not successful and only an occasional salmon is seen in the river now.

The journey down the present navigation gives no opportunity to see the old Limerick Killaloe navigation. When the Limerick Navigation Company had failed to complete the works after nearly forty years in spite of the injection of a large amount of public money, the Directors General of Inland Navigation tried to get some sense out of the board but they received no answers to their letters and were eventually told that 'the members who compose the committee for conducting the Limerick Navigation Company are all absent at present, mostly at the different watering places in England'. Eventually the Directors General reluctantly decided to take over the completion of the works but there were more problems when they tried to hand back the completed navigation to the company, who complained that further work was needed. This led to a ridiculous situation, which lasted for six years, during which time the completed navigation was impassable; the Directors General would not allow anyone to use the navigation until it was taken back by the company and so they left a temporary dam in position at Errina blocking the canal. Eventually, they were forced to buy the entire concern and the directors and shareholders were paid £17,000, which gave them a much better return on their investment than they deserved.

About twenty years later the Shannon Commissioners took it over but they carried out very limited work on this part of the navigation and made no attempt to enlarge it. This meant that although they constructed large new locks on the river, access from the sea at Limerick was still limited. Things remained in this unsatisfactory state and even when the hydro works were being carried out, no attempt was made to bring the size of the new double locks at Ardnacrusha up to the dimensions of the other locks on the river probably because at that time traffic on the river was at such a low ebb.

Because it was such an extremely difficult navigation to make, it is very interesting to inspect it today. It was made up of three stretches of canal

Limerick-Killaloe Canal: Pigeon's lock downstream of Killaloe (*Lawrence*); this area was subsequently submerged for the hydro electric scheme

alternating with sections of the river; the second lock and the lower end of the canal at Killaloe were later submerged in the 1920s by the change in water level. From the end of this canal, the navigation entered the river and passed down through Parteen and O'Brien's Bridge before re-entering the middle stretch of canal at Errina to bypass the great Falls of Doonas. When the river was in flood, navigation was extremely hazardous, a number of islands forced the water to run rapidly through narrow channels; at O'Brien's Bridge there was a steep fall of 16 inches and it sometimes took the men up to half a day to winch their boats through. In the early days before the capstan had been installed there it required 'the united assistance of all the kindly disposed people in the village' to work a boat up through the bridge. The Grand Canal Company appealed on many occasions for a lock to be built here because of the number of their boats which were damaged by striking the bridge when passing downstream. It was suggested that the boatmen should let themselves down gradually using either the capstan or a rope from a buoy above the bridge, but the company said that trying to pick up this buoy 'in a torrent of rushing water' was such a hazardous operation that the men preferred to try the lesser evil of shooting the bridge.

The middle section of canal at Errina is also very interesting. It has six locks on it, two of them double locks. We found that the best way to see it was to prevail on someone to drop you at one end and walk along it to be collected by the obliging car driver at the other end. Errina double lock at the upper end is particularly interesting because it is possible to trace signs of the fact that it was originally a triple-chambered lock, the only staircase of more than two chambers in Ireland. Because of the long drawn out building of the canal and the multiplicity of engineers and contractors involved, many of the locks ended up different sizes and this one was considerably smaller than the others. William Chapman decided to alter Erinna lock to a double instead of a triple by doing away with the middle chamber and lengthening the upper and lower ones to make them conform in size with the other locks. It was here above the lock at Errina that the temporary dam had remained for the six years while the dispute with the company was in progress. Gillogue lock, the other double lock at the south end of this canal, is also of strange construction and shows signs of alteration.

We drove on over to have a look at the old Falls of Doonas after inspecting the Errina canal. Before the hydro works they were such a splendid sight that they were considered one of the country's tourist attractions and there are many descriptions of the cascading falls which today have been deprived of most of their water and their former glory. The river falls 50 feet here in the space of about three miles and at Doonas it raced over a series of high rocks for a distance of about half a mile. Henry Inglis who visited here in the 1830s

Limerick-Killaloe Canal: Errina lock which was originally a triple chambered lock later altered to a double

Doonas Falls before the hydro electric scheme deprived them of their glory.
Lawrence

remarked: 'It offers not only an unusual scene but a spectacle approaching much nearer to the sublime than any moderate sized stream can offer even in its highest cascades.' This was always a great angling centre and in the 1870s Enright, winner of the World Fly Casting Championships, established a rod factory here at Castleconnell on the east bank which turned out his famous two-piece spliced salmon rod.

Castleconnell was the site of a stone age settlement but it took its name from an O'Connell castle built here overlooking the river, in which a grandson of Brian Boru is said to have been treacherously murdered. It became a Burke stronghold but in 1691, when the garrison was forced to surrender to the Williamite forces, General de Ginkell ordered it to be demolished; it is said that the explosion was felt in Limerick and judging by what is left today the demolition team did a good job.

In the mid-eighteenth century Castleconnell became famous for its spa water which according to Lewis's *Topographical Dictionary* 'proved very efficacious in scorbutic affections, bilious complaints, obstructions in the liver, jaundice and worms'. Robert Herbert wrote a fascinating article about the spa in the *North Munster Antiquarian Society Journal* in 1948 in which he related how the place became a fashionable resort where the wealthy denizens of the counties Limerick and Clare built handsome villas. Assembly rooms were built in 1783 for functions and earlier a Castleconnell Club was

Castleconnell village showing some of the 'villas'. *Lawrence*

founded there whose members were described in 1770 by a visitor, John O'Keefe, an actor and dramatist:

They were of the prime class of Bon Vivants and played high and drank deep; all, or most of them, having travelled, were of the chief order of high accomplishment, interior and exterior, they wore a uniform of scarlet with gilt buttons, green silk waistcoats and breeches, a green ribbon in the breast, with three 'C's' in gold.

It was obviously an excellent place to acquire a hangover with the spa water on hand.

With the turn of the century the place declined in popularity very rapidly although Lewis records that there were still 'two good hotels and a number of commodious lodgings' for those taking the waters in the 1830s. This continued to be a popular stretch of river for rowing regattas and at that time there was a rowing race held each year between the men of Clare and Limerick commencing at World's End, at the top of the Doonas falls, down the rapids and back up again, which must have been a remarkable spectacle. The name World's End was most likely a corruption of 'Worrell's Inn' but some say it is an anglicisation of a Danish name meaning the head of the falls.

At the end of the Errina canal, the navigation passed down a short length of river before entering the final stretch of canal into Limerick, which was about one mile long with two locks. There have been some moves to restore this stretch of the old navigation as a linear park, and if the locks were restored it would give access to an attractive stretch of river up towards Doonas.

The history of Limerick and its places of interest are well documented and the waters of the estuary are a different world of tides and sandbanks and great swells rolling in from the Atlantic. The sea is a no less interesting world but it is another chapter in my life and no part of my Shannon explorations. And so I will conclude my account of this great river by warning people to be careful of the estuary in 1991. I quote that well-known pair of travellers, Mr and Mrs Hall:

The mouth of the Shannon is grand beyond conception. Its inhabitants point to a part of the river, within the headlands, over which the tides rush with extraordinary rapidity and violence. They say it is the site of a lost city, long buried beneath the waves, and that its towers, and spires and turrets, acting as breakers against the tide-water, occasion the roughness of this part of the estuary. The whole city becomes visible on every seventh year, and has been often seen by the fishermen sailing over it; but the sight bodes ill luck, for within a month after, the ill-fated sailor is a corpse. The time of the appearance is also rendered farther disastrous by the loss of some boat or vessel, of which, or its crew, no vestige is ever found. In the summer of 1823 the city was last visible, and then a sail-boat, carrying a crew of fifteen men, perished.

Limerick-Killaloe Canal in the 1930s: the last lock in Limerick which was formerly a busy station

The day happened to be a Sunday, and it was reported, and of course
˙believed, that the whole fifteen were seen, about the same time, at the
parish chapel, mixing and conversing amongst their neighbours and
relatives, as they were accustomed to do in life; although, in a few hours
after, the dreadful tidings of their loss reached their families, filling the
whole community with sorrow and lamentations.

BIBLIOGRAPHY

Allen, Robert, *The Sportsman in Ireland*, London 1840.

Anon, *The Shannon Hydro-Electric Scheme*, T. C. Carroll, Limerick, n.d.

Banim, Mary, *Here and There Through Ireland*, Freeman's Journal, Dublin 1891.

Bickerdyke, John, *Wild Sports in Ireland*, Upcott Gill, London 1897.

Blakeston, Oswell, *Thank You Now*, Anthony Blond, London 1960.

Bulfin, William, *Rambles in Eirinn*, M. H. Gill, Dublin 1907.

Carlyle, Thomas, *Reminiscences of my Irish Journey*, Sampson Low, London 1882.

Clare, Wallace, ed. *A Young Irishman's Diary (1836-1847), Being Extracts from the Early Journal of John Keegan of Moate*, Sharman & Co. 1928.

Clifford, Samuel, *A Poetical Description of the Shannon*, R. Marchbank, Dublin 1786.

Cowan, John, *A Description of the Upper Part of the River Shannon*, J. & J. Carrick, Dublin 1795.

Craig, Maurice, *Portumna Castle*, Gatherum 7, Dublin 1976.

Croker, Crofton, *Researches in the South of Ireland*, John Murray, London 1824.

Cromwell, T., *Excursions through Ireland*, Longman, London 1820.

Cullen, J. B., *The Shannon and its Shrines*, Catholic Truth Society of Ireland, Dublin n.d. (1909?)

Delany, Ruth, *Ireland's Inland Waterways*, Appletree, Belfast 1986.

Delany, V. T. H. & D. R., *The Canals of the South of Ireland*, David & Charles, Newton Abbot 1966.

Delaney, V. T. H., *The Lough Derg Yacht Club, A Memoir*, Athlone 1956.

English, N. W., *Lough Ree Yacht Club 1770-1970*, Athlone 1970.

Farrell, James P., *Historical Notes and Stories of the Co. Longford*, first published 1886, reprinted Longford Leader 1979.

Feehan, John M., *The Magic of the Shannon*, Mercier, Cork 1980.

Fitzpatrick, M. J., *Shannon Lake Steamers, A Guide to the Shannon Lakes, The Duke of York Route*, Crossley Publishing Co., Dublin n.d.

Forbes, John, *Memorandums Made in Ireland in the Autumn of 1852*, London 1853.

Gardner R., *Land of Time Enough*, Hodder & Stoughton, London 1977.

Gauci, Paul, *Select Views of the Shannon*, Wm. Spooner 1831.

Goodbody, L. M., *The Shannon One Design Class, 1922-1972*, Shannon One Design Association, Longford 1972.

Gough, John, *A Tour in Ireland in 1813 & 1814 by an Englishman*, Dublin 1817.

Grose, Francis, *Antiquities of Ireland*, Hooper, London 1791.

Hall, Mr & Mrs S. C., *Ireland, its Scenery, Characters ets.*, How & Parsons, London n.d.

Harbison, John, *Guide to the National Monuments of Ireland*, Gill & Macmillan, Dublin 1970.

Harvey, R., *The Shannon and its Lakes*, Hodges Figgis, Dublin 1896.

Hayward, R., *Where the River Shannon Flows*, Dundalgan Press, Dundalk 1940.

Hennesy, William M. ed., *The Annals of Loch Cé*, London 1871.

Hole, S. Reynolds, *A Little Tour in Ireland*, Edward Arnold, London 1892.

Hughes, Kathleen, *The Church in Early Irish Society*, Methuen, London 1966.

Hughes, Kathleen and Ann Hamlin, *Celtic Monasticism - the Modern Traveler to the Early Irish Church*, Seabury Press, New York 1981.

Hutton, A. W. ed., *Arthur Young's Tour in Ireland (1776-1779)*, Geo. Bell & Sons, London 1892.

Inglis, Henry, *A Journey Throughout Ireland during the Spring, Summer and Autumn of 1834*, Whittaker & Sons, London 1835.

Joyce, P. W., *A Social History of Ancient Ireland*, M. H. Gill, Dublin 1920.

Killanin, Lord, and Duignan, K. V., *The Shell Guide to Ireland*, Ebury, London 1962.

Kohl, J. G., *Travels in Ireland in Autumn 1842*, translated from the German, Bruce & Wyld, London 1844.

Levinge, R., *A Sportsman's Guide to the Shannon*, Athlone Printing Works, Athlone n.d.

Lewis, S., *Topographical Dictionary of Ireland*, S. Lewis & Co., London 1837.

McGahern, John, *The Barracks*, Faber & Faber, London 1963.

McGarry, James P., *The Castle of Heroes on Lough Key*, Roscommon Herald, 1965.

MacLaughlin, Thomas, *The Shannon Scheme Considered in its National Economic Aspect*, Sackville Press, Dublin n.d.

MacMahon, Michael, *Portumna Castle and its Lords*, Nenagh 1983.

McNeill, D. B., *Irish Passenger Steamship Services, South of Ireland*, David & Charles, Newton Abbot 1971.

Malet, H., *Voyage in a Bowler Hat*, Hutchinson, London 1960; reprint, M. & M. Baldwin, 1985.

Malet, H., In the Wake of the Gods, Chatto & Windus, London, 1970.

Martin, Michael, ed. *IWAI Silver Jubilee 1954-79*, IWAI, Athlone 1979.

Monahan, Very Rev. John Canon, *Records Relating to the Dioceses of Ardagh & Clonmacnoise*, M. H. Gill & Son, Dublin 1886.

Murtagh, Harman, ed., *Irish Midland Studies, Essays in Commemoration of N. W. English*, Old Athlone Society, Athlone 1980.

Nash, W. J., *Lough Ree and Around it*, Athlone Printing Works, Athlone 1949.

Nowlan, David, ed., *Silver River, A Celebration of 25 Years of the Shannon Boat Rally*, IWAI, Dublin 1985.

Nowlan, Nora, *The Shannon*, Frederick Muller, London 1965.

O'Curry, Eugene, *On the Manners and Customs of the Ancient Irish*, Williams, Dublin 1873.

O'Donovan, John, *The Annals of the Four Masters*, Hodges & Smith, Dublin 1851.

O'Donovan, John, *Ordnance Survey Letters, 1837*, MS. in National Library Ireland.

O'Farrell, Padraic, *Shannon Through her Literature*, Mercier, Dublin & Cork 1983.

Otway, Caesar, *A Tour in Connaught*, Wm. Curry, Dublin 1839.

Praeger, R. L., *The Way that I Went*, Figgis, Dublin 1969.

Raven-Hart, R., *Canoeing in Ireland*, London 1938.

Rice, H. J., *Thanks for the Memory*, Athlone Printing Works, Athlone 1952.

Rice, J. H., *In the Gloaming, Chronicles of the Holles Street Club*, Sealy Bryers & Walker, Dublin 1919.

Ritchie, Leitch, *Ireland Picturesque and Romantic*, Longmans, London 1838.

Rolt, L. T. C., *Green & Silver*, Allen & Unwin, London, 1949.

Russell, T. O., *Beauties & Antiquities of Ireland*, Keegan etc., London 1897.

Scott-James, R. A., *An Englishman in Ireland*, Dent, London 1910.

Smyth, Alfred P., *Scandinavian York and Dublin*, Templekieran Press, Dublin 1975.

Somerville-Large, Peter, *From Bantry Bay to Leitrim, A Journey in Search of O'Sullivan Beare*, Victor Gollancz, London 1974.

Steele, Thomas, *Practical Suggestions on the Improvement of the Navigation of the Shannon between Limerick and the Atlantic etc.*, Sherwood Gilbert, London 1828.

Stokes, G. T., *Athlone, the Shannon and Lough Ree*, Hodges, Dublin 1897.

Stokes, William, *A Pictorial Survey and Tourist Guide to Lough Derg*, Schulze & Co., London 1842.

Thompson, David, *Woodbrook*, Barrie & Jenkins, London 1974.

Trodd, Valentine, *Banagher on the Shannon*, Banagher 1985.

Trotter, J. B., *Walk through Ireland in the Years 1812, 1814 and 1817*, Phillips, London 1819.

Wakeman, W. F., *Three Days on the Shannon*, Hodges & Smith, Dublin 1852.

Wall, Mervyn, *The Unfortunate Fursey*, Pilot Press, London 1946.

Walsh, Rev. Paul, *The Placenames of Co. Westmeath*, Dublin Institute for Advanced Studies 1957.

Weld, Issac, *Statistical Survey of Co. Roscommon*, Royal Dublin Society, Dublin 1832.

Wibberley, Leonard, *The Shannon Sailors*, William Morrow, New York 1972.

Williams, C. W., *Observations on the Inland Navigation of Ireland etc.*, Vacher & Fenn, London 1833.

Periodicals

Cairns, Conrad, 'Guns and Castles in Tipperary', *The Irish Sword*, vol. 16, no. 63, 1985.

Claffey, A. J., 'Medieval Rindoon', *Journal of Old Athlone Society*, vol. 2, no. 5, 1978.

Dowdall, N. 'A Description of the County of Longford', reproduced from a private manuscript in *Ardagh & Clonmacnoise Antiquarian Society Journal*, vol. 1, no. 3, 1932.

Foster Petree, J. 'Charles Wye Williams, A Pioneer of Steam Navigation' *Transactions of the Liverpool Nautical Research Society*, vol. 10, 1961-71.

Graham-Campbell, J. A., 'A Viking Age Gold Hoard from Ireland', *The Antiquaries Journal*, vol. 54, part 2, 1975.

Herbert, Robert, 'Castleconnell and its Spa', *North Munster Antiquarian Journal*, vol. 5, no. 4, 1948.

'Induction Valve' (pseud.), 'Motor Boating on Irish Waterways', *The Motor News*, July 1906.

Kerrigan, Paul, 'The Batteries, Athlone', *J.O.A.S.*, vol. 1, no. 4, 1974-5.

Kerrigan, Paul, 'The Batteries, Some Additional Notes', *J.O.A.S.*, vol. 2, no. 5, 1978.

Kerrigan, Paul, 'The Defences of Ireland, 1793-1815, The Martello Towers', *An Cosantoir*, vol. 34, no. 5, 1974.

Kerrigan, Paul, 'The Defences of Ireland, 1793-1815, The Shannon, Portumna to Shannon Harbour', *An Cosantoir*, vol. 35, no. 2, 1975.

Kerrigan, Paul, 'The Defences of Ireland, 1793-1815, Shannonbridge', *An Cosantoir*, vol. 35, no. 12, 1975.

Kerrigan, Paul, 'The Defences of Ireland, 1793-1815, Athlone', *An Cosantoir*, vol. 37, no. 5, 1977.

Long, J., 'The Age of the Various Stone and Bronze Antiquities found during the Shannon Navigation Operations', *Journal of the Royal Society of Antiquaries of Ireland*, vol. 11 (4th series).

Mangan, Henry, 'Sarsfield's Defence of the Shannon 1690-1', *Irish Sword*, vol. 1, 1949.

Murphy, Charlotte, 'The Limerick Navigation Company, 1697-1836' *North Munster Archaelogical Soc. Journal*, vol. 22, 1980.

Murtagh, Harman, 'The Siege of Athlone, 1690', *J.O.A.S.*, vol. 1, no. 2, 1970-1.

Murtagh, Harman, 'The Siege of Athlone, 1691', *J.O.A.S.*, vol. 1, no. 3, 1972-3.

Webb, Alfred, 'Irish Navigable Inland Waters', *Irish Monthly*, vol. 23, 1895.

'A List of Items Presented to the Museum of the Academy by the Shannon Commissioners', *Proceedings of the Royal Irish Academy*, vol. 2, 1840-4.

'The Management of the River Shannon in the 1980s, Proceedings of a Conference held in Athlone on 16-17 September 1976', *Journal of the Institute of Public Administration*, vol. 25, no. 2, 1977.

Other Sources

Minute and report books of the Directors General of Inland Navigation (1800-31) in the Public Record Office, Dublin.

Minute books of the Grand Canal Company in Heuston Station, Dublin.

Logs of trips on the Shannon.

Contemporary newspapers.

SHANNON NAVIGATION ACTS AND PARLIAMENTARY PAPERS

Acts

2 Geo. I, c. 12 (Ir), 1715, Authorised the making of a navigation from Carrick-on-Shannon to Limerick amongst other schemes.

18 Geo. I, c.6 (Ir), 1721, Appointed commissioners in the various counties to carry out navigation schemes.

3 Geo. II, c.3 (Ir), 1729, Commissioners appointed under the 1721 Act replaced by four bodies of commissioners, one for each province, and established tillage duties to finance schemes.

25 Geo. II, c.10 (Ir), 1751, Consolidated the provincial commissioners into the Corporation for Promoting and Carrying on Inland Navigation in Ireland.

7 Geo. III, c.26 (Ir), 1767, Incorporated the Limerick Navigation Company.

27 Geo. III, c.30 (Ir), 1787, Dissolved the Corporation and transferred the navigations administered by them (including the Shannon north of Killaloe) to local commissioners.

40 Geo. III, c.51 (Ir), 1800, Established a board of five Directors General of Inland Navigation who took control of all navigations adminstered by the state.

53 Geo. III, c.144, 1813, Transferred the Limerick Navigation Company's concern to the Directors General of Inland Navigation.

10 Geo. IV, c.126, 1829, Transferred the Limerick Navigation back to the re-organised Limerick Navigation Company.

5 & 6 Will. IV, c.67, 1835, Established a commission to survey the Shannon Navigation and prepare plans for its development.

2 & 3 Vict. c.61, 1839, Shannon Commissioners appointed to execute the plan.

9 & 10 Vict. c.86, 1846, Transferred the powers of the Shannon Commissioners to the Board of Public Works established in 1831 (this appears to have been a nominal transfer until the works were completed in 1850 and the Shannon Commissioners continued to present annual reports to parliament until then).

37 & 38 Vict. c.60, 1874, The Shannon Navigation Act (transferred all the property held by the Shannon Commissioners to the Office of Public Works).

48 & 49 Vict. c.41, 1885, Authorised works to be carried out on the Shannon to relieve flooding.

Irish Acts

Shannon Electricity Act, 1925, Authorised the Shannon Hydro Electric scheme.

Transport Act, 1958, Authorised CIE to withdraw their carrying service.

PARLIAMENTARY PAPERS

Irish Commons Journals

9 Sept. 1697, II, p. 190, Petition to make the River Shannon navigable. Committee appointed to consider it. No further action.

20 May 1709, II, p.586, Stephen Costello and Mortimer Heylen, who had surveyed the river, given leave to bring in heads of a bill. No further action.

27 Oct. 1761, VII, app.lxvii, Report of a committee to inquire into the state of works on the Limerick to Killaloe navigation.

1 & 15 Nov. 1763, VII, pp. 193, 219. Reports on Limerick navigation works.

20 Nov. 1767, VIII, app.ccii, Reports on Limerick navigation works.

20 Nov. 1769, VIII, app.cccxxvii, Report on progress on Shannon navigation works.

12 Dec. 1783, XI, app. cxxviii, Report on Limerick navigation works.

24 March 1785, XI, app. ccclxii, Report on the state of the Shannon Navigation.

24 Jan. 1788, XII, app. dcclxi, Present state of Limerick navigation works.

23 June 1800, XIX, app. 2, 3 & 6, Report on the Shannon navigation by William Jessop, proposal of Grand Canal Company *re* middle Shannon and report on Limerick navigation.

Imperial Parliament

1805 (169) IV, 331, Negotiations between Grand Canal Company and Directors General on middle Shannon works.

1812 (366) V, 679, 1812-13 (61) VI, 317, References to middle Shannon and Limerick navigation.

1818 (267) XVI, 457, John Killaly's report on a canal to Lough Allen.

1822 (173) XVIII, 37, Survey to be carried out on the relief of Shannon floods.

1831 (175) XVII, 519, Agreement with Grand Canal Company *re* middle Shannon.

1831-2 (731) XLV, 333, Shannon Commission's plans for river up to Portumna.

1833 (371) XXXIV, 235, Shannon Commission's plans for river north of Portumna.

1834 (532) XVII, 141, Report of Select Committee on Shannon Commission's surveys with minutes of evidence.

1836 (143) XLCII, 581, 1st Report of Shannon Commission.

1837-8 (130) XXXIV, 1, 2nd Report with survey drawings.

1837-8 (142) XXXIV, 203, 3rd Report.

1839 (172) XXVII, 1, 4th Report, part 1 with survey drawings.

1839 (208) XXVIII, 1, 4th Report, part 2 with survey drawings.

1839 (173) XXVIII, 139, 5th Report.

1840 (64) XXVIII, 533, 1841 (88) XII, 315, 1842 (71) XXIV, 341, 1843 (76) XXVIII, 253, 1844 (151) XXXI, 387, 1845 (178) XXVI, 367, 1846 (153) XXII, 463, 1847 (545) XVII, 607, 1847 (710-V) LVIII, part 3 (Index), 1847-8 (491) XXXVII, 633, 1849 (113) XXIII, 737, 1850 (407) XXV, 783, First to eleventh progress reports of Shannon Commissioners works.

1854 (91) LVIII, 201, Inquiry held at Banagher on Shannon flooding.

1859 (257) XVII, Sess, I, 245, Commander Wolfe's report on Shannon lakes.

1861 (330) LVII, 557, Inquiries held at other towns on Shannon flooding.

1863 (292) L, 701, Report by J. F. Bateman on Shannon flooding.

1865 (400) XI, 1, Report of a Select Committee on Shannon flooding with minutes of evidence.

1865 (130) XI, 57. Report of House of Lords Select Committee on Shannon flooding with minutes of evidence.

1865 (189) XLVII, 705, Report by J. F. Bateman on works left unfinished by Shannon Commissioners.

1866 (213) XI, 617, Report by Select Committee on Shannon flooding.

1867 (383) (298) LIX, 309, 327, Reports by J. F. Bateman and J. Lynam on Shannon flooding.

1867-8 (277) X, 555, Report of Select Committee on Shannon flooding with minutes of evidence.

1875 (206) XXI, 299, Inquiry into Shannon flooding and evidence taken at various towns.

1882, C.3173, Monck Commission to inquire into the system of navigation connecting Belfast, Coleraine and Limerick.

1887, C.5038, Allport Commission on Public Works.

1907, Cd.3374, Binnie Commission on Arterial Drainage.

1907, Cd.3717, Shuttleworth Commission on Canals and Waterways, Minutes of evidence on Ireland.

1911, Cd.5626, Final Report of Shuttleworth Commission.

Irish Reports

Canals and Inland Waterways Report, 1923 (minutes of evidence MS. in National Library Ireland).

Report of Drainage Commission (1938-40).

Report on River Shannon Flood Problems by Louis E. Rydell, 1956.

Committee of Inquiry into Internal Transport, 1957.

Report on the First Stage of Investigations into Shannon Flood Relief by the Office of Public Works and the Electricity Supply Board, 1961.

Navigation works	Years of construction	Approx. cost in £ stg.	Terminal points	Length in miles
EARLY WORKS (1755-1839) Shannon Navigation	1755-c. 1769	£277,650	Killaloe- Carrick	177
Middle Shannon	1800-1810	£50,431 govt. grant; £78,375 actual cost to Grand Canal Co.	Portumna- Athlone	58
Limerick Navigation	1757-1799 improvement to 1814	£110,336 up to 1814	Killaloe- Limerick	8.75
Lough Allen Canal	1818-1820	£18,805	Battlebridge- Lough Allen	4.25
SHANNON COMMISSIONERS WORKS (1839-1986) Main river	1839-1850	£584,805 (includes work on R. Fergus	Killaloe- Battlebridge	186
Boyle Water			R. Boyle (junction with R. Shannon)- Drum Bridge (R. Boyle) and Lough Key	36
Carnadoe Waters			Lough Boderg- Grange and Kilglass quays	6
River Camlin			Tarmonbarry- Lough Forbes	3.5
Scarriff River			Lough Derg- Scarriff quay	1.75
SHANNON HYDROELECTRIC (HEP) WORKS	1925-1929	navigation works part of HEP scheme	Killaloe-Limerick	8

Number of locks	Minimum size of locks	Year tonnage/ passengers (pass.)	Further developments
8 (3 flash)	Average size 80ft × 16ft (24.3m × 4.8m)	1835 9,770 tons 1835 31,562 pass.	Constructed by Coms. of In. Nav. 1785 Taken over by local coms. 1800 Athlone to Carrick and Lough Derg taken over by Directors General 1831 Transferred to Office of Public Works (OPW) 1839 Taken over by Sh. Coms.
4	as above	1835 19,475 tons average 4,000 passengers p.a.	Restoration work carried out by Grand Canal Company who administered this stretch until taken over by Sh. Coms. in 1839 (compensation £5)
11 (3 double)	74ft 9in × 15ft 2in (22.8m × 4.6m)	1836 36,018 tons 1836 14,600 pass.	Construction commenced by Coms. of Inl. Nav. 1767 Limerick Nav. Co. 1803 Taken over by Dir. Gen. 1814 Limerick Nav. Co. purchased by Dir. Gen. 1829 Restored to Lim. Nav. Co. 1839 Taken over by Sh. Coms. (compensation £12,227)
2	67ft 4in × 12ft (20.5m × 3.7m)	Limited traffic at all times. No passengers	Constructed by Dir. Gen. 1831 Taken over by OPW 1839 Taken over by Sh. Coms. 1846 (1874) Transferred back to OPW 1920s Closed to navigation because of HEP works 1978 Re-opened to Acres Lake
5	Meelick 142ft × 40ft (43.4m × 12.2m) Athlone 127ft × 40ft (38.7m × 12.2m) Tarmonbarry Roosky Jamestown Canal 102ft × 30ft (31m × 9.2m)	1840 72,062 tons. 1840 18,544 pass. 1847 121,702 tons (peak year) 1849 88,919 tons 1849 4,033 pass.	1839 Taken over by Sh. Coms. 1846 (1874) Transferred to OPW 1859 Passenger services withdrawn but summer service continued until 1862 1897 Sh. Dev. Co. recommenced passenger service
1	Knockvicar 102ft × 30ft (31m × 9.2m)	1885 41,720 tons 1910 99,500 tons 1930 67,848 tons 1950 64,678 tons	1904 Reduced to summer service 1914 Passenger service ceased 1955 CIE commenced summer passenger trips 1959/60 CIE withdrew carrying service 1963 £140,000 allocated to improve facilities and encourage hire boat firms
none			
1	Clondara 75ft × 18ft (23m × 5.5m)		
none			
1 (double	105ft × 19ft 6in (32m × 6m)	See above — a large percentage of Shannon trade to and from Limerick	Under 1925 Sh. Electricity Act Electricity Supply Board has control of water levels in consultation with OPW

Index

All page numbers in italics refer to illustrations.

230